Jane Austen
in
Hollywood

Jane Austen
in
Hollywood

Linda Troost
and
Sayre Greenfield,
Editors

THE UNIVERSITY PRESS OF KENTUCKY

Publication of this volume was made possible in part by a grant from the National Endowment for the Humanities.

Scholarly publisher for the Commonwealth,
serving Bellarmine College, Berea College, Centre
College of Kentucky, Eastern Kentucky University,
The Filson Club Historical Society, Georgetown College,
Kentucky Historical Society, Kentucky State University,
Morehead State University, Murray State University,
Northern Kentucky University, Transylvania University,
University of Kentucky, University of Louisville,
and Western Kentucky University.
All rights reserved

Editorial and Sales Offices: The University Press of Kentucky
663 South Limestone Street, Lexington, Kentucky 40508-4008

02 01 00 99   5 4 3 2

Library of Congress Cataloging-in-Publication Data

Jane Austen in Hollywood / Linda Troost and Sayre Greenfield, editors.
    p.   cm.
    Includes bibliographical references (p.   ) and index.
    ISBN 0-8131-2084-5 (alk. paper)
    1. Austen, Jane, 1775-1817—Film and video adaptations. 2. English
fiction—Film and video adaptations. 3. England—In motion pictures.
4. Women in motion pictures. I. Troost, Linda, 1957-   . II. Greenfield,
Sayre N., 1956-   .
PR4038.F55J36   1998
791.43'6—dc21   98-7882

This book is printed on acid-free recycled paper meeting
the requirements of the American National Standard
for Permanence of Paper for Printed Library Materials.

Manufactured in the United States of America

Contents

Illustrations follow page 128

Acknowledgments

First, the editors would like to thank the contributors to this volume for being so prompt in submitting articles and revisions: without such alacrity, this collection could not have appeared in so timely a fashion. Thanks also to the wonderful people at and readers for the University Press of Kentucky, who made very useful suggestions.

The University of Pittsburgh at Greensburg has provided both encouragement from colleagues and access to the World Wide Web and the various databases necessary for the production of this volume. Washington and Jefferson College deserves a large measure of gratitude for support from the U. Grant Miller Library, which unquestioningly purchased video after video as we needed them, and for support for Linda from Dr. Howard J. Burnett's Presidential Discretionary Fund. Special recognition goes to five of Linda's Washington and Jefferson students. Donna Jacobe worked efficiently in running down page references, film studio addresses, and in proofreading essays. Casey Braunstein, Amy Callipare, Meghan Daugherty, and Tiffany Peirce, all from English 355, "Jane Austen in Context," also generously donated their time to proofreading, asking no more in return than pizza and a few tomatoes from our garden. Further assistance at a crucial moment came from Jean G. Weidner, Pittsburgh regional coordinator of the Jane Austen Society of North America, who sent a lengthy and vital fax to complete strangers who sought her help in tracking down materials. At least we are strangers no longer.

For the stills from the movies and television adaptations of Austen, we would like to thank Faye Stein at the Arts and Entertainment Television Network, the publicity office of Miramax Films, Sony Pictures, and the Film Stills Archive of the Museum of Modern Art.

Deborah Kaplan's article appeared in an earlier version in *Persuasions* 18 (1996), the journal of the Jane Austen Society of North America, as did a small portion of Devoney Looser's piece. The essays by Lisa Hopkins, Kristin Flieger Samuelian, and M. Casey Diana first appeared in *Topic* 48 (1997), the journal of Washington and Jefferson College.

Introduction

Watching Ourselves Watching

Linda Troost and Sayre Greenfield

The past few years have seen a proliferation of Jane Austen adaptations. Between 1970 and 1986, seven feature-length films or television miniseries, all British, were produced based on Austen novels; in the years 1995 and 1996, however, six additional adaptations appeared, half of them originating in Hollywood and the rest influenced by it.

The boom started in the United Kingdom in September 1995 with the "wet-T-shirt-Darcy" *Pride and Prejudice* miniseries written by Andrew Davies, and crossed the Atlantic in December with the opening of Emma Thompson's high-profile adaptation of *Sense and Sensibility.* The success of both these productions lifted the art-house film *Persuasion* (written by Nick Dear and released in late September but previously aired on British television in April 1995) out of potential obscurity and brought a new—and older—audience to Amy Heckerling's Hollywood film from earlier in the summer (July), an updating of *Emma* entitled *Clueless.* The next year, 1996, was the big one for fans of Austen in the United States. *Pride and Prejudice* came to the Arts and Entertainment Network (A&E) in January, and in the same month *Persuasion* and *Sense and Sensibility* enjoyed much wider U.S. distribution. It was also The Year of *Emma*.[1] In July 1996, Gwyneth Paltrow appeared as Austen's beautiful heroine for Hollywood's Miramax Films, written and directed by Douglas McGrath, and, in November, Britain's Meridian Broadcasting produced Andrew Davies's telefilm for ITV starring Kate Beckinsale (which came to A&E in February 1997). With such competition, the BBC, which had been developing its own miniseries of the novel, put its plans "on hold for the foreseeable future" (Sawyer).

As a result of the manifold productions, Jane Austen has become even more popular. Publishers have brought out tie-in editions of the novels, Emma Thompson and Nick Dear have published their screenplays, Sue Birtwistle and Susie Conklin have written two heavily illustrated books designed to accompany writer Davies's adaptations: *The Making of Pride and Prejudice* and *The Making of Jane Austen's Emma*.[2] Membership in the Jane Austen Society of North America (JASNA) jumped 50 percent over the course of 1996 alone (4,000 members as of September 1997), and Austen-L, an E-mail list based at McGill University in Canada, has more than 600 subscribers.

The interest in Austen and in adapting her novels has, of course, been operative all through this century. Andrew Wright describes attempts to set *Pride and Prejudice* to music, to rewrite the book for the stage, and so forth, and he lists more than sixty radio, television, film, and stage productions of Austen's various works between 1900 and 1975. If the recent phenomenon has seemed more intense, one must credit, first of all, the technology that allows such intensity. In the early 1970s, global culture was not so tightly meshed as it is now nor could the marketing practices be so efficient. For instance, the only possible place on U.S. television for such BBC versions of Austen as the 1971 *Sense and Sensibility* or the 1972 *Emma* was public television's *Masterpiece Theatre*. Neither series, indeed, crossed the Atlantic. In the 1990s, however, the TV adaptations can sell not only through PBS but also the Arts and Entertainment Network (the telefilm of *Northanger Abbey* of 1986, a controversial production, was the first to combine American and British resources—the BBC and A&E). Also, the current films have an established habit of video renting and buying on which to rely. For example, the BBC sold 200,000 video copies of the 1995 *Pride and Prejudice* within a year of the first airing (Nichols), 50,000 of them in the first week (Davies). The adaptations before 1986 did not have these cultural practices so well established. After all, prior to the 1980s, few homes had VCRs in them.[3]

Technological changes have also enhanced the opportunities for hyping the films. The television and Hollywood publicity machines have become very good both at appealing to a niche audience, in ways that Deborah Kaplan explores in her essay in this volume, and at expanding that niche. Specialized TV networks, instant books of the screenplays and of the filming process, videocassettes, CDs of the soundtracks, and official websites all collaborate to allow those enamored of Austen to indulge their taste further, and at the same time, these hot spots can spark and then expand even a mild interest. Idling through the World Wide Web, a viewer may decide to check if there is anything on Austen. Suddenly she discovers references to the Austen-L mailing list, she visits the Republic of Pemberley at www.pemberley.com, and the powers of reinforcement begin their work. The privacy of reading or of renting a video becomes easily supplemented and overwhelmed by this newfound ability to use and indulge Austenian knowledge in more public locations.

Naturally, such interest can be generated by the films only because Austen's novels maintain their attractions and because the producers and writers have targeted their audience well. What in Jane Austen's novels has made them so readily adaptable to film in the 1990s, and exactly what changes have they required to be successful in this period? Investigating the Austen film phenomenon of 1995-96 along these two lines, this collection of essays sheds light on the most culturally successful features of the novels, on the six film and television adaptations, and on us, the culture that watches these adaptations.

When agreements among our contributors emerge on these issues, they do not result from any particular effort that we, the editors, have made to "scold them into harmony" (Austen 169). Indeed, disagreements on the quality of the films and the emphases of Austen's novels do occur. How faithful films are to the books and the nature of the alterations may occasion some dispute, as when Lisa Hopkins argues that the Davies adaptation of *Pride and Prejudice* diminishes the splendors of Pemberley whereas Elisabeth Ellington proposes the reverse (this differing perception may result partly from British versus American perspectives). Likewise, Cheryl Nixon emphasizes the many changes this same television adaptation has made in the portrayal of Darcy, while Lisa Hopkins and Rebecca Dickson find this small-screen translation essentially faithful to the novel. Casey Diana bucks a tendency among some other contributors toward suspicion of the films by arguing for their pedagogical usefulness. Even perceptions of how the films were received can differ: Carol Dole notes the positive reviews of Dear's 1995 version of *Persuasion,* but Amanda Collins finds the production condemned relative to the praise heaped upon Thompson's *Sense and Sensibility.* We leave decisions on such disputes to the discretion of our readers, yet the attractions of the novels as raw material for the films and certain definable tendencies in the recent adaptations do emerge from this collection.

The qualities that make Austen's novels appealing material for the large and small screen include values that, if not immutable, have been continually appreciated over the last two hundred years. Austen's characters strike a perfect balance between recognizable types and individuals with complex motivations and idiosyncratic personalities. Readers and watchers identify with them and yet cannot fully predict their behaviors. Perhaps heroines such as Marianne Dashwood and Catherine Morland push the typical end of the scale while Emma Woodhouse and Anne Elliot push the idiosyncratic end, but such differences merely broaden the appeal of the Austen canon as a whole. The concerns at the center of Austen's plots—sex, romance, and money—are central concerns in our own era. The details of developing love and the constraints of limited finances provide difficulties that lend her storylines interest for the 1990s reader of sufficient maturity—and these elements of plot, like Austen's characters, can translate to film mostly intact.

Those concerns we share with Austen and her original audience, however, cannot alone account for the burst of interest at this time. Austen also assists in her own modern-day success by providing experiences we are not used to, allowing a reactionary escapism to a simpler time as it was lived by a comfortingly wealthy and leisurely class, as Casey Diana and Suzanne Ferriss note. In her essay, Ellington posits a nostalgia for an older English countryside that renders the Austen films visually attractive to us. One might note, too, the revival of interest in both Georgian architecture (see any recent housing development) and high-waisted dresses (visit any Saks Fifth Avenue),[4] additional features of this nostalgia. Indeed, reaction against the perceived crassness of modern life may have encouraged the Merchant-Ivory films and their successors over the past decade: the appeal of nineteenth-century upperclass society to viewers who want nuance, social sensitivity, and an education—particularly in British historical detail—to count for something.

One may conclude along with Amanda Collins that this desire for a genteel past is a retreat from reality since the most successful films generally leave out those sections of society that have other, grosser tastes and ignore sections of the world with less well-known cultural patterns than England's. We seek difference, but a familiar difference, and our schooling and reading have already made the Merchant-Ivory or Austenian worlds familiar, as Rachel Brownstein (quoting Monica Lauritzen) suggests. In these films, we can hide from the uncertainties of complex twentieth-century existence, where a war in Yugoslavia or a disease in Africa may affect an island in northern Europe or the larger island of North America. Carol Dole's essay complicates this position by intimating that the appeal of Austen in our time derives not simply from the longing for a more socially restricted, elegant life but from Austen's ambiguity toward that culture and partial criticism of it. While we may desire to escape to the world of this older, genteel class, we are simultaneously uneasy about such a wish: Austen gives us the historical fantasy yet provides harsh ridicule of those who are too snobbish in their class distinctions. Therefore, to love Austen is to adore Culture (in the old, high sense of the word) but to remain aware, as she is, of some of its attendant dangers.

Among the greatest attractions of Austen's culture, whether presented by book or film, may be its devotion to manners. In recent years, we have realized that post-1960s culture has lost some of its grace, hence the rise in popularity of Judith Martin (a.k.a. "Miss Manners") and summer camps for etiquette. Our fascination with Austen taps into this fascination with social polish. We may not want to live in this world, but it is fun to visit. An appreciation of manners requires a sophisticated knowledge of social customs, a sensitivity toward others, and the self-restraint for which Rebecca Dickson directly pleads in her essay. In an era of tell-all biographies and talk shows that exploit that all-too-easy impulse for self-exposure, it is difficult not to yearn for some greater degree of reticence in society.

For reticence, however, to communicate passions effectively, as Jane Austen's novels do to the right audience, that readership or viewership must possess social confidence and cultural sophistication. Other segments of the film and television audience—perhaps those who feel constrained into unpleasant social roles or numbed into powerlessness—appreciate depictions of the individual bursting through all social restraints and all concepts of historical accuracy. For them, the adventures of Hercules or Xena, Warrior Princess, can provide a more thorough escape. But the audience educated for Merchant-Ivory's 1986 adaptation of E.M. Forster's *A Room with a View,* Mike Newell's 1992 film of Elizabeth von Arnim's 1922 novel *Enchanted April,* or Thompson's adaptation of *Sense and Sensibility* sees less need for, or possibility of, escaping cultural restrictions. This audience can do without clashes between disparate sections of society or between different nations with mutually incomprehensible social codes and objectives. It wants a game of comprehensible dimension. Limit the field to a little bit of ivory, two inches wide, and the rules become manageable and reassuring. One can acknowledge some degree of corruption in society and feel one could, nevertheless, succeed in it; there is no need to destroy the powers of "civilized" darkness and march off into the virtuous desert like Conan the Barbarian.

For such specific powers of appeal, the 1990s audience may be more open than the audience of previous decades. First, to state the obvious, the audience is largely female: at the Pittsburgh opening of Thompson's *Sense and Sensibility,* sold out an hour before its showing, the male half of this editorial team found himself in a distinct sexual minority, and at the 1997 meeting in San Francisco of the Jane Austen Society of North America, he noticed that generally only 20 percent of those attending sessions were male. Perhaps a plethora of television stations has made us all more assertive in having our particular tastes catered to, and a mainly female audience that prides itself on social sophistication may be less willing than it was in the 1970s to put up with films aimed at adolescent males. In addition, cultural winds may have blown a larger potential audience toward Austenian concerns. The election of Bill Clinton and Tony Blair to leadership in the United States and the United Kingdom respectively suggests that their political positions, combining fiscal responsibility with claims of social sensitivity, tap into a broad base—and those concerns seem remarkably central to Austen's novels.

Although the recent spate of Austen adaptations depends on novelistic

features—such as plot, character, and the general social milieu—that translate readily to film, translations too faithful to the books cannot achieve broad
enough appeal for the movie industry, even if we could agree what "faithful-
ness" to Austen might mean. In less than two hundred years, the cultural
environment has altered enough to require considerable adaptation of the
novels (how many of us these days understand the significance of owning a
barouche as opposed to a curricle?). These changes from text to film offer us
the chance for some sharp cultural self-definition. Certain alterations, of
course, derive from the shift in form. Films will shorten the stories, and even
a six-hour television miniseries must abbreviate long patches of dialogue or
the readings of letters. More important, the translation to a visual medium
encourages a far greater reliance on images: words cannot exist without a
picture. One sees this already in the 1979 BBC miniseries of *Pride and Prejudice* written by Fay Weldon. The director, Cyril Coke, cannot merely have
Elizabeth Bennet, after she has rejected Darcy, read his explanatory letter
without finding some visual equivalent. Instead, we get long shots of Darcy's
receding figure as we hear the letter being read. The 1996 McGrath adaptation of *Emma* must find some action to fill those spaces where Austen herself
simply describes the heroine's feelings—and so scenes of Emma writing in a
journal accompany her voice-over.

The unremitting images, however, provide far more than visual equivalents for Austen's text; the images inescapably change the emphasis. The matter
of costumes, for instance, makes this shift clear. Austen, writing for contemporaries who do not need the word-painting, emphatically spares us details
about clothing, but film must show its actors mostly clothed—and in historically correct costume—so it cannot avoid placing more value on a superficial concern such as fashion than Austen would. The oddness of the costume, its difference from our own style of dress, cannot help but attract our
attention, too. Often, however, directorial decisions invent images, as when
director Simon Langton and writer Andrew Davies remove Darcy's clothes in
the 1995 *Pride and Prejudice*.[5] This episode tells us more about our current
decade's obsession with physical perfection and acceptance of gratuitous nudity than it does about Austen's Darcy, but the image carves a new facet into
the text. Lisa Hopkins argues that such scenes empower women by making
men the object of the gaze, and Cheryl Nixon points out that this titillating
picture not only added symbolic depth for her students but also enlivened
the character of Darcy. Amanda Collins goes further, arguing that most of the
Austen movies (though not *Persuasion*), by their natural enough choice of
beautiful lead actors, promote the equation of human physical beauty with
worth, a Shaftesburian attitude Jane Austen seems directly critical of at times.
For instance, the splendid appearance of Gwyneth Paltrow in *Emma* can, as

Nora Nachumi indicates, undercut the satire directed against the character she plays. More generally, Deborah Kaplan worries that the emphasis on physical appearance simplifies the complexities of Austen's narration into that more associated with genre fiction. The human image is not the only change: scenery can intrude into the films as well, transforming Austenian satire on the Picturesque into an outright endorsement of the Picturesque. Moreover, this shift comes at the cost of social awareness, Ellington suggests. The simplest visual choices for a film can easily remold the values of the novels.

The delicate touch of Austen's satire may suffer much in the cinematic transformations of the novels. Nora Nachumi explores the difficulties of reproducing Austen's ironic narrator on-screen, concluding that the thoroughly modernized *Clueless* does a better job than some other films. Carol Dole notices the satire diverging to two extremes in the more faithful adaptations, with attacks on the class system becoming stronger (though perhaps less humorous) in *Persuasion* and the Davies version of *Emma* and attacks on class-consciousness growing merely superficial in the Americanized worlds of Thompson's *Sense and Sensibility* and McGrath's *Emma*. These films are not without satiric dimensions, but the directors and writers do not always seem to trust their audiences with subtlety—and perhaps with some wisdom: after all, in the movie theater or during a first showing on television, one cannot reread some previous sentence to double check for a suspected irony.

Not only the social commentary loses subtlety and balance; the passions in the stories also suffer coarsening in their compression. The emotions displayed by some characters receive considerable heightening and, as a number of contributors to this volume find, the films elevate and celebrate romance beyond any level the novels justify. Cheryl Nixon in particular emphasizes that Austen's men are modernized out of their repressions into displays of feeling. Austen generally celebrates male restraint, but film directors cannot tolerate such a value—or at least think the modern viewer cannot. And when the leading men of the films can be prodded into displaying affection toward children, so much the better, as Devoney Looser indicates, for their desirability.

If the idea and physique of the New Man of the 1990s reshapes Austen's on-screen heroes, her heroines require even greater adaptation by current films. The imprint of modern feminism on the films, however, is not any clearer than the status of feminist thought in Austen's original texts. Some of the movies at least superficially heighten the feminism to increase their appeal. Amanda Collins and Kristin Samuelian, for instance, note that Thompson's *Sense and Sensibility* creates female characters, particularly young Margaret, with whom a liberated audience can identify. Looser calls such shifts the "mainstreaming of feminism," showing heroines who can tackle physical activity, social conventions, and love all equally well. Suzanne Ferriss identifies versions of *Emma* that go in both directions, with the heavily adapted *Clueless* taking power away from the women it depicts, relative to Austen's heroines, and the two *Emma*s enhancing the depiction of women's power. On the other hand, Rebecca Dickson and Kristen Samuelian find the cinematic representations ultimately undercutting the subtle feminism Austen promoted in the novels. The late twentieth century still has not sorted out women's roles, and the on-screen depictions of Austen's characters echo the ambiguous position of women in the 1990s: feminist, traditionalist, or sometimes both, depending on whom one asks. Each screenwriter, director, and viewer sees the characters as reflecting his or her ideas of womanhood, and that may be the secret of Austen and the film adaptations: they play simultaneously to both camps and reach twice the audience. Both feminists and traditionalists can easily claim Jane Austen as their own.

Changes to Austen's texts made for the differing tastes and politics of the modern audience bring out the conflict not only between two discrete eras or philosophical stances but between two modes of reception: reading versus watching. Most of the essays in this collection will, naturally enough, favor the experience of reading (hence the decision to identify adaptations more often by screenwriter than director). To write on Austen is to be a reader, and to be a reader is to value the relative exclusivity and discipline of reading. Both fans of Jane Austen ("Janeites") and literary critics are primarily book people, and in times when we imagine that literacy is under assault, the degree of literacy required to read Austen or write criticism becomes all the more valuable by its relative scarcity. In *Pride and Prejudice*, Caroline Bingley understands that signs of reading are socially valuable, even if she does not understand how to enjoy reading itself:

> Miss Bingley's attention was quite as much engaged in watching Mr. Darcy's progress through *his* book, as in reading her own; and she was perpetually either making some inquiry, or looking at his page. She could not win him, however, to any conversation; he merely answered her question, and read on. At length, quite exhausted by the attempt to be amused with her own book, which she had only chosen because it was the second volume of his, she gave a great yawn and said, "How pleasant it is to spend an evening in this way! I declare after all there is no enjoyment like reading! How much sooner one tires of any thing than of a book!—When I have a house of my own, I shall be miserable if I have not an excellent library." [Austen 55]

Miss Bingley desires the appearance of high literacy, but she wants it on the cheap.

The problem that film adaptations of Austen's works present to a person already interested in her novels is essentially the fear of success. On the one hand, we may wish the films good commercial fortunes as a way of seconding our own appreciation, but on the other hand, this very confirmation of our taste renders our appreciation less exclusive, less a way of marking our superiority. We may both welcome and fear the invasion of the Caroline Bingleys onto our turf. In this sense, watching ourselves watching proves an exhilarating and disquieting experience, for we stand in a superior position and may well be suspicious of our own sense of superiority.

Insofar as the audience for the films consists largely of those who have already read the novels, we pay the admission, purchase or rent the videotape, or at least turn on the television to see to what extent these new versions of Austen measure up to our standards. For this audience, the films complicate the process of reading and do not replace it. The producers and distributors, however, seem to assume that seeing comes before reading, and so they picture an audience with less time, less knowledge, and less patience than the reader of Austen possesses. Of course, these hawkers of Austen may well be gathering new readers for her, too. Casey Diana's pedagogical experiment on her students portrays how the films may prepare an audience for reading, representing a shortcut to appreciation for those compelled to read one of her books or for those simply intrigued by the film into a subsequent perusal of the written texts.

However, for readers of Austen, a fear remains that these films (and the proliferating Internet websites devoted to them) may substitute for the novels. Instead of reading Austen, the Caroline Bingleys of the 1990s may just visit the Colin Firth websites and buy CDs of music from Austen's era, thinking that they are participating in High Culture. Undoubtedly the films and the spin-off products do substitute for the novels for some people, and they certainly provide a different (and complementary) experience from reading Austen's original works. The films are, by necessity, "E-Z" Austen, but we need not fear they will replace or degrade the novels. The film and television adaptations are attuned to one cultural moment as Austen's novels have proven themselves not to be. Every generation needs a film or video remake of *Pride and Prejudice* whereas Austen's novels have fit a succession of cultural moments for nearly two hundred years. That is the reason they form part of the literary canon. The films get remade because they do not inhabit a long sweep of time comfortably.

Our collection begins by looking at this sweep of time, with Brownstein's consideration of how successive remakes of *Pride and Prejudice* and *Sense and*

Sensibility have brought different aspects of Austen's novels to the foreground, appealing to the varying cultural tempers of each era. A glance at the films that have seemed less successful than the recent ones in attracting an audience may also show how the immediacy of the film medium may inhibit longer-term appeal. The 1983 television adaptation of *Mansfield Park* and the 1987 of *Northanger Abbey* certainly received less critical comment in their day than the recent films have in theirs, and their ways of fleshing out the novels may be responsible: one seems too pedantic; the other, too flighty.

Watching a film almost inevitably presents the viewer with a denser texture than does reading. As we read, we fill in spaces that the text leaves blank, and we do not all fill them in the same ways. In recognizing this distinction, we see what Roman Ingarden identifies as "the opposition of the literary work of art itself to its various possible concretizations and, in particular, to its aesthetic concretizations" (241). With varying degrees of specificity, we imagine Edmund Bertram's appearance or Northanger Abbey's servants, each according to what suits our notions. The films leave vastly less interpretive room. Who has not been disappointed, sooner or later, in some Austen character's looks on-screen? The size of the ballrooms and the mansions, the patterns of the clothes and design of the country dances, the nature of expressions that pass across the faces—all these receive definition. Even the most accurate translation of an Austen novel to film may stand at a disadvantage to the book because of its detail in the face of our various understandings or misunderstandings. Much of the indeterminacy that powers our delight in arguments about Austen gets too settled by the films.

Yet even were we united in our tastes, the filmed versions would create aesthetic problems. On the one hand, we may not want to know as much as a film adaptation gives us. The *Mansfield Park* production, for instance, takes 35 minutes to get through the first 40 pages of the novel (until the arrival of the Crawfords), about 14 percent of the film to cover the first 8 percent of the book. This section of the series provides wonderfully detailed views of the texture of life at Mansfield Park, in the sort of production that Roger Sales in his book on representation in Regency England calls "heritage" television (17-25), but at the cost of our imaginations, whether accurate or not. Moreover, while we may know that Edmund Bertram is not particularly physically striking, do we really want his earnestly bad hairstyle thrust constantly into our vision? At least in the novel, even if we had imagined him to look this way, we are mostly allowed to forget that impression.

On the other hand, any film production of a well-loved novel runs the risk of not conforming to what we may have imagined. The distinctive BBC/A&E *Northanger Abbey* introduces scenes of Catherine's gothic imaginings at length, a persistently vocalized sound track, and a cartwheeling servant lad in the garden at the Abbey. All in all, it gives us the delights of the unexpected, but it certainly leaves any devoted reader open to imagining other, perhaps more appropriate, ways of filling in the spaces in that text. The German Expressionist and Freudian elements interpolated into the film may startle not only the passionate Janeite but even the dispassionate scholar.[6]

The recent round of film and television productions, however, demonstrates by its collective success that writers, producers, set designers, costumers, composers, choreographers, food stylists, and actors can supplement the text with sights and sounds in a most appealing way. But the productions may suffer from being so fully attuned in their texture to our present tastes and imaginations that this texture will not always appeal so easily to future audiences. Once on film, those images are fixed in a way that Austen's writing (by virtue of its medium and her skill) avoids. These adaptations, then, have more to tell us about our own moment in time than about Austen's writing. In watching them, we watch ourselves.

Notes

1. The year 1996 also saw "Furst Impressions," a version of *Pride and Prejudice* aimed at children and starring Wishbone, a Jack Russell terrier. In the 1997-98 season, the thespian dog starred in a remake of *Northanger Abbey* entitled "Pup Fiction."
2. Roger Sales reports that, in Britain, *The Making of Pride and Prejudice* made the top of the nonfiction best-seller list in December 1996 (228).
3. The Austen film industry has been quick to catch on, however. The 1940 *Pride and Prejudice* appeared on video in 1985. Between 1985 and 1996, six of the seven British television adaptations produced between 1970 and 1986 were released on video. The productions from the early 1970s, none of which were shown in the United States, were obviously released to capitalize on current interest (only the 1971 BBC *Sense and Sensibility* has not made it to video, apparently because it was preempted by the 1985 production).
4. Fashion has been reluctant to revive the high-waisted dress, but Hilary Alexander credits its recent reappearance to the "sexy allure" of Gwyneth Paltrow in *Emma*. She also points to the Regency-inspired work of John Galliano for the summer 1996 *haute-couture* collection he designed for Givenchy. One should observe, however, that high-waisted minidresses were already appearing in the wardrobe of the very fashionable Cher "Emma" Horowitz (*Clueless*) the previous summer, no doubt as part of a 1960s revival rather than as an allusion to Austen.
5. Even though the BBC had just released a "heritage television" (Sales 237) production of *Pride and Prejudice* in 1989, rumors were circulating in the British press during October 1990 about a new version that would feature nudity and

"explicit sex" (Roth #589, 599, 640, 669, 733). Although the Davies version did contain some partial nudity, the explicit sex never quite materialized.

6. For an analysis of the psychoanalytic elements at work in this production, see Roberts.

Works Cited

Alexander, Hilary. "Emma's Exotic Empire." *The Electronic Telegraph* 13 Sept. 1996. Online at www.telegraph.co.uk (10 Oct. 1997).

Austen, Jane. *Pride and Prejudice.* Ed. R.W. Chapman. Rev. Mary Lascelles. 3d ed. Vol. 2 of *The Novels of Jane Austen.* 6 vols. Oxford: Oxford UP, 1966.

Birtwistle, Sue, and Susie Conklin. *The Making of Jane Austen's Emma.* London: Penguin, 1996. Includes Andrew Davies's screenplay.

———. *The Making of Pride and Prejudice.* London: Penguin, 1995.

Davies, Caroline. "BBC Pride as 50,000 Buy Austen Video." *The Electronic Telegraph* 25 Oct. 1995. Online at www.telegraph.co.uk (10 Oct 1997).

Dear, Nick. *Persuasion.* Methuen Film Series. London: Methuen, 1996.

Ingarden, Roman. *The Cognition of the Literary Work of Art.* Trans. Ruth Ann Crowley and Kenneth R. Olson. Evanston: Northwestern UP, 1973.

Nichols, Peter M. "Literary Cycle: Bookshelf, Broadcast, Video Store." *New York Times* 7 Sept. 1997. Arts and Leisure section. Online edition.

Roberts, Marilyn. "Catherine Morland: Gothic Heroine after All?" *Topic: A Journal of the Liberal Arts* 48 (1997): 22-30.

Roth, Barry. *A Bibliography of Jane Austen Studies, 1984-94.* Athens: Ohio UP, 1996.

Sales, Roger. *Jane Austen and Representations of Regency England.* With "Afterword." New York: Routledge, 1996.

Sawyer, Evelyn. E-mail to Kali Pappas. 11 July 1997. Online at www.ocf.berkeley.edu/~kip/emma.news.html (10 Oct. 1997).

Thompson, Emma. *The Sense and Sensibility Screenplay and Diaries.* Rev. ed. New York: Newmarket, 1996.

Wright, Andrew. "Jane Austen Adapted." *Nineteenth-Century Fiction* [now titled *Nineteenth-Century Literature*] 30 (1975): 421-53. Contains an annotated list of pre-1975 adaptations.

1

Out of the Drawing Room, Onto the Lawn

Rachel M. Brownstein

What gave Harpo Marx the great idea of adapting Jane Austen for the screen was "a sentimental comedy in three acts" by an Australian named Helen Jerome, a dramatization of *Pride and Prejudice* that he saw in Philadelphia on October 28, 1935. "Just saw Pride and Prejudice. Stop. Swell show. Stop," he telegraphed the powerful Hollywood producer Irving Thalberg. "Would be wonderful for Norma. Stop." The actress Norma Shearer was Thalberg's wife, who had just been nominated for an Oscar for her portrayal of Elizabeth Barrett Browning in *The Barretts of Wimpole Street;* another English Elizabeth, another evocation of a literary woman, was a natural for her. But Shearer put the project off, and then Thalberg died, and it was not until 1940 that *Pride and Prejudice* was made, starring Laurence Olivier, fresh from his brilliant successes in *Wuthering Heights* and *Rebecca.* Because MGM was reluctant to cast his real-life lover Vivien Leigh against him, Greer Garson, newly arrived from England, was given the role of Elizabeth. It was to be what Hollywood called a woman's picture, with Darcy's beautiful marble face as its focus—also a costume drama, more notable for the fancifulness and the number (over five hundred gowns by Adrian) than the truth-to-history of the clothes. (Voluminous, anachronistic, ship-in-full-sail dresses with five-foot wingspans were deliberately substituted for the "wet-nightgown" empire look of Austen's day.) But above all it was to be a comedy like the stage play Harpo enjoyed: a romp. Heaps of dirty paper flowers, plausible on the screen in black and white, decorated the sets where the Bennet virgins cavorted: the director's aim was to keep it light, bright, and pleasant. It was important to keep it British, as well. The first frame announces in print that "It happened in OLD ENGLAND," and the studio went so far as to hire the famous English novelist Aldous Huxley to collaborate with screenwriter Jane Murfin. While Huxley was somewhat distressed by his task—he acknowledged that "the very fact of transforming the book into a picture must necessarily alter its whole quality in a profound way"—he stuck patriotically, for

$1,500 a week, to the "odd, crossword puzzle job," trying "to do one's best for Jane Austen."[1]

The advertising for the film was pure Hollywood: "Bachelors Beware! Five Gorgeous Beauties are on a Madcap Manhunt!" Appreciative reviewers called it "pert," "crackling," and "brittle"; the snappy dialogue and the smart, sassy heroine were stylish, standard in screen comedies of the time. Jane Austen's plot and characters and her dialogue too were radically revised to condense and simplify ("Jane, I love him; what a fool I've been," says Elizabeth). Lady Catherine de Bourgh (played by the redoubtable Edna May Oliver, who impressed her fellow actors by swimming in the Pacific each morning before filming began) actually makes the match, here, between Darcy and Elizabeth. ("What you need is a woman who will stand up to you," she tells her nephew. "I think you've found her.")

The film diverges from the novel less predictably at the beginning than the end. The action starts in a village shop (Ford's, perhaps, borrowed for the occasion from Austen's *Emma*?) where Mrs. Bennet is buying muslin and damask to dress her daughters for the Assembly Ball, pink for Jane and blue for boyish Lizzy (this Lizzy, after the ball where Darcy rejects her, will sport a man's tie.) The business of marketing is neatly connected with that of marrying as the women look out the shop window at the "exquisite young men" who "must have come straight from court," and a sweaty Lady Lucas rushes in excitedly to announce that "Netherfield Park is let at last." (This last is pronounced to be the best news "since the battle of Waterloo"—which occurred two years after Austen's novel was published.) The Bennet ladies collect Kitty and Lydia from a Punch and Judy show in the village, and all bustle down the wooden sidewalks, the girls (count 'em: five!) like goslings behind their mother. Then comes the race home against Lady Lucas's carriage to bag the prize young men—a brilliant free translation of the theme of *Pride and Prejudice* into the language of horse-obsessed Hollywood.

Readers of the novel must balk, however, when Darcy calls Elizabeth "tolerable," and adds, "I'm in no humour tonight to give consequence to the middle classes at play." Austen is more egregiously misrepresented when Elizabeth speaks of Darcy's unwillingness to ally himself to "a family of such low descent." The novel's Elizabeth, so proud of being "a gentleman's daughter," was not quite what Hollywood wanted—any more than an Elizabeth less beautiful than her sister Jane was. Enjoying Greer Garson's perfect features and glassy composure, the camera persuades us to forget she is a decade or so older than Elizabeth Bennet's "not yet twenty." Similarly, we are meant to consider Elizabeth as a daughter of those middle classes that reliably rose up against the aristocracy in Hollywood's wartime renderings of nineteenth-century novels (cf. *Jane Eyre*), which portray OLD ENGLAND as democratic

America's ancestor. Part of the context that shaped this film was the producers' aim to get the United States into the war as England's ally: together with the formal constraints of Hollywood comedy, politics was responsible for changing Lady Catherine's mind about Elizabeth.

Why adapt *Pride and Prejudice* for the screen? Better to ask, Why not? As Harpo knew, Hollywood was always looking for plots, and certainly for variants on that reliable plot in which a charming young lady and a handsome young man find true love in spite of impediments. Austen's name recognition would not hurt sales, nor would her famous fondness for the marriage plot (she wrote six variations on it, which shows she was quite as hip as Harpo to what dependably entertains). "[W]hen a young lady is to be a heroine, the perverseness of forty surrounding families cannot prevent her," she insisted in *Northanger Abbey*. "Something must and will happen to throw a hero in her way" (16-17). Those surrounding families tend to be underrepresented in the film versions of Austen's novels, which since 1940 tend to focus closely on the heroines and the love stories, and of course the fun of thwarting the dreariness of real life, where storybook happiness hardly happens.

But the focus shifted a little away from frothy romance in the Austen films of the second half of the twentieth century. The new emphasis was on realism—and respect. The many and various Austen dramatizations that were made for television between 1952 and the late 1980s show earnest, increasing regard for both women's domestic lives and Great Literature. The women's movement of the 1970s was an influence; so were the rise of television and the (associated?) decline of reading. As one writer observes about the television serials made in England, "In adapting well-known works of fiction as a means of attracting an audience, filmmakers have in fact been relying on the appeal of a combination of familiarity with slightly mysterious remoteness and high prestige" (Lauritzen 19). Aiming at people who had not read the books but meant to, the often state-supported producers of these TV dramas claimed and maybe really thought their aim was to educate—to expose the people of Britain to their heritage, the best that had been thought and written in a more literary past. Some even meant to make viewers become readers—although the films might of course be seen, and used, as substitutes for reading, even by students required to read Austen for school. The producers relied on viewers' respect for Great Novels—and for genteel manners and upper-class accents. Audiences in America could be depended upon to respect Britishness *tout court*.

The twentieth-century notion that the novels of Jane Austen are suitable to be "taught" in school, indeed the very idea that Novels are Classics, would have startled Austen herself, who boldly argued, against established opinion, that novels should be taken seriously. In her time, novels—especially those about, by, and for women—were underrated as serious literature, and even despised. So she might, conceivably, have been heartened by seeing *Emma* and *Sense and Sensibility* presented as Classics. But surely she would have been distressed by dramatized episodes of *Pride and Prejudice* and *The Golden Bowl* and *Brideshead Revisited* that look and feel like chapters of a single interminable Classic Serial. A genre was being developed in the literal-minded literary films made for television in the 1970s and 1980s: the particulars and peculiarities of individual novels and novelists were absorbed in its overeager embrace.

Both the high seriousness and the glossy look of the literary film were intensified, and fixed, when Classic Serials met Merchant and Ivory. The complex relationship of England and America, and the almost as vexed one of movies and television, are part of the story: the producer Ismail Merchant recalled that "Jim [Ivory] used to watch BBC Television productions of Henry James and mutter, 'I can do better than that,' and 'Why should the English be doing this sort of thing, and never the Americans?'" (Long 96). (Ivory himself is an American; his partners are Indian Ismail Merchant and Polish-Jewish Ruth Prawer Jhabvala, who is married to an Indian.) The team's first adaptation of a James novel, *The Europeans* (1979), is meticulous and intelligent, also informed by respect for genteel fiction. So are their subsequent films based on novels: *The Bostonians* (1984); the three E.M. Forster movies—*A Room with a View* (1986), *Maurice* (1987), and *Howards End* (1992); *Quartet* (1981), based on a book by Jean Rhys; *Heat and Dust* (1983), from the novel by Jhabvala; *Mr. and Mrs. Bridge* (1990), which dramatizes two novels by Evan S. Connell, and *The Remains of the Day* (1993), based on the novel by Kazuo Ishiguro. The last, like *Howards End,* stars a stately home and Emma Thompson, the handsome, clever, rich, Cambridge-educated, gifted English actress who was soon to be identified with Jane Austen.[2] The distinctive Merchant-Ivory style—the deliberate savoring of elegant faces and dresses and furnishings and colors and slants of light; the focus on manners and personal relationships and country houses and greenery; the clarity of speech and importance of dialogue—makes the claim that film is Art, representational, nineteenth-century, literary Art. Virginia Woolf, in an essay on "The Cinema," expressed her fear that movies would rip off the plots of novels and vulgarize and diminish them; Merchant-Ivory stakes a claim for Film as Art by making classy films of Classic novels.

Woolf's fear was justified by the films ground out for television, such as the 1985 BBC *Sense and Sensibility.* In retrospect, it is notable for, among other things, identifying itself as "By Jane Austen." Coming back to it from the Ang Lee/Emma Thompson 1995 version ("Adapted from the novel by

Jane Austen"), one is equally astonished by its slowness and dullness. Muted colors, pearl grays and ochers, and lots of shadows insist this story is serious and meaningful—after all, above all, a Classic. In order to make the point of its high seriousness, the Dashwood women's daily life at Norland Park and Barton Cottage is rendered in pointlessly exhaustive and therefore distorting detail: they are shown unpacking their linens and stowing them in chests, as Austen's characters never have to do. Ten years later, Ang Lee could make domestic life interesting by brilliantly shifting narrative point of view, allowing us to see through Elinor's eyes and then to see Elinor, as Austen does. In 1985, simple domestic realism, therefore trivia, triumphs; the point of the film seems to be that, despite their gentility, these women are just like us and the heroines of our soap operas. So when Marianne prepares to be visited (in bed!) by Colonel Brandon, after her dangerous illness, she looks into a hand mirror and squeals, "My skin looks terrible!" Our contemporary, she accuses herself of playacting and (although she remains round-faced) of starving herself: one could read in all the papers, in the 1980s, that girls who suffer from anorexia nervosa are mostly middle-class.

Austen scholars today tend to be most interested in how the social and political life of the novelist's time informs her novels. It is amusing to think about how their own contexts, inevitably, also inform the Austen films: twentieth-century wars and politics and fashions, the technical and corporate changes in the film and television industries. Perhaps it is because context is so much talked about these days that it seems to have thickened, somehow. The Austen films of the mid-1990s are impossible to detach from it. Watching the Thompson/Lee *Sense and Sensibility* on a videocassette, one sees first of all ads for *The Sense and Sensibility Screenplay and Diaries* ($23.95) by star/screenwriter Thompson and the CD of Patrick Doyle's music for the film. (*Publishers Weekly* reported on 1 January 1996 that "the Thompson book has a first printing of 28,500 and has already gone back to press for another round of 5,000. It is a selection of both QPBC [Quality Paperback Book Club] and The Fireside Theater Book Club.") Norma Shearer's having played Elizabeth Barrett Browning made her seem (to Harpo) a likely Elizabeth Bennet; the connection between Emma Thompson and the media idea of Jane Austen is much more than casual or nominal. Thompson's aura of English literature derives not only from her having written the screenplay and the diaries but also from her prior roles in the Merchant-Ivory films, and as Beatrice in the film version of *Much Ado about Nothing* directed by her (now former) husband Kenneth Branagh; it is enhanced by Branagh's career and reputation as a Shakespearean actor and director. Modern, successful Emma's act of rescuing a female predecessor from obscurity (Austen signed herself as "A Lady") asks to be viewed as a generous star turn. From the bold beginning—the clip of the action, the clarity and intensity of the color—it is clear that Thompson's new and revised *Sense and Sensibility* is full of energy. One easily gets the picture: Jane Austen has come a long way.

Beyond the context of the tie-ins and the talk of profits that adds to the drama and glamour, beyond the context of the stars and the gossip about their private lives (Thompson's breaking up with Branagh and having a fling with Greg "Willoughby" Wise; Hugh "Edward Ferrars" Grant's getting arrested for a sex crime in Los Angeles during the filming), there are the wider contexts that we call cultural: the context of films and film buffs, of feminism and postfeminism, of cultural self-consciousness and cultural criticism, even of academic Austen criticism. The force of that last, narrowest context is easiest to illustrate: Roger Michell's directing in *Persuasion* (1995) confronts head-on, to begin with, the best-known criticism of Austen, that she failed to notice the Napoleonic Wars. Here at the beginning of the movie are demobilized sailors; over there, therefore, are the Wars themselves, of which Jane Austen, you see, was richly aware. *Persuasion* goes on to engage—as Diarmuid Lawrence's direction of *Emma* (1996) also flashily does—the other standard criticism of Austen, that she ignores the servant class, by showing us the servants looking on enviously at the gentlefolks or conspicuously easing their lives. Austen is being improved for the 1990s, her field of vision and her sympathies widened. She is being armed to defend herself against her critics, and those who know the novels and the critical controversies around them are being signaled, acknowledged, personally addressed, flattered.

It would be laughably grandiose for me to suggest that filmmakers who evoke Austen criticism seek communion with academic critics as they do with savvy film buffs, who can be depended on to observe, for instance, that the archery scene in Douglas McGrath's *Emma* (1996) harks back to a similar scene in the 1940 *Pride and Prejudice* (also not in the novel). My more modest point is that the sense of a subtext, of meanings accessible only to a chosen few, pervades the films of the 1990s. Whether it is because of what you have read about Gwyneth Paltrow (and Brad Pitt), or because of what you remember about Alan Rickman's portrayal of Valmont in the RSC *Les Liaisons Dangereuses,* or because you know the essays of Lionel Trilling (actually discussed in *Metropolitan* [1990], which evokes *Mansfield Park*), or because you do not need to be told on the screen that *Clueless* (1995) is based on Austen's *Emma,* you are invited and assumed to be in the know by the mid-1990s Austen films.

As the 1940 film reflects the element of romance in Austen's novels and the 1980s made-for-television dramas reflect her realism, these more recent movies pick up on Austen's celebrated irony. In *Sincerity and Authenticity,* Trilling, one of Austen's best readers, defines irony (with irony) as one of those words, like love, which are best not talked about if they are to retain any force of meaning—other such words are sincerity and authenticity. . . . The etymology of the word associates it directly with the idea of the mask, for it derives from the Greek word for a dissembler. It is used in a diversity of meanings, of which the simplest is saying one thing when another is meant, not for the purpose of deceit and not wholly for the purpose of mockery (although this is usually implicit), but, rather, in order to establish a disconnection between the speaker and his interlocutor, or between the speaker and that which is being spoken about, or even between the speaker and himself. [112]

To which I would say Yes, and also No. For it is a *connection with* an interlocutor that irony also depends on—someone out there who will get the allusion, read between the lines. Jane Austen is ironic when she writes, "No one who had ever seen Catherine Morland in her infancy, would have supposed her born to be an heroine" (1); this first sentence is directed at a reader who understands that Catherine, for this novel's duration, will be precisely that.

The Austen films of the mid-1990s are, like Austen's novels, ironic about romantic plots and the realities that (still) constrain women's lives. Having all come out almost at once, and being aware of that, they direct themselves at audiences equally aware—people who have read about the films and the stars in newspapers and magazines, which also feature articles about what it means that Jane Austen is the heroine of our moment. Was she or wasn't she a feminist? A snob? Is it not ironic that although we do not have a decent picture of her she is behind all these pix? That she is a celebrity as she never was in life, declared, by *People* magazine, "one of the most intriguing people of 1995"? Where earlier films ignored or elided the fact, the postmodern films insist on the irony of making a movie (that low form) of a novel by Austen (that avatar of Culture, that cultural commodity). The ads also, of course, insist—as critics have also done—on the irony of a maiden lady as the expert on women's feelings for men.

Irony is characteristic of our time: there are ironic ads that mock advertising, ironic sitcoms that are in-your-face about being sitcoms. Trilling, following Hegel, suggests that irony makes for freedom (from convention, from society), which is consonant with some views (not universal ones) of Austen as a Romantic writer, and others of her as a satirist or as a novelist detached by definition from her society, and therefore able to change the way readers see the world. But there is a significant difference between the ironic point of view from which Austen began writing in the 1790s and the ironic *style* that is widespread two hundred years later. Irony at its simplest, today, is not saying one thing and meaning another, but not being sure if you mean what you say. Austen's irony was a moralist's; postmodern irony refuses to acknowledge the moral. My point is not that Austen's novels have or illustrate simple morals—what they come to, in the end, is famously ambiguous—but that her mockery of false notions of, say, "true elegance," is based on clear, discernable ideas not only of that quality but also of the values of those who value it. The recent Austen films have a single obvious, reiterated moral: that lovers deserve to enjoy one another, as viewers deserve to enjoy movies. (*Clueless* may be an exception.) These film versions of texts that play ingeniously and ironically with categories of surface and depth (first impressions and deep self-knowledge, formal politeness and selfishness, manners and morals, words and meanings) do offer additional variations on the theme: image and text; screen action and the life behind it; Emma Thompson and Elinor Dashwood, Beatrice, Emma Woodhouse, Jane Austen, all of them bright and attractive women who were reluctant to marry. But as they cockily update her for the screen, some fall into the trap of being knee-jerk ironic about (old-fashioned, uptight) Jane Austen, and forget that she, before us, was sophisticated and subtle and very, very smart.

Notes

1. For details in the preceding paragraph and the next one, I am indebted to Kenneth Turan's article (esp. 140-42).
2. Merchant-Ivory's 1980 film, *Jane Austen in Manhattan*, deserves a note: its Austen connection is historically interesting, but it is a little off the subject here. It compares and contrasts the artifice and manners of eighteenth-century life and theater and the twentieth-century avant-garde.

Works Cited

Austen, Jane. *Northanger Abbey*. Ed. R.W. Chapman. Rev. Mary Lascelles. 3d ed. Vol. 5 of *The Novels of Jane Austen*. 6 vols. Oxford: Oxford UP, 1966.

Emma. Writer and director Douglas McGrath. With Gwyneth Paltrow and Jeremy Northam. Miramax, 1996.

Emma. Writer Andrew Davies. Director Diarmuid Lawrence. With Kate Beckinsale and Mark Strong. Meridian (ITV)/A&E, 1996.

Lauritzen, Monica. *Jane Austen's Emma on Television*. Gothenburg Studies in English 48. Göteborg, Sweden: Acta Univ. Gothoburgensis, 1981.

Long, Robert Emmet. *The Films of Merchant Ivory*. New York: Abrams, 1991.

Persuasion. Writer Nick Dear. Director Roger Michell. With Amanda Root and Ciaran Hinds. BBC/WGBH, 1995.

Pride and Prejudice. Writers Aldous Huxley and Jane Murfin. Director Robert Z. Leonard. With Greer Garson and Laurence Olivier. MGM, 1940.

Sense and Sensibility. Writer Alexander Baron. Director Rodney Bennett. With Irene Richard and Bosco Hogan. BBC, 1985.

Sense and Sensibility. Writer Emma Thompson. Director Ang Lee. With Emma Thompson and Hugh Grant. Mirage-Columbia (Sony), 1995.

Trilling, Lionel. *Sincerity and Authenticity.* The Uniform Edition. New York: Harcourt Brace, 1980.

Turan, Kenneth. "*Pride and Prejudice:* An Informal History of the Garson-Olivier Motion Picture." *Persuasions: Journal of the Jane Austen Society of North America* 11 (1989): 140-43.

Woolf, Virginia. "The Cinema." In *The Captain's Death Bed and Other Essays.* London: Hogarth, 1950.

2

Balancing the Courtship Hero

Masculine Emotional Display in Film Adaptations
of Austen's Novels

Cheryl L. Nixon

Watching Austen's Men

The exclamation, "I loved when Darcy stripped off some of his clothes and dove into the pond as he returned to Pemberley," started off a classroom discussion concerning the Andrew Davies BBC television adaptation of *Pride and Prejudice* (1995). The student explained her enthusiasm by noting that although this scene does not appear in Austen's novel, it serves to dramatize Austen's development of Darcy's character. Darcy's swim provides a dramatic visual symbol of his emotional rebirth, as he forsakes pride and moves toward a more generous love of Elizabeth. The scene makes Darcy seem "more alive" and "more human." The class concluded that while the scene is an obvious addition, it maintains the thematic thrust of Austen's plot, translating her ideas concerning character transformation into a visual vocabulary.

The same group of students, enrolled in an undergraduate seminar on Jane Austen I teach, held a remarkably similar view of the recent—and more revisionary—Emma Thompson film adaptation of *Sense and Sensibility* (1995). As with the BBC's Darcy, visually striking additions are made to the actions of Colonel Brandon. Brandon is given a dramatic rescue of the rain-soaked Marianne, a dramatic horseback ride to fetch Mrs. Dashwood to Marianne's sickbed, and a dramatic poetry reading signaling his slow conquering of Marianne's heart, among several other added scenes. While, as a group of literary critics, the class was somewhat uneasy with the liberties taken with Austen's plot, as a group of moviegoers, the class was relieved to see Austen's vision of Brandon so radically augmented. While Austen's Brandon did not seem to be a good match for the young, energetic, and emotional Marianne,

Thompson's Brandon is worthy of Marianne's love. The class consensus was clear: a "one-dimensional," "boring" Brandon had been transformed into a more "active," "desirable" one. While Austen's transformation of Darcy into a romantic hero needs only slight translation, her characterization of Brandon seems to need a complete reconfiguration. In both adaptations, however, the additions met with approval. Obviously, if my class is any indication, a "more alive" and "more active" version of Austen's heroes resonates with today's moviegoers.

My class's opinions are in good company. Louis Menand, reviewing the recent spate of Austen films in the *New York Review of Books* offers a similar analysis of the cinematic revisions of Austen's men. His essay opens with the argument that the 1995 *Pride and Prejudice* adaptation fulfills its viewers' desires precisely because it contains a crucial "enhancement": "the glamorization of Mr. Darcy" (Menand 13). Noting that "nearly all of Davies's departures from the novel involve Darcy," Menand provides the compelling argument that the added scenes, the pool-diving scene being a primary example, give Darcy a physical presence that Austen has not (13). The film adaptation succeeds because it has given Darcy "a body" (13). Menand concludes, "This is, in short, a *P&P* with extra Darcy" (13). Having proven the importance of the "erotically enhanced Darcy," Menand notes that the men in *Sense and Sensibility* must be similarly reformed (13). The "key to the . . . success" of Thompson's adaptation is its revision of the "diffident sad sack Edward Ferrars . . . and the stolid sad sack Colonel Brandon" (14). Austen "neglected" to make the men "appealing" and thus did not write a "credible romance," but the movie wisely remedies this central fault (14). The film recognizes that "the chief problem with the book is the stupefying dullness of the men the Dashwood sisters eventually pair off with" (14). To echo Menand's earlier words, the film solves the novel's problems by giving the viewer extra Edward and extra Brandon.

My class's conversations and Menand's film review come to the same conclusion: the recent film adaptations of Austen are successful because they, quite literally, "flesh out" her male characters. It is imperative that the films reconfigure the novels' romance heroes. While the success of the current adaptations reveals a timeless love of Austen, they also reveal what we, the late twentieth-century audience, do not like about Austen—or at least what the filmmaker predicts the average filmgoer will not like about Austen. Most tellingly, it is what Austen's heroines fall in love with that we do not like: the male hero. What was good enough for her female heroines is obviously not good enough for us; the films must add scenes to add desirability to her male protagonists.

Redefining Austen's Men

These observations lead me to ask two questions: first, how does the late twentieth century rewrite Austen's men and, second, what desires underlie our revisions? Answers to these two questions raise and may help to answer a third: what changes are we making to Austen when we change her representation of masculinity? The first question is rather easily answered. Both the classroom conversations and review article emphasize each film's addition of male physicality. The "sad sacks" come "alive." I don't think that these changes are concerned only with satisfying a twentieth-century lust for the body. Once it becomes obvious that each hero has been given a body, an attendant observation must be made, providing an answer to my second question. Each film's physical additions are shorthand for its emotional additions. The films use a visual, indeed a bodily, vocabulary to express what is essentially an emotional redefinition of each character.

While the male character's body is made livelier, it is more important that his emotions are made so. Darcy's dive is not a revelation of his physical abilities (he can swim!), but rather, it is a revelation of his emotional capabilities. These capabilities could be several: Darcy's dive can be read as an expression of a Romantic bond with nature, a celebration of the home where he can "strip down" to his essential self, a cleansing of social prejudices from his mind, or, as my student so nicely stated, a rebirth of his love for Elizabeth. Darcy's body is obviously not just a body, but a medium of emotional expression. The film need not tamper with Austen's words to tamper with her hero. Indeed, the BBC adaptation rewrites Austen by adding physical self-expression to a character notorious for his inability to express himself verbally. It is not only in the literal, verbal rewriting of Austen, but in the "figurative," visual rewriting that we find the most important changes made to Austen's characters and audience. Darcy's physical actions speak a twentieth-century emotional vocabulary. The visual nature of this new vocabulary presents perhaps the most radical revision of Austen's text: the visual text escapes Austen's verbal control and encourages her audience to interpret it. Is Darcy's dive an expression of his feelings for nature, for home, for society, or for Elizabeth? The viewers are asked to question male emotional expression and provide their own answers. To provide a preliminary answer to my second question then, it seems that added scenes uncover our desire for a specific revision of Austen's heroes. We want masculine emotional display that encourages our interpretation.

Seeing ourselves in the film interpretations serves to reintroduce my third question: how does our modern-day desire for emotional display reconfigure Austen's representation of masculinity? Each film captures a conflict central to Austen's project: the male protagonist's complex attempt to maintain social restraint while evidencing emotional expression. Courtship offers the hero a paradoxical challenge in that he must follow normalizing rules of public behavior in order to create uniquely personal emotional connections. Courtship forces the hero, not only the heroine, to negotiate the demands of a long list of dichotomous behaviors: the private and public, personal and social, physical and mental, emotional and reasonable, sentimental and rational, expressive and repressive. Each film's emphasis on emotional expression upsets Austen's resolution of these dichotomies. The films prematurely resolve rather than heighten these conflicts; masculine emotional display makes the final pairing of hero and heroine obvious, removing the narrative suspense of a relationship hindered by social restraint. By reconfiguring these conflicts and their resolution, the films remove the most interesting challenges Austen places before her male characters. The challenge is not only if the hero will win the heroine, but how he will do so. The hero's educative process may be less obvious than but nonetheless parallel to the heroine's: the hero proves his masculinity by learning to regulate his emotions in accordance with the constraints dictated by a public courtship.

The films endow Austen's courtship romance protagonists with emotional display emphasizing our current notions of "romance" rather than late eighteenth-century understandings of "courtship." A brief consideration of Austen's heroes reveals that masculine emotional restraint, and not display, provides proof of the heroes' worthiness. Fitzwilliam Darcy, Edward Ferrars, Colonel Brandon, Henry Tilney, Edmund Bertram, George Knightley, and Captain Frederick Wentworth each accept specific societal strictures against emotional display. Darcy refuses to make public his role in Lydia's marriage, although it would reveal his continued affection for Elizabeth. Edward refuses to betray his lack of feelings for Lucy Steele and plans to keep his promise to marry her. Brandon restrains his emotions and allows Marianne to display hers by not warning her away from Willoughby. Tilney, Edmund, Knightley, and Wentworth all enjoy extended close social or familial contact with but do not overtly display their love for the female protagonist, evidenced by the fact that each heroine is kept guessing to the very end of the novel as to her prospects for matrimony. In fact, each of these men lectures against or openly critiques his beloved's patterns of emotional display. Each hero equates courtship with emotional restraint and proves his worth by enacting that equation until a climactic event forces an emotional display that, in turn, forces courtship into marriage. For Austen, even this marital reward is characterized by restraint; while the film adaptations of *Emma* and *Persuasion* each end with an emotional, physical kiss, the novels do not indicate any such a display.

The recreation of these heroes as emotionally expressive characters is inconsistent with Austen's character development and, more importantly, is at odds with Austen's own critique of sensibility. The mid-to-late eighteenth-century "cult of sensibility" positioned an emotions-based formation of the male subject against the Enlightenment model of a reason-based male subject. Sensibility has a complex cultural definition in the late eighteenth century but, generally, the individual characterized by sensibility must demonstrate "the faculty for feeling, the capacity for extremely refined emotions and a quickness to display compassion for suffering" as well as "an innate sensitiveness or susceptibility revealing itself in a variety of spontaneous activities such as crying, swooning, and kneeling" (Todd 7). To prove his sensibility, then, the individual must physically display his emotions. The "novel of sensibility" enacts these values by emphasizing the hero's "capacity for refined feeling" (Todd 8), and its male readers are likewise encouraged to express their "cultivation of feeling" and "feelings of delicacy" (Barker-Benfield 145). Central to the novel of sensibility is an emotional display that connects character to reader: sensibility "stops the story to display this feeling in the characters and elicit it in the reader in its physical manifestations of tears and trembling" (Todd 8). It is exactly this valuation of emotional display that Austen wrote against. As critics such as Marilyn Butler make clear, Austen's novels are a conservative reaction against the literature of sensibility and a reassertion of a rational rather than emotional construction of both character and reader (Butler 7-17).

In *Sense and Sensibility* and *Northanger Abbey,* most notably, Austen warns her characters and readers against sensibility's excessive display of emotion. Anne Mellor devotes a chapter to Austen's "rational woman," demonstrating that "Austen portrayed the heroines of her novels, *not* as the women of passionate sensibility" but as "women of *sense*" (52-53). If the "good sense and self-control" (58) of Austen's women embodies the notion of "rational love" (55), certainly their male partners duplicate these qualities. Austen's emotionally extravagant, supporting male characters such as Wickham, Willoughby, John Thorpe, Henry Crawford, Elton, and William Elliot are punished by social censure and a lack of marital fulfillment. If the male protagonist displays a lack of emotional restraint, he is similarly punished but also reformed and ultimately rewarded. While Darcy's first, selfish marriage proposal is met with rejection, his second, more tentative and solicitous proposal meets with success. Brandon tells of his heart-wounding attachment to the sentimental Eliza, but he has conquered these past emotions and can thus help Marianne reorder hers. Edward Ferrars is constrained by a past emotional excess—his engagement to Lucy Steele—and proves his worth by rationally accepting that constraint. Socially-dictated emotional restraint heightens the suspense of masculine development and the suspense of court-ship ordering.

While Austen's male protagonists prove their worth by meeting a de-mand for social restraint, they prove their worth to moviegoers by meeting a demand for emotional display. Both the novels and films enact their respec-tive time periods' visions of the correct balance between emotional display and restraint: Austen's vision of the late eighteenth century favors restraint; the films' vision favors display. The differences between the two could be seen as revealing "what we got wrong about Austen." Instead, I believe the differences reveal how we today use Austen to reveal ourselves to ourselves; at a most basic level, this seems to be exactly how Austen would have wanted her readers to use her. Our revisions of Austen reveal our calculated, if not rational, determination to create "masculine balance" according to our own emotions-based criteria. And yet, our revisions reveal that we continue to look to Austen when we want help in creating our ideas of masculinity.

The material added to Austen's novels by the film adaptations of *Pride and Prejudice* and *Sense and Sensibility* answer Austen's invitation to define "balanced" masculinity. Austen's titles encourage her interpreters to recog-nize the value of equilibrium; society must avoid valuing the extremes of pride and prejudice and sense and sensibility. Her chosen plots create struc-tural unity; the courtship plot's marriage conclusion unites the differences of two into one. And her characters' internal contradictions become harmo-nized; the male and female protagonists engage in a conduct-booklike pro-cess of self-reformation. Yet when seeking to define the "balance" that Austen dictates for today's readers, the idea proves nebulous. As an examination of literary criticism demonstrates, we look to Austen for "balance" while we reconfigure Austen's work to evidence our changing definition of it.

Although literary criticism lauds Austen's novels for achieving many forms of balance, it has not specifically addressed Austen's vision of balanced masculinity. The recent film interpretations fill this gap in literary criticism: the cinematic revisions of Darcy, Edward Ferrars, and Brandon reveal how we in the late twentieth century envision masculinity's reconciliation of so-cial restraint and emotional display. The films demonstrate our rejection of Austen's equation of masculine equilibrium with courtship restraint and evi-dence our insistence that the romance hero attain harmony with himself and the heroine through the expression of emotion. The scenes added to *Pride and Prejudice* and *Sense and Sensibility* cast the male protagonists as individu-als constructed by their emotions. Each is remade as a character of sensibil-ity. In the adaptations of *Pride and Prejudice* and *Sense and Sensibility* of the 1990s, each hero displays his struggle to achieve the emotional expression which will bring him into balance; each demonstrates this struggle by physically displaying the emotions he cannot speak. The films are consistent with the literary criticism in portraying Austen as actively demonstrating the desirability and attainability of balance, yet they recreate the masculine form that Austen's balance takes. The films equate Austen's vision of masculinity with our own.

If we look at these films closely, we can see what we want to see in Austen: a balanced form of masculinity on display. We can also see how her writing unbalances our expectations of masculinity, and we can see how her notions of masculinity are unbalanced by our revisions of her novels.

Finding Literary Balance in Austen

Austen's literary critics have long been interested in her ability to balance competing demands. For example, Ian Watt's monumental *The Rise of the Novel* emphasizes Austen's formal balancing act by positioning her as the literary heir of both Richardson and Fielding. Her "technical genius" is her ability to balance the differing narrative forms of two authors "whose apparent divergences can in fact be harmoniously reconciled" in her writing (Watt 296). She is lauded for her ability "to combine into a harmonious unity the advantages both of realism of presentation and realism of assessment, of the internal and of the external approaches to character" (Watt 297). Similarly, Wayne Booth's *Rhetoric of Fiction* devotes a chapter to *Emma,* exploring Austen's use of narrative distance to balance the reader's judgment of and sympathy for the heroine. On the formal level of authorial voice, Austen "reinforce[s] . . . the double vision" of the reader, ultimately bringing our like and dislike of Emma into alignment through both the structure of narration and the plot of courtship (Booth 256). Austen ultimately unifies these competing demands through the marriage of Knightley and Emma. Their marriage "fulfils every value embodied in the world of the book. . . . It is a union of intelligence; of 'reason,' of 'sense,' of 'judgment.' It is a union of virtue: of 'good will,' of generosity, of unselfishness. It is a union of feeling: of 'taste,' 'tenderness,' 'love,' 'beauty'" (Booth 259). As these brief quotations from Watt and Booth reveal, Austen criticism rests on the foundation of Austen's "balance," "unity," and "harmony."

Austen's critics have located these ideal qualities in her representation of gender. Joseph Boone provides a recent analysis of the formal unity achieved by Austen, emphasizing the balance created between the male and female characters. In a chapter uncovering the desire for "perfect harmony" in the courtship narrative, Boone explores *Pride and Prejudice* and "the feeling of most readers that this union [between Darcy and Elizabeth] *truly* balances the claims of self and society for its protagonists—a rare feat in the history of the marriage tradition" (83, 90). Providing a compelling dissection of the novel's "symmetrically balanced structure" (91), Boone emphasizes the formal perfection of a novel in which the unity between male and female is reflected within the unified plot structure (96). More recently, Glenda A. Hudson argues that Austen's vision of gender relationships "makes a case for balance in male/female relationships" (109). Examining Austen's reliance upon intrafamilial "siblinglike unions" between male and female (101), Hudson contends that "Austen creates an harmonious synthesis of roles and values as a solution to problematic gender politics," and that these "sibships" ultimately create "relatively egalitarian communities" (107-8). According to these critics, Austen achieves a near utopian equation of the sexes. While balance is achieved between gendered subjects, very little is said of the balance which must be located within the masculine subject in order for this larger equation to be achieved.

As Hudson reveals, Austen's feminist critics have adopted the language of "balance," "unity," and "harmony" to suggest that Austen creates a courtship balance between men and women precisely in order to critique her culture's inability to assign these terms to women's relationships with men. Nancy Armstrong's brilliant interrogation of the social contract reveals its reconfiguration as a sexual contract in which men's political and economic control of the public sphere is equalized by women's domestic control of the private sphere. Just as for Watt, Booth, Boone, and Hudson, Armstrong's Austen provides hope that balance is attainable. For Armstrong, Austen's *Emma* presents us with the relationship "between Emma and Knightley, a union that magically stabilizes the community" (153). The novel embodies the hope that "the conflict between male and female did not require the conversion of the one to the other's system of values after all; it simply required finding the right kind of currency to represent what was in the interest of both" (151). This currency is a language of kinship, discovered through reading, which will "set out to discover . . . the private reality underlying *all* social behavior, even that which belonged to the domain of the public and masculine, i.e., political, world" (158). Armstrong's reading of Austen could be seen as utopian; here, Austen imagines a route away from social division and toward a private, feminine form of unity left unrealized by the social contract. The film adaptations can be seen as enacting this twentieth-century vision of Austen: the individual can reveal the personal, emotional reality that underlies all social, publicly defined behavior. In the figure of the emotional male, the filmgoer can, to repeat, "discover . . . the private reality underlying *all* social behavior." The films make Armstrong's reading of Austen a reality.

Like Armstrong, Patricia Meyer Spacks demonstrates that equilibrium between emotional expression and social restraint provides equilibrium between the masculine and feminine spheres. But Spacks complicates Austen's promises of balance by proving Austen's courtship resolution's utopian assertion of unity to be self-consciously fictional. Austen simultaneously "construct[s] fictions of ideological harmony" and "suggest[s] harmony's high costs" (203). In other words, although Austen does resolve her culture's central conflicts—and Spacks provides a list of polar opposites very similar to those we are exploring: "reason/feeling, masculine/feminine, history/romance, desire/control" (203)—Austen also betrays her knowledge that courtship's marriage resolution masks social divides that cannot be so easily bridged. Spacks explains, "The vision of harmony between 'masculine' and 'feminine,' between the drive toward power and toward intimacy" (and I would add here the expression of both social restraint and emotional excess) "allures [Austen] but does not entirely persuade" her (203). Spacks argues that Austen's novels question the harmonies they seem to evidence: "the anomalies of male-female relations in *Sense and Sensibility* raise questions about the nature of society's (and books') harmonious arrangements" (218). While many critics praise Austen for enacting a perfect balance between courtship's form and content, thus convincing her reader that utopian balance is possible, Spacks reveals the strain that underlies Austen's balancing act. This strain points to the inherent impossibility of creating the utopian unity Austen's readers so desperately want.

While Spacks unveils "harmony's high costs" (203) to emphasize the "unfairness" (216) of the female character's powerless position in relation to men, I believe her argument can be applied to the film adaptations' depiction of men. If we accept Spacks's argument, Austen self-consciously reveals the inadequacy of art in its attempt to resolve all dichotomies. And yet, in her very act of writing, Austen also reveals art's unstoppable urge to create resolution. While fiction may only be creating fictions of balance, this activity reveals fiction's need to attempt to locate that balance. Austen's fiction may be self-consciously exploiting a gap in the act of representation which the films can exploit in turn. If Austen's novels rewrite late eighteenth-century reality by self-consciously masking its divisions, the films are similarly rewriting the novels' "reality" by masking the divisions in Austen's writing. If the twentieth-century reader feels an emotional imbalance within Austen's male characters, the films are then doing what all good fiction attempts to do: they are attempting to mask imbalance with balance.

Adding Masculine Balance to Austen: Extra Darcy

In the film adaptation of *Pride and Prejudice,* then, Darcy must be brought into balance. According to the literary critics cited above, this ideal of Austenian balance could take many forms: the film can attempt to maintain narrative unity by translating Austen's authorial voice into a cinematic vocabulary, to maintain formal unity by pushing a more obviously structured courtship plot, to maintain social unity by creating connections between the public and private and by revealing the feminine underlying the masculine, or to maintain a self-reflective fictional unity by revealing Austen's masking and unmasking of reality's imbalance. Ultimately, I believe the 1995 BBC film accomplishes the first three by giving Darcy a new physical vocabulary to express his emotional attraction to Elizabeth. The very addition of this vocabulary reveals the fourth: screenwriter Davies's rewriting of Austen reveals the necessity of masking and unmasking the imbalance between Austen's and the twentieth century's constructions of masculinity.

In Davies's screenplay of *Pride and Prejudice,* Darcy is cast as an awkward hero tortured by an excess of emotions he cannot express. With his tousled dark hair, smoldering eyes that stare deeply into middle space, and a pained self-consciousness in social situations, he is convincingly reimagined as a vaguely Byronic hero. A brooding loner who can neither physically contain nor verbally express his inner emotional battles, Darcy engages in a roster of physical activities that do not appear in the novel but which convey these battles to the viewer. The film's additions envision Darcy playing billiards, bathing, fencing, and swimming. As Darcy's pursuit of Elizabeth becomes more certain, his physical activities are increasingly replaced by meditative stares which, in turn, become increasingly direct; this expression of longing peaks when he spends a tumultuous night pacing back and forth to his window while attempting to write a response to her rejection of his marriage proposal. Darcy's physical activities reveal the violence of his emotions while his longing stares restate his inability to express verbally those emotions. While Darcy displays emotional restraint, he physically displays that which he is restraining. Darcy's physical activities create a cinematic form of self-expression, a dialogue between his mind and body that runs throughout the entire film but is absent from the novel.

Darcy's restraint is one which his emotions place on his emotions, rather than the restraint placed on them by society. Darcy's early responses to Elizabeth emphasize the physical activity of this restraint. One of the first scenes added to Austen's novel occurs when Elizabeth visits Jane at Netherfield. After playing nurse to Jane, Elizabeth comes downstairs and, searching for the Bingley party, walks down a corridor and peeks into a lighted room. She has mistaken the room and awkwardly interrupts Darcy, who is playing a solitary game of billiards. As the startled Darcy jerks up from his game, the film strikingly frames his body between the edge of the billiards table below and the large rectangular chandelier above. His body is visually trapped, just as he is trapped in a face-to-face confrontation with Elizabeth. They exchange no words, and Elizabeth quickly exits. A glower creases Darcy's brow as he turns back to his game and agitatedly sinks a red billiard ball with a loud, violent smack. The intensity of his response is out of order with Elizabeth's interruption, and the viewer is encouraged to ask why. Is Darcy angry at Elizabeth's interruption, signaling his dislike for her? Is he flustered at Elizabeth's interruption, signaling his attraction to her? Is he castigating himself for his inability to speak to Elizabeth? The only conclusion that can be made with any certainty is that Elizabeth provokes an emotional reaction.

Darcy's physical reactions to Elizabeth quickly order themselves into an easily interpreted grammar of emotional signs. In the next fabricated Netherfield scene, Darcy's physicality is emphasized as a complement to Elizabeth's, signaling an emotional connection between the two. The film intercuts images of Darcy taking a bath with images of Elizabeth frolicking with a large dog. Darcy's uninhibited physicality mirrors Elizabeth's. After seeing the naked Darcy being bathed by a servant while lounging and sighing in a large tub, we see Elizabeth walking outside and coming upon a large dog, which she laughs at and immediately starts to chase. This image is interrupted by that of the bathing Darcy, getting out of the tub and being helped into his robe. While still wet and tousled, Darcy peers out the window at Elizabeth, who is tugging at a stick in the dog's mouth. Darcy longingly gazes at Elizabeth for a lengthy space of time. Each character's natural self is revealed; each is removed from his or her constraining societal role, enjoying an unguarded moment and reveling—sighing and laughing—in bodily pleasure. At this early stage in the film, when the novel still has Darcy and Elizabeth bristling at one another, the viewer cannot help but feel that the two are connected both physically and emotionally.

After Elizabeth rejects his marriage proposal, Darcy turns to physical exercise as if to chastise the flesh for its desires. When placed in the context of earlier scenes, this physical behavior can only be an expression of his continuing love and not an exorcising of it. In a most noticeable addition to Austen, Darcy engages in an intense fencing match with his fencing master. He fights with great force and noise, sweating and panting with exertion. After being praised by his master, he turns away with a brooding stare. Looking deep into himself and speaking only to himself, he exclaims, "I shall conquer this." It is obvious that Darcy is expressing his desire to conquer his love for Elizabeth—not, say, to conquer a weakness in his fencing technique.

This emotional dialogue with the self is best expressed by physical exertion. Unlike the film, the novel does not express Darcy's continued emotional struggle; when he and Elizabeth are separated, the reader learns nothing of his thoughts or actions. While the novel leaves the reader, like Elizabeth, uncertain of Darcy's emotions, the BBC adaptation allows no such questioning of the relationship.

These added scenes of masculine physicality are easily equated with their unspoken emotional content: Darcy's growing and continuing love. The film's interest in Darcy's bodily struggle with his emotions is best evidenced by the scene in which he writes a letter responding to Elizabeth's rejection of his first marriage proposal. In the novel, the letter's text is given to the reader after it has been received by Elizabeth; its content is, in effect, voiced by Elizabeth because the reader reads it as Elizabeth reads it. In contrast, the film gives the viewer the text of the letter as Darcy is writing it. The letter is read aloud by Darcy, not Elizabeth. The mental activity of reading is translated into the physical activity of writing. The letter is no longer a symbol of Elizabeth's misinterpretation and reevaluation of the past "text" of Darcy. Rather, the letter becomes a means of showing Darcy's emotional depth and conveying his struggle at self-expression. A quiet scene of silent reading in which the female reader is being persuaded becomes an emotionally charged scene of masculine writing in which the writer argues his case. The activity of letter-writing creates another opportunity for Darcy to express his internal self through external activity—and another opportunity to note that this is how the twentieth century, and not Austen, expresses masculinity.

Immediately after being rejected by Elizabeth, Darcy returns to his aunt Lady Catherine's Rosings Park. He avoids the gathered party and rushes upstairs, breathing heavily and entering his bedroom in an agitated manner. He immediately sits down at his desk and starts to write. After a few sentences, he is overcome by emotion and sets his pen down. He stands up and walks over to the window, deep in thought. The film chooses not to show him composing his letter in a rational, removed fashion, but to display him composing his letter as part of deeply personal, and perhaps cathartic, process of reliving his past. While gazing out of his window, a set of flashback scenes reminds Darcy of his troubled relationship with Wickham, displaying their shared childhood, shared time at school, and Darcy's later pursuit of the nearly-eloped Wickham and his sister, Georgiana. Back at his desk, these flashing images cause Darcy to break off his narrative—the closing of his eyes and leaning back of his head express his overwhelming emotions. The letter-writing scene ends with a disheveled Darcy washing his face and groaning, the implication being that he has been up all night composing his missive. He returns to his room and violently, even painfully, extinguishes his candle with his bare fingers, although the snuff is pointedly lying next to it. His physically torturous night reflects his tortured emotions.

While these scenes are characterized by emotional excess, Darcy's physical actions also demonstrate restraint. Darcy's silent staring out of a window serves as a repeated motif in the movie, becoming a visual shorthand for a retreat into his feelings for Elizabeth. Darcy quite literally turns his back on any gathering to watch Elizabeth come and go at Netherfield, Rosings Park, and Pemberley; he similarly turns his back on any gathering that discusses Elizabeth's charms or faults. He refrains from showing any emotion to the others, yet the viewer can again see this show of physical restraint as an expression of emotion.

Darcy's intense stare becomes more and more interactive over the course of the film, drawing Elizabeth into it. Most strikingly, when Darcy and Elizabeth have reunited at Pemberley, the film collapses together several drawing-room conversations, creating a scene in which Elizabeth helps Georgiana with her piano playing. Darcy stares lovingly at Elizabeth, who overlooks Georgiana at the pianoforte; she raises her head and confidently looks back at him, and they exchange telling smiles. The exchange of looks is interrupted by Caroline Bingley's mention of Elizabeth's family, "Are not the militia removed from Meryton? They must be a great loss to *your* family." The speech repeats Austen's words (*Pride* 269) and adds a cruel mention of Wickham's name, which does not appear in the novel. The remarks discompose Georgiana, but, to Darcy's great admiration, Elizabeth smoothes over the moment and puts Georgiana at ease. Later that evening, after the guests have retired, Darcy takes a candlelit walk back to the music room, leans on a mirrored fireplace, and looks longingly at the pianoforte. A flashback allows him to relive the image of Elizabeth's smiling face. While the essence of Austen's drawing-room conversation has been maintained, the film adds a nonverbal series of glances, smiles, and flashbacks which become the focus of the scene.

The "extra Darcy" presented in these scenes is extra emotion. Darcy's added physical display of emotion provides a radical revision of the masculine balance Austen advocates between personal expression and social restraint. For example, in the film adaptation, Elizabeth's rejection of Darcy's first marriage proposal can be read as a rejection due to his inability to voice his full emotions. Compared with his doting stares, billiard playing, bathing, fencing, and swimming, Darcy's proposal seems restrained; although he expresses his love, he is unable to put his hidden emotions into a verbal vocabulary that matches the intensity of his physical vocabulary. His private desires are held back by public considerations of social inequality. Viewing the film, we feel Elizabeth is right to reject him; he has not given full expression to the depth of the emotions we, the audience, know him to have. In contrast, the novel can be read as constructing the scene according to completely opposite dictates. Darcy's proposal is rejected because he has displayed too much of his emotions rather than too little. Darcy does not show proper courtship restraint and propose according to proper social form; after Elizabeth rejects him, he himself says, "These bitter accusations might have been suppressed, had I with greater policy concealed my struggles, and flattered you into the belief of my being impelled by unqualified, unalloyed inclination. . . . But disguise of every sort is my abhorrence. Nor am I ashamed of the feelings I related" (Austen, *Pride* 192). In contrast to the film, which places the same verbal expression within the context of emotionally charged physical expression, the text positions this verbal expression as an unexpected outburst from a character who has displayed almost no emotion in any form. Austen's Darcy has suddenly displayed too much emotional freedom: he expresses his love openly and then openly states the frustrating barriers his love has overcome. Is Darcy's proposal too expressive, as the novel might have it, or not expressive enough, as the film has it? The answer is both; he exists as both in two different *Pride and Prejudice* texts. Masculine emotional display has been envisioned differently by each; it provides a telling example of how Austen's "balance" has been reformulated and paradoxically maintained by today's audience, an audience that expects masculinity to evidence balance through emotional display.

Adding Masculine Balance to Austen: Extra Edward and Brandon

Betraying the same desire to add twentieth-century emotional substance to Austen's male characters, Thompson's *Sense and Sensibility* makes substantial revisions to the two heroines' suitors by replacing scenes of restraint with those of connection. Edward Ferrars's capacity for emotional expression is emphasized by giving him a new relationship with Elinor's youngest sister, Margaret. In addition to displaying all of the charms of the twentieth-century father, Edward also attempts to display the sensitivity of a twentieth-century husband. In several added scenes, he attempts to, but never quite succeeds in, expressing his love of Elinor. Thompson's Colonel Brandon follows Austen's dictate by creating an awkward, reserved, middle-aged-but-seeming-older man. But Brandon's capacity for emotional display is emphasized by casting him as the unfairly disadvantaged suitor who imitates the actions of his successful rival, Willoughby. Rather than using Brandon's distant reserve as a foil to Willoughby's exuberant sensibility, as the novel does, Thompson's Brandon serves as Willoughby's foil simply by having him do all that Willoughby does, just not so well. Most interestingly, the movie creates a visual logic whereby both Edward and Brandon express affection through metonymic gift exchange. In several added scenes, each gives his beloved physical objects which become his substitute in the courtship. Each suitor's emotions are displayed by the objects they give: Edward gives a handkerchief and atlas; Brandon gives flowers, a pianoforte, and poetry. The film adds a physical language of love in which the exchange of objects from hero to heroine represents the exchange of emotions.

Very early in the film, Edward proves his emotional worth to Elinor by forming a strong paternal bond with Margaret, who has just lost her father. Margaret barely appears in the novel, and she certainly neither provides a proving ground for Edward's emotional capabilities nor presages Edward's emotional connection to the Dashwood family. Yet in the film's memorable, completely fabricated introduction of Edward's character, he proves his extraordinary powers of perception and sympathy by discovering the emotionally distressed Margaret and forming an instant bond with her. Within hours of meeting the Dashwood family, while on a tour of Norland's library, Edward notices movement under a library table and watches as a child reaches out from underneath to pull an atlas under it. He tells the family of Margaret's location, and Elinor then tries to rationally talk Margaret out from under the table. In contrast, Edward sees the situation from the child's perspective and immediately knows that he must appeal to Margaret's emotions rather than to her reasonable understanding of social propriety. Pretending that the child is not there, he appeals to her love of geography by asking Elinor if she knows where the source of the Nile is located. Edward engages Elinor in a playful geography guessing game, which has its desired result: Margaret cannot help but show off her geography expertise—"The source of the Nile is in Abyssinia"—and comes out from under the table to do so (Thompson 44). Edward emotionally connects to Elinor through the figure of Margaret.

The atlas becomes a metonymic reminder of Edward's connection to the Dashwood family, as he has promised to carry the atlas to Margaret once they have moved from Norland to Barton Cottage. The gift of the atlas and the gift of Edward's visit become synonymous; Margaret constantly reminds the audience of their equation by expressing her desire to receive both. It is therefore a great disappointment when the atlas arrives at Barton Cottage, sent by mail and not carried by Edward. The gift is given but it is not physically presented by the person it represents. From this moment on, Elinor questions Edward's emotional connection to her.

The movie tempers Edward's awkward social restraint with his open display of affection for Margaret; his shyness comes not from his inability to express emotion but from his sheepish understanding that he has shown rather too much. After the library scene, the film's next fabricated scene displays Edward and Margaret playing at fencing. Playing on the lawn with fake swords, Edward is teaching Margaret how to lunge when he realizes that Elinor is watching them from her window. Embarrassed to be caught at such child's play, he waves to her, at which point Margaret takes advantage of his distraction and stabs him with her sword. The scene is a very funny addition, but this humor adds emotional elements to Edward's character that are nowhere in the novel: a connection to children, a playful sense of humor, and a display of familial affection. This sense of emotional depth is maintained throughout the next few scenes, as Edward makes several references to playing along with Margaret's fantasy that she will become a pirate and he will serve as her cabin boy. Even in serious conversations with Elinor concerning their hopes for the future, Edward demonstrates his capacity for familial connection by joking that his future will be spent "swabbing" the decks of Margaret's pirate ship (Thompson 50).

The film adds several scenes to the beginning of the novel, fabricating a rich web of emotional connections between Elinor and Edward. Elinor is displayed crying over Marianne's piano-playing of their deceased father's favorite song. Edward comes upon the teary-eyed Elinor and, recognizing her need for support, offers her his handkerchief which she then keeps. Embroidered with Edward's initials, ECF, the handkerchief becomes a physical reminder of Edward's emotional bonds (Thompson 45). Once they are apart, for example, Elinor sits on her bed and gazes longingly at the handkerchief. This simple scene is a major revision of Edward and Elinor's relationship (there are no such symbolic ties), of Edward's capacity for self-expression (he never gives Elinor a personal item), and of the character which the novel positions as the embodiment of "sense" (Elinor never meditates on her emotions for Edward in such an obvious manner). The film gives the hero and heroine a means of expressing emotions that the novel leaves unrepresented. Later in the film, the handkerchief's meaning shifts as Elinor's understanding of Edward's emotions becomes more complex. While speaking with Lucy Steele, and hearing of Lucy's engagement with Edward for the first time, Elinor's fears are confirmed when Lucy pulls out a handkerchief, embroidered with the telltale ECF, to dab her nose. The handkerchief becomes a physical display—and the film has Lucy rather purposefully display this proof of her story—not of Edward's love of Elinor but of Edward's betrayal and love of another (Thompson 126).

These symbols of affection are given further meaning by Edward's many attempts, and failures, to communicate his love; his physical effort at attempting to speak calls attention to the voice he does not have and the emotions he does have. The film creates several scenes in which Edward seems on the verge of avowing his affection to Elinor and in which his emotional struggle is physically represented by verbal inadequacy. Before Elinor leaves Norland, Edward starts to explain his engagement with Lucy, but is interrupted before he can explain his complex emotional position. Edward can only fumble for words; after proclaiming, "There is something of great importance I need . . . to tell you—about—about my education," he stutters, "and there, I—that is to say, he has a—" and is interrupted in midsentence by his sister Fanny (Thompson 60-61). Later, when the Dashwoods have traveled to London, Edward unexpectedly visits Elinor after not having seen her since his departure from Norland. He enters the drawing room and quickly begins to explain his absence, not realizing that Lucy Steele is seated in the rear of the room. He is able only to spit out, "Miss Dashwood, how can I—" before Elinor calls attention to Lucy's presence (Thompson 158). The next words to this fabricated statement are left unspoken, but can easily be surmised as being something like "apologize for myself" or "explain myself." The film wants Edward to express his inexpressible emotions and adds scene upon scene of near-confession. Without adding lengthy soliloquies to Austen's text, the film successfully signals Edward's emotional tumult. When Elinor tells him that Brandon is giving him a parish living, Edward proclaims Elinor his friend and simply says, "Forgive me" (Thompson 171). He does not explain what he is asking forgiveness for, but the audience can assume that he is apologizing for encouraging Elinor's emotions while being engaged to another woman. In their simplicity and forthrightness, these added words signal Edward's inexpressible emotions.

As in Davies's construction of Darcy, Edward's emotions must be displayed but can rarely be expressed verbally. Thompson consistently implements an ingenious strategy of having her heroes attempt and fail at verbal communication (even these attempts are not figured in the novel) while they attempt and succeed at symbolic physical connection. Both Edward's and Brandon's affections are introduced by Thompson's visual grammar of metonymic exchange. While Austen does equate the exchange of physical objects with the exchange of affections in other novels—think of Fanny Price's necklaces in *Mansfield Park*—she does not use this representative strategy in *Pride and Prejudice* or *Sense and Sensibility*. For Thompson, it becomes the primary means by which she can add emotional complexity to Edward and, more obviously, to Brandon. For example, just as Edward's love for Elinor is symbolized by his gifts of the atlas and handkerchief, Brandon's early courtship of Marianne is symbolized by his giving her a knife to cut reeds and, later, a lawnbowling ball at a party. This process of metonymic substitution extends to flowers, a pianoforte, a volume of Spenser's verse, and finally the substitution of Brandon himself for Willoughby.

Colonel Brandon is *Sense and Sensibility*'s figure of emotional restraint,

if only because he wishes to dampen the affections between the two characters of sensibility, Marianne and Willoughby. He is rewarded with the marriage to Marianne precisely because he is this "thing apart" from them: a
rational, reasonable, socially respected, and emotionally reformed man. And
yet the film reconfigures this lover's triangle, making Brandon "a part" of the
emotional communication shared by the other two. As in Austen's novel,
Willoughby represents emotional expression, specifically the false emotional
display of sensibility. Departing from Austen, the film remakes Brandon into
a standard-bearer of true emotion. But, crucially, he must express his honest
emotion through physical displays which mimic the form of sensibility. In
having Brandon mimic the physical shorthand for emotional depth that we
see Willoughby enacting, the film slowly erases the emotional distinctions
between the two. As Willoughby loves Marianne's music, so does Brandon;
as Willoughby brings flowers, so does Brandon; as Willoughby reads poetry,
so does Brandon. The two are no longer opposites but instead parallel one
another.

In the film, Brandon first sees Marianne while she is playing a pianoforte at the home of her mother's cousins, the Middletons. Brandon hears her
singing upon entering the house, is slowly drawn toward the music room,
and comes to rest against the door at the back of the room, gazing in rapture
at the beautiful woman and her beautiful song. In contrast, in the novel,
Brandon has spent the full evening with the family, has been labeled "silent
and grave" and "an absolute old bachelor" (Austen, *Sense* 34), attended to
Marianne's playing as part of the group, and "heard her without being in
raptures" (35). But, as in the BBC characterization of Darcy, his film-created
stare is meant to be read as one of emotional expression: it is love at first
sight, physically displayed but unexpressed verbally. This scene of music-
enhanced love foreshadows another addition at the end of the film, in which
Brandon proves his love by sending Marianne a pianoforte. Although the gift
is addressed to the family, both she and the family read it as a gift sent to her
alone. The letter accompanying the instrument instructs her to learn an enclosed song by the time Brandon returns. Marianne's affection is tested by
this exchange of physical signs of love. She accepts his gift and immediately
begins to practice the requested music; an exchange of marriage vows will
soon follow.

Throughout the film, a series of new scenes makes direct comparisons
between the courtship practices of Willoughby and Brandon. The film forces
Brandon to play the role of a Willoughby-like suitor, a role which he never
approaches in the novel. The day after Marianne has fallen, twisted her ankle,
and been rescued by Willoughby, Brandon comes to the Dashwood cottage
to inquire after her health. He comes bearing a bouquet of flowers, which

Marianne accepts; the flowers are quickly handed over to Elinor and placed in a vase out of Marianne's sight. When Willoughby is on his way up the cottage walk, Brandon is quickly dismissed and Marianne must be reminded to thank him for the flowers. As Brandon walks past Willoughby, he very pointedly notices that Willoughby is carrying a bouquet of flowers to give to Marianne. Willoughby gives Marianne her flowers while noticing that she has been given a bouquet before his. He hands over his bouquet, which is similarly placed in a vase by Elinor but then placed on a ledge by Marianne's side, so that she can continue to gaze at it. Marianne voices a metonymic substitution of the flowers for their bearers that makes her comparison between the two suitors clear: when Willoughby hands her the flowers, she exclaims, "*These* are not from the hothouse," and, "I have always preferred wild flowers!" (Thompson 96). Willoughby is equated with the wildflowers he has brought; his affections seem natural, open, and wildly attractive. Brandon is equated with the hothouse flowers; to Marianne, his emotions feel unnatural and forced, just as the flowers' growth has been "forced" in the stuffy atmosphere of a greenhouse. Brandon is recreated as a demonstrative suitor who equates physical exchange with emotional exchange; in this way the film "forces" him to become a character unnaturally similar to Willoughby. Indeed, he takes on Willoughby's attributes to make obvious the differences between them, demonstrating the varying rates of success with which the same courtship techniques are met.

At the end of the movie, the transformation of Brandon into an emotionally expressive, Willoughby-like character is complete. Most significantly, Brandon rescues Marianne from the rain in a scene that parallels Willoughby's rescue of the rain-drenched Marianne after she twists her ankle. The film's sequence of events completely rewrites Austen's version of Marianne's illness. In the novel, Marianne's illness is the culmination of "[t]wo delightful twilight walks . . . all over the grounds . . . assisted by the still greater imprudence of sitting in her wet shoes and stockings" (Austen, *Sense* 305-6), which exacerbate the symptoms of a "heavy cold" (305). In the film, as soon as she arrives at the Palmers' estate, Marianne is driven by an irrational desire to take a lengthy walk in the rain to see Willoughby's home, yet another instance of Thompson's use of metonymic substitution. She climbs a hill which overlooks Willoughby's rambling Combe Magna (which is geographically impossible in the novel), recites Shakespeare's sonnet 116, and calls Willoughby's name to the distant mansion. When the Palmer group starts to worry about her absence, Brandon searches the grounds for her (including the hothouse!). He returns with the wet and deathly ill Marianne in his arms. Brandon has performed the ultimate metonymic substitution: he has substituted himself for the courtship hero. The elderly, staid, and emotionally repressed Brandon is accepted as a believable substitute for the youthful, vigorous, and emotionally expressive Willoughby.

In this saving of a rain-soaked Marianne, the paralleling of an earlier scene involving Willoughby with the same scene featuring Brandon is used to great effect. This substitution of Brandon for Willoughby is made doubly obvious by the addition of scenes in which Brandon reads poetry to Marianne, a purposeful doubling of Willoughby and Marianne's first meeting in which they recite Shakespeare sonnets to each other. Toward the end of the film, as Marianne recovers, Brandon is displayed reading Book 5 of *The Faerie Queene* aloud to her. The camera lingers on the scene, and, with Brandon sitting with his back to the camera, the viewer is not sure if the figure is Willoughby's or Brandon's. The film encourages the viewer to equate Willoughby and Brandon. The camera slowly circles the couple, revealing Brandon and the growing intimacy between the two as Brandon recites, "For there is nothing lost, but may be found, if sought," and encourages Marianne to find her lost romantic hero in himself (Thompson 187). Marianne asks him if he will come read to her again tomorrow; when he responds, "No—for I must away," Marianne pleads, "You will not stay away long" (Thompson 188). Brandon's transformation into an emotionally expressive hero is complete.

Edward and Brandon have been successfully recast; they are emotionally distant heroes who are transformed into emotionally expressive heroes who are always physically present, if only through the objects that represent them. The characters' desirability is constructed out of a new emotional capacity signaled by physical presence. In contrast to Austen's novel, the film presents Edward and Brandon as potential matches for Elinor and Marianne from their introduction onwards. As the heroes' attempts at emotional display increase, the viewer's desire that they win the sisters' love increases. While each couple's eventual marriage fulfills our twentieth-century notions of balance, this masculine emotional display removes the uncertainty and suspense from Austen's cautionary courtship tales. More important, the film has reconfigured the ideal hero; he is no longer a representative of social restraint but is an embodiment of emotional display.

Concluding Masculine Balance in Austen: Absent Willoughby

Watching these film adaptations, I cannot help but conclude that sensibility has won its battle. The debates that Austen saw herself entering—those between private and public, personal and social, physical and mental, emotional and reasonable, sentimental and rational, expressive and repressive—have today been ceded to the side of the emotional. The qualities Austen sought to mediate against—the personal, physical, emotional, sentimental, and expressive—have been given their strongest allies in the films made from her texts. Perhaps this should not be surprising given the formal demands of the translation from novel to film. The mental experience of reading a novel has been translated into the more emotionally manipulative experience of physically viewing a film. The courtship hero is sympathetic because he expresses the qualities aligned with an emotional construction of the viewer. The audience can feel best for a male who feels. Or, to be more accurate, the audience feels most for a man who struggles to display his feelings.

This conclusion is best evidenced by the film *Sense and Sensibility*'s radical revision of the events surrounding Marianne's illness. In the novel, while Marianne is deathly ill and Elinor waits for the appearance of her mother, Willoughby enters the scene. Austen uses a cliffhanger introduction to his reappearance; in the last sentence of Volume 3, Chapter 7, Elinor is described as hurrying to meet the expected Mrs. Dashwood: "She rushed forwards towards the drawing-room,—she entered it,—and saw only Willoughby" (*Sense* 316). This reappearance of Willoughby is a shock to both Elinor and the reader. This emotional reintroduction of Willoughby leads to the next chapter, in which Willoughby confesses his continued love for Marianne, his loveless marriage, and his libertine actions. His affecting story convinces Elinor of his intention to marry Marianne before his past history precluded him from doing so. Elinor "betray[s] her compassionate emotion" at hearing such a story (*Sense* 329); indeed, the figure of sensibility is able to win the sympathy of the figure of sense. She forgives Willoughby for his abhorrent behavior and continues to meditate upon "his influence over her mind" (*Sense* 333). Emphasizing Willoughby's ability to cause Elinor mental confusion, Austen signals the dangerous power of an emotionally expressive male.

Paradoxically, in a movie that has revised Austen by adding more emotion to her characters, the character who represents that sensibility is cut out: this scene of Willoughby's return and his emotional exchange with Elinor is removed. The disturbing power of Willoughby's emotions are replaced with a reassuring display of Brandon's emotions. The extent to which the twentieth-century audience needs an emotional hero is revealed by the extent to which we must remove an emotional hero who does not prove to be a hero. In Austen's novel, Willoughby's emotional capacity does not lead to a happy union with Marianne but signals the instability of their romance. The movie must show him as a real villain. The film discards Austen's ambiguous scenes proving the danger of Willoughby's emotional power and rehabilitating him in both Elinor's and the reader's minds. In short, the film will not allow Willoughby to do what its heroes cannot do: express his emotions verbally. If Austen's dramatic display of Willoughby were added to the film, his emotional power would again throw into relief the emotional weakness of Edmund and Brandon. The coding of Willoughby's emotional display as "dangerous" would complicate the newly expressive figures of Edward and Brandon.

Thompson obviously thought it best to allow Willoughby to remain a coldly calculating character who abandons Marianne and to avoid complicating his character with proof that he continues to display attractive emotions. Extra Edward and Brandon is not enough; for Austen's novel to appear balanced, Willoughby must be absent. Masculine emotional display must be unambiguously positive. Austen's portrayal of the evil influence of excessive masculine emotional display is removed by the film, proving that it is the valorization of those very emotions that has unbalanced Austen's novels.

Works Cited

Armstrong, Nancy. *Desire and Domestic Fiction: A Political History of the Novel.* New York: Oxford UP, 1987.

Austen, Jane. *Pride and Prejudice.* Ed. R.W. Chapman. Rev. Mary Lascelles. 3d ed. Vol. 2 of *The Novels of Jane Austen.* 6 vols. Oxford: Oxford UP, 1966.

————. *Sense and Sensibility.* Ed. R.W. Chapman. Rev. Mary Lascelles. 3d ed. Vol. 1 of *The Novels of Jane Austen.* 6 vols. Oxford: Oxford UP, 1966.

Barker-Benfield, G.J. *The Culture of Sensibility: Sex and Society in Eighteenth-Century Britain.* Chicago: U of Chicago P, 1992.

Boone, Joseph Allen. *Tradition Counter Tradition: Love and the Form of Fiction.* Chicago: U of Chicago P, 1987.

Booth, Wayne C. *The Rhetoric of Fiction.* 2d ed. Chicago: U of Chicago P, 1983.

Butler, Marilyn. *Jane Austen and the War of Ideas.* Oxford: Oxford UP, 1975.

Hudson, Glenda A. "Consolidated Communities: Masculine and Feminine Values in Jane Austen's Fiction." In *Jane Austen and Discourses of Feminism.* Ed. Devoney Looser. New York: St. Martin's, 1995. 101-14.

Mellor, Anne K. *Romanticism and Gender.* New York: Routledge, 1993.

Menand, Louis. "What Jane Austen Doesn't Tell Us." *New York Review of Books* 1 Feb. 1996: 13-15.

Spacks, Patricia Meyer. *Desire and Truth: Functions of Plot in Eighteenth-Century English Novels.* Chicago: U of Chicago P, 1990.

Thompson, Emma. *The Sense and Sensibility Screenplay and Diaries.* Rev. ed. New York: Newmarket, 1996.

Todd, Janet. *Sensibility: An Introduction.* London: Methuen, 1986.

Watt, Ian. *The Rise of the Novel.* Berkeley: U of California P, 1957.

3

Misrepresenting Jane Austen's Ladies

Revising Texts (and History) to Sell Films

Rebecca Dickson

A consumer's prefatory note to filmmakers: in spite of the dismayed nature of this article, please understand just how much I enjoyed each of the recent Austen-based productions. *Persuasion, Pride and Prejudice, Sense and Sensibility,* and *Emma* are all delightful visual and audio experiences. Beautiful settings, witty and lively dialogue, lovely costumes, clever irony, and more—overall, they are all well done. Directors and screenplay writers, I paid money to watch these movies. If an Austen-based film appeared in theaters, I saw it at least once and later purchased it on video. I even purchased the BBC video of *Pride and Prejudice,* all six volumes of it, for some $100.00. I *like* these films. Allow me to articulate my fervent desire that moviemakers will continue to make such fine films—whenever Hollywood and the BBC make films of this quality, I vow to spend a substantial amount of money on each.

I start with this message because, somewhat obviously, films are a product like anything else sold in our consumer-driven world, and products need markets. Just as obviously, filmmakers must carefully consider what makes a film sell, and selling an Austen-derived film—to producers, production houses, and audiences—is a daunting project for today's screenwriters and directors. Austen's early nineteenth-century culture and our own contemporary Western world are separated by nearly two centuries of continuous social and technological change, which makes her world downright foreign to our own, and Americans do not tend to like foreign films, no matter what language they are in. And while Austen takes some 300 to 450 pages to unfold her story, the typical screenplay is only about 100 pages long; a screenwriter must do a lot of squishing to fit an Austen tale into a two-hour film. On top of these difficulties, the average moviegoer has become a somewhat demanding flicker-brain who expects movement and action to happen quickly on the screen. In Austen, movement and action simply do not happen quickly. The writer and director of an Austen-based film can slow their films down considerably of course (few teenaged boys will choose to check out an Austen-based film, so chase scenes and gory violence are not necessary); still, both writer and director must consider the audience's expectations and sensibilities. Therefore, they will add humor, pull out a few scenes, shift a theme or two.

Therein lies the danger. Shift an element from Austen's novel and a screenplay writer may lose a vital portion of the novel's meaning. The strength of the recent Austen adaptations is that, for the most part, they follow her texts carefully (the BBC/A&E's recent production of *Pride and Prejudice* sticks to Austen's plot like glue, which perhaps explains why, in my opinion, it is the best of all the recent Austen adaptations). But two films stray from Austen's intent with ill effect: Nick Dear and Emma Thompson revised Austen's texts when they wrote their respective screenplays *Persuasion* and *Sense and Sensibility*, and in so doing, they have undermined the quiet feminist force of both works. Austen's muted protofeminist themes were vitally important in her time and still have their use today. It is disappointing that the writers either did not see the effects of their changes or assumed those effects irrelevant. Selling a film cannot be worth the damage done, especially in the case of *Sense and Sensibility*.

The damage done to *Persuasion*, though disappointing, does not ruin the film. In fact, when I emerged from the theater after seeing *Persuasion*, I thought it one of the best films of the year. Amanda Root is perfectly cast as Anne Elliot, and Ciaran Hinds makes a fine Wentworth. Nick Dear and director Roger Michell also present an effective symmetry, both aesthetically and thematically, as the film opens and closes with dialogue and images of the sea. Their presentation of the British Navy is especially noteworthy, given its importance not only to the novel but to Britain when Austen was alive. And the dialogue, cinematography, and costumes all work well.

I like everything about this film, actually, but for the portrayal of Elizabeth Elliot. Actress Phoebe Nicholls is not at fault here—physically she is a believable Elizabeth, and she acts her part well. No, the mistake of Elizabeth Elliot lies with screenplay writer Nick Dear, and the mistake is her heavily exaggerated coarseness. One can see why he translated Elizabeth as he did: it is fun to despise the indolent, carping Elizabeth of the film. Her portrayal is humorous, and exaggerating her selfishness creates a more clear foil for Anne. But Elizabeth's portrayal misleads viewers about the nature of women's roles in the early nineteenth century, the same century that witnessed the beginning of the feminist movement. If one does not understand women's roles of the time, one may overlook the feminist movement's achievements. Dear does not appear to have considered this as he reshaped Elizabeth's character.

Dear's *Persuasion* opens in an elegant room at Kellynch Hall. Sir Walter Elliot, Lady Russell, Mr. Shepherd, Mrs. Clay, and Elizabeth have met to discuss Sir Walter's debts. Most of the people in the room behave with the decorum expected of the gentry: Sir Walter struts about with fine bearing, Mr. Shepherd addresses Sir Walter respectfully, Lady Russell speaks discreetly and modestly, and Mrs. Clay flatters Sir Walter most appropriately. Mrs. Clay and Lady Russell are models of virtue as they perch primly upon their chairs and listen attentively to the gentlemen. Not so with Miss Elizabeth Elliot, the eldest of Sir Walter's daughters, who has been the mistress of Kellynch Hall since age sixteen. She sprawls on her chair with legs stretched out in front of her, somewhat reminiscent of a high-school football player in drag, munching on bonbons. Never mind that gentlemen are in the room, as is Lady Russell, a dignified older woman who has helped to rear Sir Walter's children. And yet there Elizabeth slouches, hovering over her box of chocolates. When she speaks, she does so with her mouth full, and we never see her offer anyone else in the room any sweets. She even sucks her fingers provocatively (presumably she is licking off every morsel of chocolate) and later emits a shrill laugh so unwarranted that the sycophantic Mrs. Clay cannot help but look at her askance. As the others discuss the financial duress that threatens to oust the family from their home, Elizabeth remains disengaged. She only becomes interested in the conversation when Lady Russell presents some figures to help the family retrench; she sits up as her father considers Lady Russell's budget. He scans it, rejects it, then hands it to Elizabeth. Elizabeth gives it a once-over, disgustedly throws it to the floor, glares at Lady Russell, then resumes her slumped position over the bonbons.

Elizabeth's indolent shrillness does not end with the first scene. When we see her later in Bath, she still lounges, she is still indolent, and, during a scene at the dining room table, she becomes surprisingly unpleasant. Elizabeth, Mrs. Clay, Sir Walter, and Anne discuss Mr. Elliot, who has of late been visiting Sir Walter and his entourage. When Anne reports that she has seen Mr. Elliot at Lyme, Elizabeth doubts her report. When Anne maintains she did see him, Elizabeth becomes shrill. "Well, I do not know," she loudly and mysteriously exclaims, "It might have been him, perhaps" (Dear 58). The viewer wonders why she is suddenly angry, but receives no explanation. A few scenes later, the viewer is again confused by Elizabeth's harshness with Anne. Elizabeth sits nervously with her father before their visit to the Dowager Viscountess Dalrymple. As Anne enters the room, Sir Walter requests her presence on their visit to the fine Lady D. Anne is willing to go but is unimpressed with the upcoming outing. Elizabeth flares at this. She angrily shrieks at her sister: "A Viscountess, she is a Viscountess!" She glares at Anne a moment, then adds coldly, "And family" (Dear 64). By this time, the viewer wonders just how emotionally balanced Elizabeth is—in both of these scenes, she appears on the verge of a loud, long fit. The viewer who has read the book is wondering where this shrieking woman has come from, for she does not appear anywhere in Austen's novel.

Informal as our own time is, Elizabeth's behavior would still be considered indelicate in the presence of company; during Austen's time, Elizabeth's actions would certainly draw censure. Never in all of Austen's novels do we watch a young woman act as rudely as does Elizabeth in the first few minutes of Dear's version of *Persuasion*. Not even the silly and impetuous Lydia Bennet of *Pride and Prejudice* slouches in front of visitors or insults a respected friend of the family. Austen's characters always keep their tempers; when they are irritable or out of sorts, they remain in their rooms. Austen's characters disagree in private, never with others present (consider, for example, Lady Catherine de Bourgh's argument with Elizabeth about Mr. Darcy or Mr. Knightley's frequent arguments with Emma—the arguers are always alone).

In Dear's defense, the reader/viewer is supposed to disapprove of Elizabeth. From the first pages of the novel, we are to loathe Sir Walter and to dislike Elizabeth. But we are not to think her an embarrassment to anyone, which Dear's Elizabeth would have been to her family and acquaintances during Austen's time. Austen's Elizabeth is vain, self-involved, and unfeeling toward Anne, but she is not the lolling, loud, and unbalanced social disaster Dear portrays. Indeed, she is quite the opposite:

> Thirteen years had seen her mistress of Kellynch Hall, presiding and directing with a self-possession and decision which could never have given the idea of her being younger than she was. For thirteen years had she been doing the honours, and laying down the domestic law at home, and leading the way to the chaise and four, and walking immediately after Lady Russell out of all the drawing-rooms and dining-rooms in the country. [*Persuasion* 6-7]

Austen tells us later that "Elizabeth was certainly very handsome, with well-bred, elegant manners" (*Persuasion* 140).

Austen's Elizabeth does not match Dear's because he has overlooked what we know of women's history. A nineteenth-century woman born into the gentry would not slouch in a chair and treat her guests rudely. She would not sit with legs splayed out in front of her like a "commoner" with guests present, she would not eat in front of others who were not eating, nor would she speak with her mouth full—whatever she might do in private, she would not act this way with two gentlemen and an older, respected lady present. She did not dare. As Deborah Kaplan tells us, Jane Austen and her friends and relatives complied with early nineteenth-century expectations of women. In general, they were submissive to the wishes of their fathers, husbands, and/or brothers, and always behaved with careful attention to the impressions they made on others (Kaplan 17-61). Ladies of the gentry managed their houses and managed their children; although they did not scrub floors or change diapers, they did supervise such work. If they did their task well, they developed a reputation for capability that was as much achievement as most gentlewomen could hope for (Robinson 190-99). For complex reasons that space will not allow me to discuss fully here, they did not complain about these circumscribed roles; suffice it to say that to complain was considered unseemly and unfeminine, and, more importantly, they received something in return for their dependence on their husbands: social prestige and financial security. There was also the problem of image. When Austen was alive, a woman who did not act in a submissive, domestic manner was assumed to be of a lower social order; therefore, gentlewomen tried to act in a dignified manner that bespoke their cultivated civility. The letters, diaries, and books that thousands of nineteenth-century women left behind suggest that gentlewomen kept their unhappiness about their place in the socioeconomic hierarchy to themselves or discreetly shared complaints with female friends in letters or in private conversations. Women were extremely careful about their social personas; they did not want anyone to describe them as indolent or shrill because indolence and shrillness were associated with the working classes.

A young woman of the gentry risked much in letting down her decorum. Kaplan gives several examples of what happened when a woman of the gentry acted in an unrestrained manner. A girl or woman who was self-willed might be ostracized, as happened with Hester Wheeler, an adolescent acquaintance of the Austen circle. Though the details are sketchy, young Hester had the unfortunate tendency to speak her mind. She was thus considered a social disgrace. To keep her from sullying the characters of good girls, she was sent away to distant relatives (Kaplan 53). Even a noblewoman was vulnerable to censure if she did not follow social rules. Kaplan tells of Lady Frances Honywood, another acquaintance of the Austens, who challenged both her culture's expectations of women and her family's male head. Lady Honywood's son had promised her late husband (his father) to take care of her financially in the manner to which she was accustomed; after his father's death, the son refused to honor his promise. Lady Honywood tried publicly to shame him into helping her financially. She even published an account of how he treated her in hopes that he would attend to her. As a result, she was ostracized from her social circle—she, the daughter of a viscount, the wife of a baronet. No one appeared to sympathize with her: even her daughter was wary of showing regard toward her socially ostracized mother (Kaplan 54-56). Lady Honywood could not get away with unacceptable behavior—no woman of the gentry could. Jane Austen would have known this, as would Elizabeth Elliot; vain and self-involved Elizabeth may be, but she does not push the limits of feminine behavior at any time in the novel.

In portraying Elizabeth as openly shrill, indolent, and self-serving, however humorous she may be, Dear suggests that women faced fewer pressures to conform than they actually did in the early nineteenth century. He implies that women had the freedom to think only of themselves when they did not. This is dismissive of women's achievements later in the century, when they dared to challenge male authority and, ultimately, to win women's suffrage. It took courage for women to step out of the carefully circumscribed roles they had been assigned. If those women had had the room to be socially disgraceful that Dear gives Elizabeth Elliot, their actions would not have been so necessary, so impressive, nor so important.

Dear's presentation of Elizabeth also overshadows the subtle accomplishment of the book: Anne Elliot's and Sophia Croft's quiet espousals of protofeminist opinions. In Austen's lifetime, if a woman embraced the fledgling women's movement, she was quickly labeled as a bluestocking or emotionally unstable. Austen was fully aware of this. Thus she was careful to express her own discontent about women's roles subtly: Sophia Croft mildly but earnestly protests when her brother Captain Wentworth declares that women cannot handle a sea voyage (*Persuasion* 69-70), and Anne quietly but repeatedly points out to Captain Harville that women are not allowed much in their culture (*Persuasion* 232-36). Both women speak respectfully but firmly; both are polite but adamant. Both women defend the capabilities of women and imply frustration with the limitations put upon them. These are protofeminist complaints. Indeed, Anne Elliot's argument with Harville is the most obvious feminist statement in all of Austen's works. That it must come from the meek Anne Elliot, who is self-sacrificing and careful to follow her culture's prescriptions for female behavior, suggests how risky it was to harbor or express feminist thoughts in Austen's time: if a woman wished to voice frustration with the limitations placed on women, she had to do so gently, unostentatiously. Exactly as Austen's Anne Elliot does in *Persuasion*.

But in the nineteenth-century world Dear portrays in his film, this soft-spoken feminist suggestion loses its force, for if Elizabeth has the freedom to be a social disgrace, as Dear suggests, then gentlewomen have the freedom to espouse feminist frustration without censure. Thus Anne's achievement is undermined by the outrageous behavior Elizabeth exhibits throughout the film. Anne's quiet feminism is important, both because it is an early published expression of doubt about male authority and because gentlewomen read Austen: if she quietly complained about women's circumscribed roles, her female readers likely took note.

Presumably Dear thought the film would sell better if it presented a more obnoxious Elizabeth than the novel portrays. Whether a more obnoxious Elizabeth was necessary is hard to say; one would hope that viewers who would want to see an Austen-based film are savvy enough to understand her subtle cues. But what is clear is that Dear thought exaggeration necessary. In his perception, the Elizabeth of the novel, who could run a household admirably but still be self-absorbed and vain, was too subtle for today's filmgoers to vilify. So Dear sharpened the picture, and in so doing, revised not only Austen's texts but key aspects of what we know of women's history.

Given that films are one of the primary educators of the American public (one learns about the Irish problem from *Michael Collins,* about a South American dictator from *Evita,* about the Holocaust from *Schindler's List*), one might as well get a period piece like *Persuasion* correct. It is awfully unfair to ask that directors get the facts straight, but the lessons of human history may still have meaning after all, so directors should perhaps try to be mostly accurate. And who knows? A more subtle presentation of a character like Elizabeth just might train viewers to recognize subtlety.

But Dear's screenplay is considerably more subtle than Emma Thompson's version of *Sense and Sensibility.* Though overall the film is entertaining and visually impressive, I emerged from the theater after seeing *Sense and Sensibility* disappointed. It was not because Emma Thompson was too old for the part or because she and Hugh Grant were mismatched or because Alan Rickman's Colonel Brandon did not seem fit for Kate Winslet's Marianne. No, none of these common complaints bothered me at all. I was instead concerned that I had apparently read the book upside-down, or screenplay writer Emma Thompson did, because Elinor was all wrong. Not in her particulars: Thompson's Elinor is mature, kind, intelligent, and perceptive; she is our Elinor Dashwood, sensible and true. But in the film, Elinor is also repressed. Yes, she is repressed, that late twentieth-century sin against all that is normal in human nature. In this sense, Thompson follows the novel; it is true that Austen's Elinor does not broadcast her feelings. She is dutiful to the expectations of women in the nineteenth century: she controls her anguish when she must leave her family home and her admirer Edward Ferrars; she hides her shock and despair when she learns Edward is engaged to the silly Lucy Steele. She even controls her frustrations with her younger sister

Marianne, who provides the vital lesson of the novel as she transforms from a naive, romantic, overly emotional girl into an adult capable of reason. In Austen's *Sense and Sensibility,* Elinor's self-restraint is an achievement. But in the film, that self-restraint needs correction. Therefore, in Thompson's *Sense and Sensibility,* it is Elinor who transforms and "faces herself," not immature and self-involved Marianne—the exact opposite of what Austen intended.

In order to get an unbiased perception of the film *Sense and Sensibility,* I asked a friend of mine what she thought the film's central point was. This friend is well educated and an avid reader, but she had not read *Sense and Sensibility.* After telling me it was a period piece that depicted the difficulties of romance in the last century, she said the following: "It's about a woman finding a comfort level with her own emotions. She finds something new in herself. She grows up."

This last comment was exactly what I had seen going on in the film, and it had bothered me. I asked who was the woman who had to find a "comfort level" with her emotions, who had to grow up? "Elinor," my friend replied. What did Marianne learn in the film? I asked. "Nothing, except that some men are jerks. Marianne learns a typical lesson about romance, but Elinor learns about herself. She takes care of others until she has to take care of herself, and then her character evolves." Does Marianne's character evolve? "No. Elinor's character evolves. Elinor has to learn to face herself and her emotions."

Such an interpretation comes as a surprise to a viewer who has read the book because Elinor is one of Austen's protagonists who does not need to transform over the course of the novel. Somewhere, somehow in her life previous to the novel, Elinor learned to be responsible, judicious, and compassionate. She is no emotionally excessive Marianne, who must learn that love and life are not nearly as simple as she thinks they are. No, Elinor is complete: she pays attention to others, advises her mother, and helps rear her younger sisters. She falls in love and discovers that her love is already engaged, but there is no lesson involved in that heartbreak; Elinor is already whole. She rarely complains and is careful not to assume she knows answers when she does not. She is suspicious of Willoughby before anyone else is and sees through Lucy Steele. Because of her emotional grounding, she is able to nurse her sister through a dangerous illness. She takes care of herself, and she is able to attend to the needs of others, be they emotional or physical. Even those critics who prefer Marianne's romantic expressiveness must agree that Austen presents Elinor as a complete character who need not change to meet the challenges of plot.

Perhaps this last trait is what concerned Thompson, for today one is supposed to consider oneself first and others later; purportedly, a person who considers others does not get the promotion, does not broker the big deal, does not get the house with the swimming pool. I do not mean to suggest that our own age is more mean-spirited than Austen's age (the early nineteenth century's socioeconomic hierarchy was downright vicious), but our general cultural lessons do seem to be more obviously self-oriented. Thus Elinor is repressed by our standards, and only when she is unrepressed can she receive Austen's reward of a happy marriage; only when she faces her emotions can the film end. This is what modern filmgoers expect from a film: repression must be eradicated in a protagonist, especially if the protagonist is female. Therefore, Thompson has our Elinor break down three times in the film. The film is not about Marianne's epiphany and growing-up process; it is about the importance of not being repressed.

We learn early in the film that talking of one's emotions is admirable. Margaret announces she likes Mrs. Jennings because she "talks about things" (Thompson 74), implying that the Dashwoods do not, which we are to construe as a sign of repression. We also watch Colonel Brandon reprimand Elinor when she complains that her sister "set[s] propriety at naught" and that "Marianne does not approve of hiding her emotions" (Thompson 107). Colonel Brandon disagrees—he thinks Marianne unspoiled. Elinor responds that Marianne is "rather too unspoilt, in my view. The sooner she becomes acquainted with the ways of the world, the better." While in the book Colonel Brandon only begins to remonstrate with Elinor and tell his own story (and then, in an ironic aside, Austen tells us how Marianne would have romanticized such a tale), in the movie, Colonel Brandon gets the final word. He tells Elinor not to wish Marianne to change, which again suggests that Marianne's emotionally excessive character is more acceptable than Elinor's reserved one.

Throughout the film, Marianne is continually after Elinor to express her feelings in regard to Edward Ferrars. When the expressive Marianne learns Edward is engaged to Lucy Steele, she is shocked that Elinor has for months hidden her heartbreak and despair. Marianne demands to know why Elinor did not tell her of Edward's engagement earlier. She asks of Elinor: "Always resignation and acceptance! Always prudence and honour and duty! Elinor, where is your heart?" (Thompson 167). Finally Elinor loses her composure— she speaks harshly and loudly with Marianne, telling her that she does have feelings, enough so that even Marianne would be satisfied. Marianne is stunned; she stands next to the door, hurt and betrayed by her older sister's outburst. We viewers get the feeling that somehow this has been important for Elinor—she needed to express herself as forcefully as she does. We approve when we see her anger and frustration as she snaps at her sister. This, we nod approvingly, is a woman who is moving beyond repression.

This, of course, is very unlike the book, in which Marianne says nothing slighting about "resignation and acceptance . . . prudence and honor and duty." Elinor does admit to Marianne that she has known for some time that Edward was engaged; she explains that she had not complained about it because she had a duty to keep her promise to Lucy. She adds that she also kept silent in order not to upset her family; she explains that she loves not only Edward, but also her mother and sisters, and she "was glad to spare them from knowing how much [she] felt" (Austen, *Sense* 263). It is not that Elinor does not have emotional storms; she does, but she does not broadcast her anguish. Marianne, of course, is astonished to hear that her sister has kept such heartbreak to herself; she also doubts the depth of Elinor's regard. But Elinor convinces her of her deep feelings, and they engage in "tenderest caresses" (264) while Marianne is emphatically apologetic about her own self-centered suffering:

> Oh! Elinor . . . you have made me hate myself for ever.—How barbarous have I been to you!—you, who have been my only comfort, who have borne with me in all my misery, who have seemed to be only suffering for me!—Is this my gratitude!—Is this the only return I can make you?—Because your merit cries out upon myself, I have been trying to do it away. [*Sense* 264]

It is an important scene, for it is the beginning of Marianne's transformation into a person who can think of the feelings of others along with her own.

But Thompson instead convinces us that Elinor needs transforming, for she keeps requiring cathartic outbursts of her. Elinor's second breakdown takes place as Marianne lies ill. Elinor is deeply worried about her sister, for, as he is leaving the doctor says that Elinor should "prepare [her]self" (Thompson 183), we are to assume for Marianne's death. Again we watch Elinor struggle to maintain her composure. She speaks incoherently to Marianne's still form, a speech that is difficult for the viewer to follow: "Marianne, please try—I cannot—I cannot—I cannot do without you. Oh, please, I have tried to bear everything else—I will try—but please, dearest, beloved Marianne, do not leave me alone" (Thompson 184). The scene perplexes the viewer: what exactly is Elinor promising to do for her sister? The novel does not help solve this mystery—Elinor makes no such promise in the novel. She does not need to, for Austen's Elinor does not feel herself repressed or lacking somehow. She has nothing to apologize to Marianne for as her sister hovers near death.

Unlike the film, Austen's novel has little melodrama about Marianne's illness, even when she develops a dangerous fever. Never does Elinor break down; she just sits with her sister until she is well. Elinor is content when her sister improves, but she is too mature and too tired to be instantly ecstatic over Marianne's improvement. Austen's admiration of a character such as Elinor's is obvious as she describes Elinor's state after her sister improves:

> Elinor could not be cheerful. Her joy was of a different kind, and led to anything rather than to gaiety. Marianne restored to life, health, friends, and to her doating mother, was an idea to fill her heart with sensations of exquisite comfort, and expand it in fervent gratitude;—but it led to no outward demonstrations of joy, no words, no smiles. All within Elinor's breast was satisfaction, silent and strong. [*Sense* 315]

Elinor does not allow her emotions to bounce between despair and cheerfulness in a matter of moments; she feels deep, quiet contentment over her sister's survival, not a passing moment of superficial cheer. She handles her emotions carefully. Obviously, she recognizes their volatile nature and does not trifle with them, nor does she allow them to trifle with her. This is a mature, capable woman.

But this same woman must break down once more before her character has "evolved" in the film. This takes place in one of the final scenes. Edward visits Barton Cottage. The Dashwood women have been inadvertently misled: they believe Edward has married his longtime fiancée, Lucy Steele, but it is his brother, Mr. Robert Ferrars, who has married the fun-loving Miss Steele. When finally Elinor understands this, she breaks down into loud, wailing tears in front of Edward, her family, and the movie audience. It is downright embarrassing, for Elinor's is not an attractive cry. It is a miserably pent-up one, one she cannot control, full of snorts and roars. She does eventually break into a smile, but she has to engage in a torrent of sobbing before Thompson allows her that. Presumably many people in the audience are smiling—ah, the strong, reserved woman is broken. Now she can be happy. Now the film can end.

Needless to say, Austen gives Elinor some privacy for her cry. When Austen's Elinor learns Edward Ferrars is an unmarried man, she rushes from the room to cry alone. Austen allows her that dignity. Thompson does not.

Certainly a reserved protagonist is a difficult sell these days. America likes its heroines to have no secrets, and since America's film-consumer base is an influential one, American expectations dictate what heroines will be like, even British ones. But is it not possible that Austen's central theme in *Sense and Sensibility* could be of use to our late twentieth-century world? I am going to say something decidedly unpopular here: I like the plot as presented in the book. Marianne the unrepressed should still have to grow up, not Elinor. I like Elinor as the most mature person in the novel, and—here comes what is bound to be unpopular—I like that she can control herself emotionally. A certain amount of self-restraint in a person is an overlooked quality these days. How refreshing it is to meet someone who does not immediately recount the excruciating details of his or her former substance abuse, recent divorce, expectations for a new relationship, sexual concerns, and work problems. How impressive it is to find a person who, though obviously feeling a mighty amount of emotion, can still think of the needs of others and attend to them. I have long thought that America the Boundary-less could benefit from a few more Elinors; thus my respect for Jane Austen: she condones emotional control.

Elinor obviously feels powerful emotions. As we read the novel, we learn that she conceals her feelings because she does not want to make her family more miserable than they already are. After all, as *Sense and Sensibility* unfolds, the family is dealing with the death of the father and income provider, the loss of their family home, a move into an unfamiliar area, vastly curtailed living expenses, obnoxious neighbors and relations, and several romantic upheavals. Austen's Elinor understands her mother and sisters need a respite from emotional scenes, so she keeps her troubles to herself. But she recognizes her own despair; she cries frequently in the novel (see 182, for example). Although she is alone when she weeps, Elinor is not denying her emotions. But those emotions do not dictate her behavior. Thus, throughout the novel, Austen continually holds up Elinor as a model for women to follow. I have always willingly followed Austen's prompts—Elinor is one of my role models.

Is Elinor repressed? It depends on how one defines repression. If repression means not to recognize or admit to one's own emotions and impulses, this is certainly a bad state. Denial usually fails as a coping strategy. But if repression means to recognize one's emotions and impulses, yet not to allow those emotions to dictate one's actions, well, a film heroine who can repress her emotions a bit might serve our angry, gun-toting populace well.

Thompson's translation of Elinor Dashwood has a surprising antifeminist element to it. Note that it is the strong woman who breaks, not the immature, malleable one. This is confusing, given that when Marianne becomes dangerously ill, we are to attribute her illness partially to her unwillingness to harness her emotional response to Willoughby's treachery. Not only does Elinor break down in Thompson's screenplay, but she also is more dependent on men than Austen's Elinor. Austen created a strong, perceptive Elinor who is a complete creature when we meet her: no man contributes to her maturation; no Willoughby indirectly teaches her the ways of the world (Elinor seems to know about the world's Willoughbys before her sister meets her dashing young man); no Colonel Brandon teaches her about the wonders of a willful nature; no male doctor tells her to prepare herself emotionally for her sister's death. When Thompson offers us an Elinor who must come emotionally unglued in the film, she erases much of Elinor's achievement. The complete Elinor becomes a struggling girl-woman who is shaped by a man's actions. As Susan Morgan tells us, Austen was engaged in a unique project. Unlike most novelists of her day, she pondered the possibility of a woman who is not formed by a man's attentions, by a man's desire for her and sexual attraction to her. Thus we do not find sexual intrigues in Austen's novels. While some critics see this as a fault in Austen's works, I agree with Morgan that the absence of sexual intrigues in Austen's works is important. If sexual attraction is off the page, then a protagonist must grow up on her own without the catalytic penis to prompt her personal evolution (Morgan 352). Elinor somehow grew up all by herself. She became a savvy, capable woman without a father (and basically without a mother). But Thompson makes Elinor more dependent on a man's advice (Colonel Brandon's) and a man's actions (Edward's) in order to make her face herself. Elinor the Capable crumbles. Any viewer who has read the book is disappointed to see that happen.

But facing one's emotions sells, right? Thompson's version of *Sense and Sensibility* has been popular with female audiences. It had a good run at the theaters and is a popular video. In order to sell the film, Thompson shrinks our strong and self-sufficient Elinor into a girl-woman with unexpressed emotions who must learn to demonstrate them. To get a man and to enjoy a happy ending, Thompson's screenplay suggests, a woman must break several times. Now that is a different *Sense and Sensibility* than Jane Austen intended.

Nick Dear and Emma Thompson apparently think subtle, quiet self-sufficiency will only go so far with modern audiences, thus the excessive Elizabeth Elliot and emotionally eruptive Elinor Dashwood of their respective screenplays. Their assumptions leave Austen's muted feminist leanings backstage; indeed, in *Sense and Sensibility,* the protofeminist elements are nearly obliterated. I have a gnawing feeling that this is what sells—the muting of feminist suggestions, even in films made for women. I suppose this reveals much about our late twentieth-century culture: even after nearly two hundred years, any feminism must be carefully packaged if one wants to sell a story.

Works Cited

Austen, Jane. *Persuasion.* Ed. R.W. Chapman. Rev. Mary Lascelles. 3d ed. Vol. 5 of *The Novels of Jane Austen.* 6 vols. Oxford: Oxford UP, 1966.

————. *Sense and Sensibility.* Ed. R.W. Chapman. Rev. Mary Lascelles. 3d ed. Vol. 1 of *The Novels of Jane Austen.* 6 vols. Oxford: Oxford UP, 1966.

Dear, Nick. *Persuasion.* Methuen Film Series. London: Methuen, 1996.

Kaplan, Deborah. *Jane Austen among Women.* Baltimore: Johns Hopkins UP, 1992.

Morgan, Susan. "Why There's No Sex in Jane Austen's Fiction." *Studies in the Novel* 19 (1987): 346-56.

Persuasion. Writer Nick Dear. Director Roger Michell. With Amanda Root and Ciaran Hinds. BBC/WGBH, 1995.

Robinson, Lillian S. *Sex, Class, and Culture.* Bloomington: Indiana UP, 1978.

Sense and Sensibility. Writer Emma Thompson. Director Ang Lee. With Emma Thompson and Hugh Grant. Mirage-Columbia (Sony), 1995.

4

Austen, Class, and the American Market

Carol M. Dole

As each new Jane Austen production reaches the market, culture critics and film reviewers have struggled to understand this sudden fascination with a world nearly two centuries in the past. Widely divergent theories have been proposed for the outpouring of such adaptations on big screen and small in the 1990s.

Film industry watchers point out how easily the novels of a writer who is "her own script editor" can be brought to the screen (Lane, "Jane's World" 108) and note the hunger in some segments of the audience for an alternative to "big-screen explosions and computer wizardry" (Maslin).[1] Among cultural analysts, one set of theorists proposes that we are in search precisely of what we have lost, of a "comforting, orderly world" (James) where a strict system of manners like that operating in Jane Austen's novels might help us avoid being "bewildered by the moral and social universe" (Rothstein).[2] In contrast, many of the filmmakers involved in the Austen projects point to their relevance to today's world: *Sense and Sensibility* screenwriter/star Emma Thompson insists, "people are still concerned with marriage, money, romance, finding a partner" (quoted in Kroll 67), and director Ang Lee asserts that there are restraints today just as in Austen's world (quoted in "Austen Anew").

This variety of opinions suggests that adaptations of Jane Austen's novels hold a mirror up to our own society even while not seeming to do so. Beyond the Empire-style dresses and baronial estates is an inflexible and complex social system that may be more like our own than we can easily acknowledge. This essay will argue that one of Jane Austen's chief fascinations for American audiences in the 1990s is her keen analysis of the vicissitudes of class, a topic which American films in particular have resisted confronting openly.

In *The Imperial Middle,* his 1990 study of class in America, Benjamin DeMott argues that film participates in a myth of classlessness promulgated by American culture at large. Like political speeches and Polish jokes, films engage in the American habit of "talking class while denying explicitly or implicitly that class is meant" in an effort to cope with the national paradox "that they belong to a class society that is nevertheless highly gratified by its egalitarian ideals" (DeMott, *Imperial* 26). Both in his book and in a 1991 article in the *New York Times,* DeMott demonstrates how routinely class barriers are obscured in recent Hollywood films. One method of disposing of class barriers is to demonstrate that "social strata are evanescent and meaningless" ("In Hollywood" 22), as in *Dirty Dancing* (1987), *Pretty in Pink* (1986), and other teen films where a merit-based order replaces the original class lines. Another is to show class boundaries to be easily permeable. In the hit *Working Girl* (1988), for instance, Melanie Griffith is able in just months to shed her Staten Island accent, her working-class boyfriend, and a position in the secretarial pool to take over her boss's position and lover. Likewise, in the 1990 blockbuster *Pretty Woman,* the raucous prostitute played by Julia Roberts is transformed in just days—with the aid of a shopping spree and a lesson in table manners—into a discreet woman who can win a wealthy CEO. In other films, such as *Driving Miss Daisy* (1989) and *Platoon* (1986), class issues are raised only to be dismissed (DeMott, "In Hollywood" 22).

American films, by and large, participate in the national dogma of individual achievement that has helped us remember the name of Horatio Alger long after boys stopped reading his books. This ethic of individualism, combined with our democratic ideals, fosters a myth of classlessness deeply ingrained in our culture. Jane Austen, with her sharp sense of class distinctions and scant tolerance of social climbers, would at first glance seem unlikely to appeal to the mainstream American movie audience. In fact, however, the "notorious instability of her novelistic irony" (Poovey 173) gives Austen's treatment of class a doubleness that makes it uniquely appropriate material for audiences trained to evade their own strong class assumptions.

Jane Austen's novels are very particular about the determinants of class—money most of all, but also landed estates, titles, family position, and inheritance rules—which are essential to their courtship plots. In spite of her almost unparalleled attentiveness to class issues, however, Jane Austen's attitude toward class divisions is notoriously hard to pin down. Depending on the critical winds, it has been easy at different times to see her as altogether apolitical, as clinging to the tradition of a responsible landed class, or as slyly critical of the gender and class divisions of her society. Moreover, as Tony Tanner and other critics have argued, the attitudes embodied in Austen's novels changed over the course of her career, moving from the early vision of a harmonious traditional world represented by Darcy's estate Pemberley, to the implication in *Persuasion* that the old social order had lost its usefulness as a guide to proper behavior. The sheer number of seemingly valid interpretations of Austen's class attitudes produces a flexibility that, together with the doubleness of her ironic tone, allows filmmakers considerable latitude in their own treatments of class in her novels.

This latitude is a boon, for in adapting Austen's novels it is impossible to evade the question of class. True, in some ways the novels are surprisingly silent on these matters: the working class and even household servants are notoriously absent from Austen's domestic fictions, and there is barely a mention of her era's Luddite riots and wars and economic upheavals in the wake of the industrial revolution. Her concern is with a very limited population, described by Raymond Williams as "an acquisitive, high bourgeois society at the point of its most evident interlocking with an agrarian capitalism that is itself mediated by inherited titles and by the making of family names" (115). In spite of her silence on more overtly political events, in the plots of Jane Austen's novels the "complicated interaction of landed and trading capital" forms the "true source of many of the problems of human conduct and valuation, which the personal actions dramatise" (Williams 115). Thus it is impossible for a filmmaker to separate off the courtship plots, and the self-definition they entail, from issues of class.

Recent film adaptations of Jane Austen's novels have taken differing approaches to class, but those approaches correspond quite closely to the nationality of the filmmakers.[3] The solidly British productions take the hardest look at class, while the mainstream American films tend on the surface to ridicule class snobbery but on a deeper level to ratify class divisions.

Persuasion (1995), one of the two recent Austen films that are thoroughly British—with its director (Roger Michell) and screenwriter (Nick Dear) coming from the British theater world and most of its actors drawn from the Royal Shakespeare Company—is the only version to insistently draw attention to class issues.[4] The film provides striking visual testimony to the workings of the British class system. Although like *Sense and Sensibility* and two versions of *Emma* this adaptation is a costume drama, it is the only one that exposes the raw edges of everyday life in Regency England. Even its wealthy characters are shown to have bad teeth and unkempt hair, and to live in poorly lit houses. More significant in our context is that it gives its viewers a glimpse of the working classes that Austen never provides.

The film makes it impossible to ignore the fact that the indolence of the Elliots is purchased by the labor of numerous servants and dependents. As Sir Walter enters his coach for the journey to Bath, close-ups of the assembled servants produce an effect quite opposite to grand parade: their stony faces and gliding eyes invite us to meditate on their likely feelings toward their master, who insists that "a Baronet must be seen to live like a Baronet" (Dear 4), even when deeply in debt. Later, in the Elliots' rooms in Bath, the slouching postures of Sir William and Elizabeth only throw into starker relief the statue-like poses of the menservants arranged against their walls like furniture.

Unlike the novel, the film version of *Persuasion* does not just indict the snobbish Elliots: it also reminds us that even the more likable upper-class characters feed off the labor of others. The hunting scene is less notable for proving our hero to be a good shot than for exposing the purely recreational and rather silly nature of the hunt, as beaters are shown at the labor of producing easy shots for their masters. Likewise, field workers are pictured laboring outside Kellynch Hall as Anne takes her departure (in a pig cart, being "only Anne"), and in the scene of the Musgrove sisters' stroll on the seacoast at Lyme, the presence of fishcutters in the foreground hints that most women are not at similar leisure.

With all these visual reminders of pervasive class differences, *Persuasion* does not, like the more American adaptations of Austen, either erase or belittle concerns about class. Nor does it covertly reinstate class values through the final disposition of the characters. The source material makes it possible to maintain a truly consistent criticism of a class system that imposed harmful barriers. Of all Austen's novels, *Persuasion* is least respectful of class traditions. Indeed, as Tanner has argued, this last complete novel betrays a "crisis of values" in which all traditional forms of authority are undermined, among them any correlation "between social title and social role" (217).

The lampoon of aristocratic snobbery evident in earlier novels, most obviously in *Pride and Prejudice*'s treatment of Lady Catherine de Bourgh, becomes more scathing in *Persuasion* as it turns on the heroine's own sisters and father, who "never took up any book but the Baronetage" (Austen, *Persuasion* 3). More important, the very plot of the novel turns on the heroine's regret about a class-based decision she had made eight years before. Under the advice of her motherly friend Lady Russell, Anne Elliot at 19 had broken an engagement to Frederick Wentworth, a naval officer who "had nothing but himself to recommend him" (*Persuasion* 26). At 27, she does not blame herself or Lady Russell for the decision, but she has realized that Lady Russell was in error and that her own acquiescence had caused her years of unhappiness. *Persuasion* is a novel that endorses marriage for love even when in conflict with prudential considerations, including class. With traditional social values in disarray, class boundaries are called into question, producing a form of class mobility unknown in Austen's earlier novels. Only in this novel is the heroine paired with a hero who does not belong to a landed family, a naval officer who has taken advantage of the Napoleonic Wars to achieve fortune on the basis of his merits without regard to his birth.

Simply by following the novel's plot, then, the film automatically indicts the practice of choosing one's spouse based largely on considerations of

rank and money. To this basic stance, the film adds a twentieth-century egali-
tarianism by making two significant changes to Austen's story in order to
vilify class-conscious characters who are somewhat milder in the original.
Austen's Lady Russell may have somewhat too much "value for rank and
consequence" (*Persuasion* 11), but she is nonetheless a sensible woman who
is deeply concerned about Anne's welfare. In contrast, the Lady Russell in
Nick Dear's screenplay, who pushes Anne to marry her father's heir and tries
to derail an important conversation between Anne and her rediscovered lover,
seems far more concerned with making Anne a prudent match than with
making her happy. Likewise, Anne's cousin and suitor William Elliot is more
nefarious in the film. Austen's Mr. Elliot is capable of marrying in large part
for money (as he did his first wife) or for rank (as he hopes to preserve his
claim to the baronetcy by marrying Anne), but he also acts in part out of a
genuine attraction to Anne. The film makes the class-conscious Mr. Elliot
more of a blackguard, a wastrel who conceals his ruin while trying to repair
his fortunes through marriage.

  Although it received glowing reviews, *Persuasion*—which arrived in
U.S. theaters before *Sense and Sensibility* popularized Austen—was confined
to the art-house circuit and did only modest business. Its criticism of the
British class system may not have deterred Americans from enjoying it, but
the Hollywood tradition (not to mention Merchant-Ivory) has trained mainstream audiences to expect from costume dramas a prettification that *Persuasion* lacks. *Sense and Sensibility* (1995), a more international production that
combined other cultural perspectives with Hollywood gloss, was able to capture both a large audience and recognition at the Academy Awards.

  The wide appeal of this film to American audiences is enabled in part
by its ambiguous treatment of class values, an ambiguity inherent in the
book. In this early novel, Austen is characteristically forthright in condemn-
ing greed and snobbery (most obviously combined in Fanny Dashwood) but
also makes clear that money and rank cannot be ignored. Austen uses the
dichotomy between her two heroines to stress the dangers of either excessive
prudence or, more pointedly, excessive individualism. Marianne's unbridled
desire for Willoughby is more blamable than Elinor's self-denial and even more
dangerous than Willoughby's decision to marry for money, for Marianne's refusal to acknowledge class-related motivations brings her to the brink of death.

  One of the reasons for the success of the film adaptation is the balance
achieved by representing the claims of both sense and sensibility through
assembling filmmakers from diverse backgrounds. British actress Emma
Thompson crafted a script in which class retains its overt role in the plot and
in which prudence is preserved as a positive value. Taiwanese director Ang
Lee, accustomed to depicting the clash of cultural norms and individual de-

sire in films like *The Wedding Banquet* (1993), brought a respect for the importance of social restraints. Producer Lindsay Doran, both a lover of the book and a child of the Hollywood studio system, persuaded Sydney Pollack's production company to undertake the film, thus guaranteeing that the film would be made palatable to American audiences.

For the benefit of audiences unfamiliar with the intricacies of the British class system, *Sense and Sensibility* exaggerates the apparently small class differences between Elinor Dashwood and her lover Edward Ferrars. After all, Americans might wonder, why should Mrs. John Dashwood be so upset at the thought that her brother Edward might marry into the same family as she had? As Emma Thompson crafted the screenplay, executive producer Sydney Pollack insisted that Indianans like himself should be made to understand such basics as "why Elinor and Marianne couldn't just go out and get a job" (quoted in Thompson 265), so the film is careful to demonstrate that there *is* a social distinction between Edward, an eldest son slated to inherit considerable wealth, and Elinor, whose father had been legally enjoined from leaving his daughters any interest in the Norland property. After their father's death displaces them from Norland Park, the film shows the Dashwood sisters enduring at their new home hardships never suggested in the novel: they shiver from the inadequate heat at Barton Cottage and huddle around a table, worrying about the household bills. Whereas in the novel Marianne brought her own "handsome pianoforte" with her to Barton Cottage (Austen, *Sense* 26), in the film she must suffer from the loss of music until her admirer Colonel Brandon searches out an instrument small enough to fit into their tiny parlor.

In spite of this exaggeration of the lovers' difference in financial position, however, in the end, the film underplays the consequences of the class distinctions so important to the novel. Although in the film Elinor does mention that Edward may be unable to marry "a woman of no rank who cannot afford to buy sugar" (Thompson 84), the question of rank becomes rather insubstantial because Thompson omits the character of Lord Morton's daughter, who appears in the novel as the Ferrars family choice for Edward. As for money, foreshortening does the trick. Although the film depicts many earlier episodes at a leisurely pace and (wisely) takes the time to flesh out Austen's rather thin portrayal of Edward, it ends abruptly after Edward makes his declaration to Elinor. She is never given an opportunity even to reply before the scene cuts to the triumphal wedding procession that concludes the film. Gone are Edward's successful attempts to reinstate himself in his mother's graces in order to establish "an income quite sufficient to th[e] wants" of himself and his bride (Austen, *Sense* 374), and the small living that Brandon grants Edward is assumed—unlike in the novel—to be adequate to a family's needs. In the film, prudential problems are magically resolved by a close-up of an emblematic image, the glittering coins that Colonel Brandon tosses into the sky in the final scene. It is raining money—why worry?

Thanks to screenwriter Emma Thompson, who believes that the main question of Austen's novel is "can love survive without money?" (255), the film retains a conversation between Elinor and Marianne suggesting that Willoughby would probably have been unhappy even had he married the woman he loved because, without Miss Grey's fortune, he could not have maintained his expensive habits. However, whereas Austen's novel is imbued with the sense that a competence is necessary to maintain a happy marriage, the film is open as well to the more romantic reading that Love is All. The shot of a brooding Willoughby watching Marianne's wedding from afar, which carries far more visual power than the sisters' earlier conversation, acts as an argument for the primary importance of love. The sheer attractiveness of the youthful actors playing Marianne (Kate Winslet) and Willoughby (Greg Wise) speaks the claim of passion.

While the international group of artists who crafted *Sense and Sensibility* made only minor modifications to accommodate the modern valuation of individualism over social restriction, they did leave the film open to at least the possibility of a reading that denies the validity of class distinctions. They were able to do so because, through its sympathetic portrait of Marianne, Austen's novel recognizes the claims of Romantic individualism. Not so her later *Mansfield Park*.

Of all Austen's completed novels, *Mansfield Park* seems the least likely to yield an enjoyable film adaptation, since "there is scarcely one of our modern pieties that it does not offend" (Trilling 127). Its heroine, Fanny Price, a passive character found by many critics and readers to be priggish as well, proves her moral goodness by refusing to act in a household play. Moreover, the novel's dour tone matches its vision of a society in decline. Mansfield Park, the gracious home of Sir Thomas Bertram, "seems a citadel in a turbulent world" (Poovey 213). It is, however, threatened not only by outside forces—the faulty morality of London as represented by the Crawfords, the threat of financial loss suggested by Sir Thomas's trip to Antigua and exemplified by the ignoble Prices—but by internal problems that have led to the fecklessness of Sir Thomas's heir and the shame of his daughter. In spite of these internal problems,[5] the traditional landed estate provides a worthier exemplum of proper living that any available alternative—as Fanny recognizes in Portsmouth when she longs to leave her parents, avoid Mary Crawford, and return to the Park.

Given the novel's dark tone and charmless heroine, it is hardly surprising that *Mansfield Park* has not joined the wave of direct Austen adaptations for the big screen (so far, there has been only a 1983 BBC miniseries). But the novel has served as a major source for a low-budget independent film that *Newsweek* praised as "an American movie that actually talks about class (a much bigger no-no than sex and violence)" (Ansen 61): Whit Stillman's *Metropolitan* (1990). In spite of excellent reviews and a screenplay that merited an Academy Award nomination, the film never made it out of the arthouse circuit—whether because of its modest production values and lack of stars or because it contained too much frank talk about class for the comfort of mainstream audiences.

Stillman's riff on *Mansfield Park* has rarely been noticed in the corpus of Austen films. Although the film's bright and affectionate satire is more characteristic of Austen's other works, the many allusions to *Mansfield Park* in the film's dialogue mark it as a loose adaptation of Austen's most somber novel.

A study of young members of the Eastern elite, *Metropolitan* has little plot, but its chief characters are borrowed from *Mansfield Park*. Austen's virtuous heroine becomes Audrey Rouget, who is almost as retiring and principled as Fanny Price, whom she likes so much. Tom Townsend, a penniless Princeton student who embodies Fanny's outsider status, plays Edmund to Audrey's Fanny. Like Edmund, he is blinded to Audrey's love by the fascinating but dangerous Serena (read Mary Crawford). Of course he ends up with the better woman.

Whit Stillman borrows Jane Austen's preoccupation with the fate of a threatened class to give structure to his autobiographical examination of America's gentry. His film, set during a debutante ball season in the recent past, features glossy Park Avenue debs and their escorts at a constant round of afterparties where they philosophize about the decline of their class. As Stillman had in real life, his characters suffer what he has termed "mansion syndrome" (quoted in Stanley 9). "Inside the mansion," Stillman explains, "things are safe and nice. . . . If you go outside and try to accomplish something, you have nowhere to go but down" (Stanley 9). This theory is not unlike Austen's portrayal of Mansfield Park as a haven from a dangerous and changing world. But where the ideology of Austen's age encouraged most gentry to live a life of relative leisure and thus allowed for retreat into the mansion, the modern American work ethic demands some public occupation. Most often this takes the form of entry into the marketplace, where capitalist competition becomes more important than pedigree or manners— a hierarchy beginning to emerge in Austen's time. *Metropolitan*'s young socialites have not yet tested themselves against the world, but they worry about the specter of downward mobility. Like the Bertrams, they are imperiled both by the forces of the outside world and by their own internal dissolution: Frank drinks too much, Nick is plagued by drugs, the young women are vulnerable to the sexual predations of Rick Von Slonocker (a baron, Austen's requisite bad aristocrat), and several suffer from neglect by absent fathers.

Like Austen's novels, *Metropolitan* recognizes both the realities of class and the absurdities of over-respect for class, poking fun both at Tom Townsend's socialist dream of classlessness and at his friend Charley's terrors that his elite class is doomed to extinction. And, again like Austen, it makes a case for manners and similar modes of social regulation. Based on his reading of Lionel Trilling, Tom Townsend argues that Jane Austen's condemnation of young people doing a play is "near ridiculous from today's perspective," but the hurtful consequences of a game of "Truth" soon show how right Audrey was to insist, like Fanny, that social proprieties serve a purpose.

Although dissolution of the gentry class threatens in *Metropolitan* as it does in *Mansfield Park,* a genial and forgiving satire reminiscent of early Austen informs the film's look at class. Tom's habit of propounding Fourierism in a tuxedo draws a smile rather than the scorn similar hypocrisies could expect in *Mansfield Park.* Tom's insistence on socialism seems charming because we know he is a "public transportation snob," as his new friend Nick accuses, in large part because he cannot afford a cab. Nor can we take too seriously Charley's insistence that the Upper Haute Bourgeoisie (a name he finds more distinguished than "preppie") is doomed, particularly after a middle-aged WASP he encounters in a bar tells him that some UHBs make it and some do not. Charley rejects any evidence that undermines his theory of class doom, but the older man's observation returns us to a very American belief in individual achievement. Likewise, the film ends by taking its characters down a peg. After a pricey cab ride from Manhattan to the Hamptons, during which Tom confesses to Charley that he has abandoned socialism, the film's final shot is of three UHBs (who have never needed to learn to drive) in a far less privileged position: hitchhiking. The film's protagonists seem to be heading straight for the vicissitudes of DeMott's imperial middle class.

In spite of its uncharacteristically direct discussion of class issues, then, *Metropolitan* ultimately engages in the characteristic American retreat from acknowledging the permanence or final importance of class divisions. Tom, Audrey, and Charley do not ultimately take refuge in the mansion, like Fanny and the Bertrams; they are last glimpsed on the road, with little certainty of where they will end up. More importantly, the film's tone is one of bemusement. Although it respects the painful confusion of these children of privilege, the film also derives most of its comedy from their hyper-consciousness of class standing. Their passionate interest in class theories is, finally, silly—as silly as Tom Townsend's belief that reading Trilling on Austen is better than reading Austen's actual novels, since that way you get the book and what to think of it at the same time.

An Austen novel that invites a similarly humorous take on class assumptions is *Emma,* which has recently inspired three very different adaptations, two American and one British. *Clueless* (1995), Amy Heckerling's farcical spin on Austen's novel, is set in a Beverly Hills high school in the 1990s. In contrast, Douglas McGrath's lighthearted *Emma* (1996) is bedecked with period costumes, picturesque British locations, and all manner of British supporting players. But its roots are nonetheless in Hollywood, with its American star Gwyneth Paltrow (daughter of Blythe Danner and Bruce Paltrow), a Texas-born writer (McGrath again) with a *Saturday Night Live* pedigree, and a studio (Miramax) that consented to the deal so it could snare Paltrow for *The Pallbearer* (Giles 67). Like McGrath's film, the telefilm adapted by award-winning dramatist Andrew Davies and directed by Diarmuid Lawrence is a costume drama, but this British *Emma* (1996) is darker in tone than its rivals and somewhat different in attitude.

Although a British television production seems natural enough given the BBC's history of adapting nineteenth-century novels, on first blush it might appear surprising that not one but two American studios chose to target the most consistently class-conscious of Jane Austen's novels. However, the doubleness of this novel's attitudes toward class meshes perfectly with contradictory American attitudes, which combine the rhetoric of equality with the practice of social stratification based on education, income, race, and ethnicity.

On its most obvious level, Austen's *Emma* is a witty satire whose chief target is snobbery. It features the usual Austen suspects—in this novel it is the vulgar Eltons who are ridiculed for their sense of superiority—but also takes the finer risk of investing its own heroine with seriously problematic attitudes toward class. Emma is perfectly capable of declaring the yeomanry to be "precisely the order of people with whom I feel I can have nothing to do" (Austen, *Emma* 29) or of being insulted that the vicar of Highbury should have "the arrogance to raise his eyes to her" in a proposal of marriage (135). One of the most important lessons Emma must learn in the novel is the error of her own false sense of class superiority.

Accompanying the novel's attack on snobbery, however, is an underlying attitude that class distinctions are proper and even beneficial. The novel's most famous scene, the climactic Box Hill episode where Emma pokes fun at an impoverished gentlewoman, provides an occasion for Mr. Knightley to school Emma about class proprieties:

> How could you be so unfeeling to Miss Bates? How could you be
> so insolent in your wit to a woman of her character, age, and
> situation? . . . Were she a woman of fortune, . . . I would not

quarrel with you for any liberties of manner. Were she your equal
in situation—but, Emma, consider how far this is from being the
case. She is poor; she has sunk from the comforts she was born
to. . . . (Austen, *Emma* 374-75)

If the righteous Mr. Knightley's advocacy of *noblesse oblige* suggests a conservative attitude toward class, so too does the final disposition of the characters.
The novel's happy ending involves each character's marrying another of similar
status: Knightley and Emma belong to the most elevated families in the country; Harriet, financially secure but illegitimate, is matched with the prosperous
farmer Robert Martin; Frank Churchill marries a woman whose family has lost
its money but who has been raised to an elegance like his own.

　　Intimate relationships other than marriage are also seen to properly
take place within class boundaries. One of the primary lessons that Emma
must learn by the end of the novel is that "[b]irth, abilities, and education"
had marked Jane Fairfax, not Harriet Smith, as the proper associate for her,
and that the friendship with the right class of woman would have "spared
[her] from every pain which pressed on her now" (Austen, *Emma* 421). Much
of that pain springs from her failure to bow to Mr. Knightley's insistence that
her protégée Harriet Smith had no claims "either of birth, nature or education, to any connection higher than Robert Martin" (*Emma* 61)—a lesson
borne out by the discovery that Harriet is the illegitimate daughter not of a
gentleman, as Emma had insisted, but of a tradesman. Harriet's eventual engagement to Martin is seen to rightly draw her away from Hartfield, "which
was not to be regretted.—The intimacy between her and Emma must sink;
their friendship must change into a calmer sort of goodwill; and, fortunately,
what ought to be, and must be, seemed already beginning, and in the most
gradual, natural manner" (*Emma* 482). The ambiguous voice of this passage,
as Mark Parker has pointed out, allows for multiple interpretations:

　　　Emma can generate two readings of class: a progressive one, which
　　　emphasizes the insidious workings of class in Emma's disposal of
　　　Harriet; and a reactionary one, which sees and accepts this work-
　　　ing as part of the price of social stability. Each reading turns on
　　　assumptions about the narrative voice: whether it is silently in-
　　　dignant . . . or simply complicit. [358-59]

The disposal of Harriet and similar passages in *Emma* have provided persua-
sive evidence for critics who regard Austen as "ultimately an apologist for the
landed classes" (Tobin 425). Of all Austen's novels, perhaps, *Emma* is most
open to strongly divergent readings of class.

Both American film versions of *Emma* take full advantage of the slipperiness of Austen's text in devising approaches that will both pay tribute to our ideology of classlessness and reinforce the class structures on which we implicitly rely.

McGrath's *Emma* attacks class notions through humor of a different order from Austen's, with an "anachronistic snap bordering on irreverence" (Maslin). His film winks at the silly class notions of these folks, and he is not afraid to underline his point with a sight gag. When Harriet visits the poor with Emma, the visit degenerates into comic shtick, with Harriet knocking down baskets and bumbling over the food. When Knightley explains that he just wants to stay "here where it's cozy," the camera pulls around to reveal that his snuggery is an enormous manor. As Anthony Lane observes, the director seems to have decided that the "hierarchies of Highbury life are a complete joke" ("Dumbing" 76). Little effort is made to communicate the pressures of rank on interpersonal relations. Some reactions are elided— Emma's indignation in the novel that Elton would aspire to her becomes in the film dislike born of shame for her own error—and most are made to seem simply Emma's silliness, as when she insists the Coles are beneath her while pining ostentatiously for an invitation to their party. Since the gradations of rank remain largely unexplained, any character's attention to those gradations seems foolish snobbery.

The film's *mise-en-scène* also undercuts hierarchies. Pairs of characters, regardless of their rank relationships, are routinely positioned within the frame in a lateral configuration so that neither figure is dominant. Harriet and Emma are repeatedly shown seated on opposite sides of the fireplace, or walking side by side toward the camera; Knightley and Emma, or Elton and Emma, are often captured in two-shots. Since Harriet bows her head into Emma's lap in one scene, Emma must make a similar gesture in another. Doorways, window seats, and other symmetrical backdrops further emphasize the symmetry of the characters' positioning. This relentlessly symmetrical composition visually reinforces the film's egalitarian views.

Although most of the plot remains intact, the film erases what may be the most problematic passage of the novel: Emma's final disposal of Harriet as a friend. In McGrath's version, the estrangement between the two women is fleeting; when Emma's announcement of her engagement is seen in dumb show through a window, Harriet appears to rush out of the room, but the very next scene has the two warmly reuniting over the news of Harriet's own engagement. The sequence ends with an embrace, then cuts to the closing wedding scene, where Harriet is one of the few friends that Emma kisses as she leaves the church. Nothing in this version suggests that difference in rank will ultimately separate the two women or that Emma should instead have chosen Jane Fairfax as a friend. Indeed, the gap between Mr. and Mrs. Knightley and Mr. and Mrs. Martin is narrowed by the costuming of Martin more as gentleman than as laborer and by Knightley's declaration that Martin is "a good friend."[6]

And yet, in spite of its egalitarian tone, the film reinscribes class values as well. For one thing, its source material necessitates that class boundaries will prevail. Unless it is to diverge sharply from the book—never a safe venture when one is adapting a literary classic—the film must end with all of the characters finding mates within their own classes. But in addition the filmmakers evoke imbedded American reverence for the appurtenances of upper-class life. The film's cinematographers and set decorators fill the screen with gleaming furniture, graceful white tents on spacious green lawns, and "bowers of suspiciously rosy apples" (Lane, "Dumbing" 76), further idealizing a locale of imposing manors and picturesque views. Out of doors, the perpetual sunshine invites sleeveless frocks year-round, except when a veil of snow is needed to complete the Christmas cheer; indoors, fires give a golden glow to dinner tables heaped with silver and delicacies—tables that, as Gertrude Himmelfarb observes, are "far too lavish for the squirearchy of a small town like Highbury" (75). In spite of its raillery of the class system that produces these privileged people, the film's seductive spectacularizing of upper-class luxuries works to endorse such a system. Moreover, the filmmakers obscure the human cost of such luxuries; unlike the British film *Persuasion,* this American film makes almost invisible the working-class labor that produces this world of leisure. Tea tables with silver services seem magically to appear on the lawn without human intervention, and even the Box Hill picnic admits only a fringe of servants glimpsed in long shot.

The contrast between McGrath's visualization of the Box Hill picnic and that in the British telefilm *Emma* is revealing. Whereas the American version barely acknowledges the necessity of servants to produce an elaborate meal far from the road, the Lawrence/Davies telefilm points up the realities of such an outing. Servants are shown clinging to the outside of a lumbering cart full of hampers and other requisites, and a dramatic shot captures them struggling up the hill with chair and tables for their masters' comfort. The film even allows us to glimpse the contrast between the servants' simple meal and the gentry's bountiful platters of food, snowy tablecloths, and stemmed glasses.

The Box Hill sequence is typical of the British adaptation of *Emma.* The British telefilm provides constant visual reminders of the number of workers needed to sustain the leisure of its principal characters. Transitions between scenes characteristically turn on the movement of servants bringing in letters or opening doors or unpacking luggage. While Emma and Harriet chat, two

maids silently attend to the ladies' hair. Although most often the visual depictions of servants seem casual, at times they can be pointed: a bewigged
servant is seen repeatedly stooping to move Mrs. Elton's knee cushion to
each strawberry plant even while she rhapsodizes about the delight she takes
in the "simple and natural" act of gathering the fruit for herself.

Reminders of Highbury's class divisions are scattered throughout the
British *Emma*, testament to screenwriter Davies's interest in what he has called
"the fears and evasions of the aristocracy and gentry, living in such close
proximity to the great unwashed" (quoted in Birtwistle and Conklin 13). En
route to Miss Taylor's wedding, the Woodhouse carriage passes squalid cottages that house large families. The film begins and ends with thieves breaking into Mr. Woodhouse's chicken coop, a reminder that hunger, and the
violence it breeds, are abroad in the land.

But the effect of the film's depictions of the lower classes is more one of
providing "social context" than one of pillorying the characters for the era's
class divisions (Davies, quoted in Birtwistle and Conklin 13). Whereas *Persuasion* invited the audience to identify with servants and laborers by featuring them in close-up and implying their dissatisfactions, this *Emma* takes a
more neutral approach, making us aware of the presence of the lower classes
through full or long shots but never allowing them subjectivity. The film
even minimizes its own exposure of poverty. The squalid cottages' momen-
tary appearance on-screen is undercut by competition from the credit titles
and by a recurrent underbeat of the sprightly music that accompanies the
entire wedding sequence. Nor do we see the inside of such a cottage since
Emma's visit to the poor is eliminated from this adaptation. The chicken-
theft scenes, with their strutting cocks and stolen hens, invite an alternative
comic reading through their positioning near marriage/engagement sequences,
especially in light of Mr. Woodhouse's lament that he has lost "six good hens
and now Miss Taylor." And although during production the director asked
the food stylist to create a dramatic difference between the servants' food and
the gentry's at the Box Hill picnic (Birtwistle and Conklin 44), the more
rustic lunch is barely discernible in a fleeting long shot.

This downplaying of the darker side of the early nineteenth-century
class system is necessary given the imperative to present Emma as "faultless
in spite of all her faults" (Austen, *Emma* 433) to an audience schooled to
more egalitarian notions (whether practiced or not). Davies and Lawrence
thus opt for what Parker termed the "progressive" reading of class in this
ambiguous novel: not only Emma's snobbery but also her value for rank
distinctions are presented as flaws she must renounce before her marriage
with Knightley.

The invented scene that closes the film, the harvest supper, presents a fantasy of genial class intermingling that has no precedent in Austen's novels. After a lyrical scene of workers bringing in the harvest while children scamper among sheaves of hay, Knightley's tenants are invited to mingle with the gentry at a bountiful banquet. The impossible Mrs. Elton, whose snobbery in the novel is considerably magnified in this film, serves as scapegoat by so unattractively embodying Emma's erstwhile class attitudes: we are meant to despise her when she complains, "Are we to sit down with hobbledehoys?" even while smiling down on the arriving workers. In contrast, Emma herself very publicly seeks an introduction to Robert Martin—a moment underlined by a sudden silence on the soundtrack—even though Martin's costuming and inarticulateness in this film clearly differentiate him from the "gentlemen." Emma's new willingness to cross class boundaries is dramatized in the dance that concludes the sequence. Although the segregated seating at the meal had been in accordance with the class habits of the time, the dance of the three newly engaged couples flouts historical accuracy in favor of an image of class harmony.

The British film, then, joins the American one in criticizing class prejudices and in retaining our sympathy for Emma by implying the continuation of her friendship with Harriet across class barriers. However, the British version does not engage in the doubleness of the American version. In contrast to McGrath's film, Lawrence's telefilm neither glorifies class privilege nor ignores its price. Although the rich folk of Highbury are seen to live in enormous houses, the labor needed to maintain those houses is everywhere apparent. Without losing the good humor of Austen's novel, this twentieth-century adaptation quietly recognizes the human cost of maintaining the social arrangements she depicts.

As many critics have noted, Amy Heckerling's less overtly faithful rendition of *Emma* actually achieves a satirical edge that brings it much closer than the other adaptations to the spirit of Austen's novel. Heckerling cut free of her source so completely that most of the theatrical audience for *Clueless*— which was marketed for teenaged girls but became a sleeper hit (Weinraub)— had no idea that the film had any relation to Jane Austen.[7] Although the only overt reference to its source is a single character's name (Elton), *Clueless* takes its characters and plot almost directly from Austen but at the same time transforms Austen's world so thoroughly that it achieves a satire perfectly attuned to our times.

Both the film's general setting, Beverly Hills, and its specific setting, a public high school, offer rich opportunities for class-based satire. The target of the general setting is conspicuous consumption. All the characters seem to live in mansions and own hot cars, whether they have a driver's license or not. The satire is broad to the point of being farcical. Cher, the glamorous fifteen-year-old equivalent of Emma, sees no reason to learn to park a car since "everywhere you go, you've got valet." She is motherless due to a tragedy during "a routine liposuction." This skewering of the moneyed classes, however good-natured, is characteristic of the American privileging of middle-class values that DeMott describes. At the same time, it is akin to Austen's ridicule of the pretensions of the Eltons and of Emma's own excesses.

Counteracting this broad satire, however, is an admission of the existence of distinct classes in modern American culture. But like some other American films that address class issues—such as John Hughes's *Pretty in Pink* or *The Breakfast Club* (1985)—the examination of class in *Clueless* uses a high school setting to disguise its operations. In reality, public high schools give many Americans one of their few opportunities of associating closely with people of different classes—unlike the workplace, where managers are hardly encouraged to eat lunch with maintenance workers—but popular culture treatments of high school social stratification tend to disguise class as clique. Economic forces and ethnic or racial divisions are mystified, as these cliques are reputed to be based on style or interest. Cher shows her awareness of the vital importance of this hidden class system as she introduces Tai, the transfer student she has taken under her wing as Emma took Harriet, to the school's cliques: Alaina's group, who think only about the TV station; the "Persian Mafia," who all drive BMWs; the popular boys (the only acceptable high school boys for a friend of Cher's to date); and the "Loadies," drug-users and class-cutters that "no respectable girl actually dates."

Clueless is, then, able to provide a corollary to the complex hierarchies of Highbury, with similar prohibitions against crossing class lines to form intimate relationships. But any discomfort with suggesting that America at large has so rigid a class system is done away with, not only through the assumption that this culture is confined to teenagers, but through changing class markers. The racial divisions that are so deeply imbricated in our class hierarchies are barely evident at Bronson Alcott High School. Cher and Dionne, white and black best friends, are almost interchangeable: both are extremely popular, both live in enormous mansions, both are bad drivers, both dress to the hilt, and both, as Cher explains, are "named after great singers of the past who now do infomercials." True, Dionne's boyfriend is African American— an unspoken admission that the rules for sexual relationships might be more stringent than for other friendships—but he is also one of the aristocrats of the school, one of the "popular boys." The only hint of classification by race or ethnicity comes from the dark hair and the moniker of the "Persian Mafia"—a group implied to be not Americans at all, and thus outside the American class system.

The film also works to erase one of the most fundamental determinants of status in America: economics. This erasure is most evident in the treatment of Tai and Travis, the film's equivalents of Harriet Smith and Robert Martin. Tai arrives at her new school bearing some of the markers of a lower class—a New York accent, flannel shirts, and a generally unsophisticated effect. Her style of dress might suggest that she lacks the economic resources to buy the sort of vast designer wardrobe that Cher and Dionne sport, but in the film, her propensity for flannel is used only as a visual indicator that she is a natural Loadie. Her constant questions about where she can get drugs seem naturally to affiliate her with the Loadies, who dress the same way she does. Tai is quickly marked as a match for Travis, the most prominent of the Loadies, not only by their mutual interest in flannel and drugs, but by a shared love of Marvin the Martian and a common propensity to tumble down stairs. No hint is ever given of the economic status of either; their houses are not shown, and money is never discussed.

When Cher resolves to transform Tai into a popular girl (the high school's upper class), she first warns her to stay away from Loadies like Travis and then performs a makeover on Harriet. Cher is shown snipping at her own clothes to come up with a chic outfit for Tai, but after that first day, Tai is well stocked with stylish outfits as if by miracle—there is no transformative shopping trip à la *Pretty Woman,* because such a shopping trip would necessitate attention to economics. Under Cher's tutelage, Tai, with the advantage of mysterious origins, slips through the class barrier. But she is still not acceptable to Elton, who when Cher reveals her plan to match them, exclaims much like his namesake, "Why would I go with Tai? . . . Don't you know who my father is? . . . Me and Tai, we don't make sense. Me and you—that makes sense." The parallel episode in Austen's novel functions to reveal both Emma's snobbery and Elton's indelicate class ambitions; this version is used to condemn snobbery on anyone's part and to belittle Elton's undemocratic insistence on dating/marrying into his own class.

Although in Cher's outcry against such snobbery the film pays lip service to free movement across classes, it nonetheless reinscribes Austen's maintenance of class boundaries by final couplings based directly on those in *Emma.* Heckerling made major changes to Austen's plot by writing out Jane Fairfax, making the Frank Churchill character gay, and introducing Dionne and her boyfriend Murray, so she could certainly have changed Tai's final partner to someone other than Travis. Instead, she justifies their coupling by invoking one of the few widely accepted class dividers in America (one also important to Austen): intelligence/education. The one place Cher had failed in her makeover of Tai was in improving her vocabulary. Although Cher's own idea of intellectual stimulation is reading *Fit or Fat,* she is impressively articulate and is able to correct Josh's pretentious girlfriend on a point in

Shakespeare (albeit thanks to her fascination with Mel Gibson). The natural intelligence that shines through her mall-obsessed ignorance marks Cher as a worthy partner for Josh (the Knightley character), a college student given to reading Nietzsche. IQ also demands the coupling of Tai and Travis; she cannot multiply seven times seven and he cannot recall how many steps are in his twelve-step program.

Even though it maintains a class system, *Clueless* asserts an American faith in class mobility nowhere suggested in Jane Austen's book. Travis and Tai may be destined for each other by class background, but neither is left to wallow among the Loadies. Travis's expertise at skateboarding gives him a claim to Cher's attention—in the tradition of *Dirty Dancing*—and his twelve-step program frees him from the drugs that ostensibly defined his lower-class group. Tai's obsession with drugs inexplicably disappears, and she wins popularity on her own terms through her notoriety after an attack in the mall. Most significantly, although they have a temporary estrangement Cher does not drop Tai the way Emma drops Harriet in the novel. The final scene at the teachers' wedding provides an egalitarian view of Dionne and Murray, Cher and Josh, Travis and Tai seated together at a table dressed in their best. Costuming points to some differences in class level—Tai wears a blue dress that does not rival Cher's and Dionne's slicker pink outfits, and Travis sports a T-shirt under his black tie—but the character proxemics testify that they are indeed equals.

Both American film adaptations of *Emma,* then, take advantage of the double readings enabled by Jane Austen's irony in order to simultaneously deny and reinscribe class strictures—a doubleness that characterizes all of the American adaptations of Austen's novels. To differing degrees, *Clueless, Metropolitan,* and McGrath's *Emma* all deny class restrictions in a manner consistent with DeMott's analysis of the American myth of classlessness. The cross-class friendships in these films suggest class boundaries to be permeable, and the doctrine of individual achievement that underlies the updated adaptations corresponds to the American ethic of self-determination. Moreover, all three films use humor to belittle as snobs any characters who betray their awareness of usually unspoken class divisions, thus invalidating class talk.[8]

At the same time that they deny the efficacy of class barriers, however, these American films aestheticize the upper-class lifestyle in a manner consistent with the American ethic of achievement but not with its myth of classlessness. In doing so, they form a contrast to the more British adaptations of Austen's novels. The Michell/Dear *Persuasion,* with its critical examination of class exploitation and its refusal to prettify the lives of the gentry, not only echoes but emphasizes the novel's questioning of rigid class divisions. The Lawrence/Davies *Emma* interprets Austen's novel as progressive in its class attitudes, and does so without undermining its own message through a mindless celebration of upper-class life. With its mixed cultural influences, the Lee/Thompson *Sense and Sensibility* gives serious consideration to class-linked social restrictions before magically erasing them in its final scenes. In the end, however, that film too adheres to DeMott's dictum for American films ("In Hollywood" 22): "Class dismissed."

Notes

1. Louis Menand additionally points out that the Austen films provide much needed roles for women, and Fay Weldon notes that "Austen is not expensive to make" (15).
2. Rothstein sees a parallel between the Austen craze and contemporaneous phenomena such as the best-seller status of William Bennett's pedagogical tales and the importance of "family values" in recent political debates, all of which suggest a longing for manners. Evan Thomas makes a similar argument. Elayne Rapping suggests that "a world in which there were rules of conduct, rules of morality, rules of virtue and character" can be particularly attractive to today's young women because of its promise that "once one mastered and followed those rules, one would . . . be rewarded with love, fulfillment, security, and peace of mind" (37)—which can look very appealing in contrast to the "rocky" (38) life of women in the postfeminist age. Other commentators object to this valorization of a more decorous age. *Forbes* editor Susan Lee points out "all the hypocrisy those good manners concealed," and insists that the "quiet acceptance required of Austen's heroines is rather repellent." British writer Martin Amis notes that some of the Austen fever in his own country is "a blend of disembodied snobbery and vague postimperial tristesse" (32).
3. My study is confined to feature-film length adaptations only, whether released to theaters or televised. Director Diarmuid Lawrence's *Emma* is a telefilm; the 1995 *Persuasion* was telecast in England but first released in the United States as a 103-minute theatrical film; all the other adaptations I discuss are theatrical releases. I have not included the miniseries productions, since their greater length invites the inclusion of details that other adaptations omit and thus makes a valid comparison more difficult.
4. Although *Persuasion* was co-sponsored by a public television affiliate in the United States, I class it as British based on its BBC production and its British creators and actors. Likewise, I categorize Lawrence's *Emma* as British because of the nationality of its cast and creative team, in spite of the fact that this British ITV television production received some of its financing from the American A&E network.
5. Actually, the landed estate is even less viable than it appears since Sir Thomas's economic power relies on his holdings in Antigua, and the "illusion of traditional paternalism" cannot be sustained by the Caribbean "plantation economy, in which both land and labor were fully commodified" (Stewart 26).

6. This term has more implication of egalitarian intimacy than Knightley's explanation in the novel: "[Martin] knows I have a thorough regard for him and all
   his family, and, I believe, considers me as one of his best friends" (Austen,
   Emma 59).
7. Ironically, the video of the more overtly faithful McGrath film of *Emma* was
   marketed not as a Jane Austen adaptation but as "a lighthearted comedy . . .
   based on the story that inspired the hit movie *Clueless!*" (video cover).
8. This statement might seem inapplicable to *Metropolitan* since its characters repeatedly discuss class. However, the film to some extent undermines such talk
   by poking fun at the earnest cluelessness of the speakers. Stillman slyly shows
   he knows the rules of class obfuscation in American film by having Charley,
   who in his circle of friends worries most vocally about the demise of his elite
   class, explain to an outsider that "there is very little social snobbery in the
   States. I mean it's considered unacceptable. There's almost a national taboo
   against it."

Works Cited

Amis, Martin. "Jane's World." *The New Yorker* 8 Jan. 1996: 31-35.
Ansen, David. "In a Class by Themselves." *Newsweek* 27 Aug. 1990: 61.
Austen, Jane. *Emma.* Ed. R.W. Chapman. Rev. Mary Lascelles. 3d ed. Vol. 4 of *The
    Novels of Jane Austen.* 6 vols. Oxford: Oxford UP, 1966.
————. *Persuasion.* Ed. R.W. Chapman. Rev. Mary Lascelles. 3d ed. Vol. 5 of *The
    Novels of Jane Austen.* 6 vols. Oxford: Oxford UP, 1966.
————. *Sense and Sensibility.* Ed. R.W. Chapman. Rev. Mary Lascelles. 3d ed. Vol.
    1 of *The Novels of Jane Austen.* 6 vols. Oxford: Oxford UP, 1966.
"Austen Anew." *The New Yorker* 21-28 Aug. 1995: 55.
Birtwistle, Sue, and Susie Conklin. *The Making of Jane Austen's Emma.* Penguin:
    New York, 1996.
Clueless. Writer and director Amy Heckerling. With Alicia Silverstone and Paul
    Rudd. Paramount, 1995.
Dear, Nick. *Persuasion.* Methuen Film Series. London: Methuen, 1996.
DeMott, Benjamin. "In Hollywood, Class Doesn't Put up Much of a Struggle."
    New York Times 20 Jan. 1991: sec. 2, pp. 1+.
————. *The Imperial Middle: Why Americans Can't Think Straight about Class.* New
    York: William Morrow, 1990.
Emma. Writer and director Douglas McGrath. With Gwyneth Paltrow and Jeremy
    Northam. Miramax, 1996.
Emma. Writer Andrew Davies. Director Diarmuid Lawrence. With Kate Beckinsale
    and Mark Strong. Meridian (ITV)/A&E, 1996.
Giles, Jeff. "Earth Angel." *Newsweek* 29 July 1996: 66-68.
Himmelfarb, Gertrude. "The Many Faces of Emma." *Civilization* Dec. 1996/Jan.
    1997: 74-75.

James, Caryn. "Austen Tale of Lost Love Refound." Review of *Persuasion*. *New York Times* 27 Sept. 1995: C18.

Kroll, Jack. "Jane Austen Does Lunch." *Newsweek* 18 Dec. 1995: 66-68.

Lane, Anthony. "Jane's World." *The New Yorker* 25 Sept. 1995: 107-8.

———. "The Dumbing of Emma." *The New Yorker* 5 Aug. 1996: 76-77.

Lee, Susan. "A Tale of Two Movies." *Forbes* 4 Nov. 1996: 391.

Maslin, Janet. "So Genteel, So Scheming, So Austen." Review of *Emma*. *New York Times* 2 Aug. 1996: C1.

Menand, Louis. "What Jane Austen Doesn't Tell Us." *New York Review of Books* 1 Feb. 1996: 13-15.

Metropolitan. Writer and director Whit Stillman. With Carolyn Farina and Edward Clements. New Line Cinema, 1990.

Parker, Mark. "The End of Emma: Drawing the Boundaries of Class in Austen." *Journal of English and Germanic Philology* 91 (1992): 344-59.

Persuasion. Writer Nick Dear. Director Roger Michell. With Amanda Root and Ciaran Hinds. BBC/WGBH, 1995.

Poovey, Mary. *The Proper Lady and the Woman Writer: Ideology as Style in the Works of Mary Wollstonecraft, Mary Shelley, and Jane Austen*. Chicago: U of Chicago P, 1984.

Rapping, Elayne. "The Jane Austen Thing." *The Progressive* July 1996: 37-38.

Rothstein, Edward. "Jane Austen Meets Mr. Right." *New York Times* 10 Dec. 1995: sec. 4, pp. 1, 14.

Sense and Sensibility. Writer Emma Thompson. Director Ang Lee. With Emma Thompson and Hugh Grant. Mirage-Columbia (Sony), 1995.

Stanley, Alessandra. "'Metropolitan' Chronicles Preppy Angst." *New York Times* 29 July 1990: H9, H14-15.

Stewart, Maaja. *Domestic Realities and Imperial Fictions: Jane Austen's Novels in Eighteenth-Century Contexts*. Athens: U of Georgia P, 1993.

Tanner, Tony. *Jane Austen*. Cambridge: Harvard UP, 1986.

Thomas, Evan. "Hooray for Hypocrisy." *Newsweek* 29 Jan. 1996: 61.

Thompson, Emma. *The Sense and Sensibility Screenplay and Diaries*. Rev ed. New York: Newmarket, 1996.

Tobin, Mary-Elisabeth Fowkes. "Aiding Impoverished Gentlewomen: Power and Class in *Emma*." *Criticism* 30 (1988): 413-30.

Trilling, Lionel. "*Mansfield Park*: The Opposing Self." Rpt. in *Jane Austen: A Collection of Critical Essays*. Ed. Ian Watt. Englewood Cliffs, N.J.: Prentice-Hall, 1963. 124-40.

Weinraub, Bernard. "A Surprise Film Hit about Rich Teen-Age Girls." *New York Times* 24 July 1995: C10.

Weldon, Fay. "Jane Austen and the Pride of Purists." *New York Times* 8 Oct. 1995: H15, H24.

Williams, Raymond. *The Country and the City*. New York: Oxford UP, 1973.

5

Jane Austen, Film, and the Pitfalls
of Postmodern Nostalgia

Amanda Collins

The producers of culture have nowhere to turn but to the past:
the imitation of dead styles, speech through all the masks and
voices stored up in the imaginary museum of new global
culture.

—Fredric Jameson,
Postmodernism or, The Cultural Logic of Late Capitalism

The only reason people want to be masters of the future is to
change the past.

—Milan Kundera,
The Book of Laughter and Forgetting

Consider the case of the 1995 film *Persuasion.* The videocassette of this film may be purchased in two versions. The differences between these versions have nothing to do with the film or the videocassette. The videos are exactly the same. The differences lie in the boxes that house the videotapes.

The first, which is an adaptation of the poster that advertised the film, depicts the film's stars, Ciaran Hinds and Amanda Root, poised for that long-awaited kiss that so shocked Janeites and historical purists. They seem to be holding hands and the shot is nearly full length, showing everything but their feet. Instead of the Bath street scene that was the background for the kiss in the film, the pair are flanked by a rose arbor, a flower bed and, in the distance, the sturdy facade of Kellynch Hall, where the film's heroine, Anne, was raised. Superimposed across the top of the rose bower are the words

"Jane Austen's Persuasion, A Film By Roger Michell." The lonely bit of blue sky hovering over Kellynch Hall is branded with the obligatory "Two Thumbs Up" of Siskel and Ebert, and the very bottom of the tableau is emblazoned with *Time's* opinion that *Persuasion* is "The Best Picture of the Year."

The second box is identical to the other—with one exception. It has become a video version of the oft-reviled "bodice ripper" cover, which takes its name from the sexually explicit love scenes featured in the romance novels of the late 1970s in which the hero often ripped the bodice of the heroine's gown in the heat of passion. Instead of Ciaran Hinds in Wentworth's rather dapper naval uniform and Amanda Root in the pretty yellow gown that suited her portrayal of Anne Elliot, we see another couple on the verge of a kiss. This couple is in a state of dishabille that would disturb the Janeites far more than the chaste kiss depicted in the film. The gentleman, whose hair is very obviously several shades lighter than that of Ciaran Hinds—he is, in fact, not Ciaran Hinds at all—wears a naval uniform which seems somehow less formal than that worn by Hinds in the film. Perhaps this informality stems from the pose that this unknown hero has adopted. His head tilted in midair, the intended destination of his puckered lips seems to be the arched neck of the lady he holds in his arms. She, too, is wearing a less constricting outfit than her counterpart on the other box. Her off-the-shoulder, low-cut gown reveals the creamy expanse of her shoulders and upper chest to decided advantage. Her hair is less confined than Amanda Root's chignon-imprisoned locks. This woman's hair, also significantly lighter than her counterpart's, flows wantonly over her shoulders. The most significant difference between this picture and the other, however, has to do not with its content but with where it can be seen. The first box is that which would accompany the videocassette if you were to purchase it; the other is what customers see at the rental store. The same film—different packaging.

Those of you who have seen the film are aware that this passionate scene never occurs in the film. In fact, it never occurred in any Jane Austen adaptation in recent memory. But neither did the first. The first may seem closer to the "real thing" because it can boast of picturing actors who are actually *in* the film, but it too is never seen in the film itself. Both of these boxes are prime examples of the postmodern phenomenon known as *simulacra,* what Jean Baudrillard calls "a real without origin, or reality" (203).

The significance of these boxes as simulacra is not in the fact that they obscure the "real," but in the fact that they have become another type of "real": the *hyperreal.* They are the models, the copies of something that does not exist. There is no scene in the film that these pictures recreate. They are not *re-creations* but *creations.* Thus, we have two different scenes on these boxes, neither of which occurs anywhere but on those boxes, yet they are supposed to be representations of what occurs in the film. But unlike a representation, which means "to present again," these boxes do not present something *again:* they present it for the first time. They are a new presentation disguised as *re*-presentation. Therein lies the hollow nature of the simulacrum.

The idea of the simulacrum becomes even more complex when applied to the use of classic novels in film. Roger Michell's production of *Persuasion* (screenplay by Nick Dear), released several months before Ang Lee's 1995 film version of *Sense and Sensibility* (screenplay by Emma Thompson), did not enjoy nearly as much publicity or success at the box office as the latter. In fact, *Persuasion* was made as a telefilm by the BBC and was released theatrically only in the United States. As such, it was not a particularly popular selection among critics looking for films to review. But as soon as the public fascination with Austen adaptations became obvious, critics hurried to include reviews of *Persuasion,* which they had previously ignored, in their film reviews of *Sense and Sensibility.* This juxtapositioning of the two films led to a curious trend among critics to praise the "pretty" 1995 film version of *Sense and Sensibility* and to condemn the "gritty" 1995 film *Persuasion.* This seems to indicate a public privileging of the romantic over the realistic. It also seems to indicate a preference for the "hyperreal" over the "real."

According to Fredric Jameson, "the new spatial logic of the simulacrum can now be expected to have a momentous effect on what used to be historical time" (198). In deference to Jameson's assertion about "historical time," I think it might be useful to examine the ways in which history has been adapted for the 1990s in this series of films adapted from the novels of early nineteenth-century novelist Jane Austen. Specifically, I will look at the ways in which these adaptations have both embodied and rewritten the words Jane Austen set to paper nearly two hundred years ago, attempt to make some sense of the cultural climate in which these adaptations are flourishing, and also try to determine to what extent these films have appropriated the work of Jane Austen for the purposes of fulfilling a societal need for nostalgia. Then perhaps we can come to some understanding of the ways in which the postmodern desire for the "hyperreal" is changing our perceptions of the past.

In her review of *Sense and Sensibility* for the *New Statesman and Society,* Lizzie Francke wrote of the recent trend in film adaptations of nineteenth-century novels: "The nineteenth century is revisited and played out and revisited over and over again [in these films]. Not as a stale fixation, but with some of its expectations and frustrations aired now seeming, sadly, all too recognizable" (43). What this quotation reveals is the underlying rhetoric, which pervades most reviews of such films, that seems to equate films set in the nineteenth century with the nineteenth century itself. In the films, the nineteenth century is not "an ever-fixèd mark" (to borrow from the Shakespearean sonnet quoted in the film *Sense and Sensibility*) but a fluid thing that can be transformed into something "all too recognizable." In a manner similar to the ways in which the Victorian bourgeoisie, according to Michel Foucault, changed not only its perceptions and beliefs about its collective body, but also the body itself (152), so too have we postmoderns changed not only our perceptions of history but history itself. The rhetoric of these film reviews implies that history is whatever we make it.

This rewriting of history is evident in the dichotomy set up between positive reviews of *Sense and Sensibility* and the negative reviews of *Persuasion*. In several of the most articulate reviews, Emma Thompson's adaptation of Austen's novel is described as nothing short of miraculous. Yet, often in the same review, Nick Dear's screenplay for *Persuasion* is implicitly criticized because it has not been "adapted" enough.

In his glowing review of *Sense and Sensibility*, Richard Alleva writes that in the novel, Edward Ferrars is a "[stick] walking about in [a] frock [coat]" (15). He unabashedly praises Thompson's transformation of Edward in the film into a man "we believe Elinor is right to love . . . and that's what counts" (16). Admittedly, Austen's characterization of Edward has been problematic for both readers and literary critics from *Sense and Sensibility*'s first publication, and not without reason. It does seem difficult at times to accept such a perceptive and intelligent heroine as Elinor giving her love to a man whom even she describes with such damning praise as "his address is certainly not striking; and his person can hardly be called handsome, till the expression of his eyes, which are uncommonly good, and the general sweetness of his countenance, is perceived" (Austen, *Sense* 20). However, Alleva's praise of Thompson for her transformation of Edward's character in the screenplay seems to devalue the novel and promote not only the adaptations that must occur in the transition from the page to the screen, but also the "re-writing" of Austen to fit audience preferences. "What counts" is that we can approve of Elinor's love for Edward, not that we see a portrayal of Edward as Austen wrote him.

This privileging of audience approval over the written text is also evident in Alleva's criticism of Amanda Root's performance in *Persuasion,* as "almost self-effacing" (16). He is not alone. In fact, much of the blame for the failure of *Persuasion* as a film seems to have been placed by critics on Root's head. Among the complaints regarding her performance were "she lacks the charm with which even much *homelier* performers have been known to enchant an audience" (Simon, rev. of *Persuasion* 58, my emphasis); "she has pleasant eyes but a grim mouth . . . and a countenance that doesn't invite speculation" (Kauffmann, rev. of *Persuasion* 26). In a manner very similar to those who praised Emma Thompson for changing the character of Edward to win audience appeal, these critics seem to denigrate Amanda Root's performance as Anne Elliot for being too close to Austen's characterization of Anne in the novel: "A few years before, Anne Elliot had been a very pretty girl, but her bloom had vanished early; and as even in its height, her father had found little to admire in her (so totally different were her delicate features and mild dark eyes from his own); there could be nothing in them now that she was faded and thin, to excite his esteem" (*Persuasion* 6). Given the performance Root gives in the film, which seems to be an accurate portrayal of a woman who has lost her "bloom," the criticism of her acting ability and her looks seems directed not at her but at Jane Austen herself. Just as readers objected to Austen's handling of Edward, film viewers protested over her depiction of Anne as self-effacing. Again, "what counts" is that the audience should approve of and be engaged with the characters, and sometimes achieving that approval involves rewriting the fiction of the past to suit the needs of the present, since what is being altered is not history or historical fact but a fiction written in the past.

This privileging of the hyperreal over the original text of Austen's novels seems to be part of a trend that Jameson describes as "the insensible colonization of the present by the nostalgia mode" (199). This "nostalgia mode," according to Jameson, is one in which "the past as 'referent' finds itself gradually bracketed and then effaced altogether leaving us with nothing but texts" (199). The idea of a "bracketed" past seems eminently applicable to Alleva's other objections to *Persuasion:*

> the drizzly (and lovely) photography, the anachronistic music (Chopin, among others), the generally hushed quality of the soundtrack, and the almost self-effacing performance of Amanda Root (of, to be sure, a self-effacing heroine) nudge it a little further into the nineteenth century than the sensibility of Jane Austen belongs. (16)

What is particularly interesting about this passage is the idea that Jane Austen does not "belong" in the nineteenth century. Alleva disregards the notion that the novel *Persuasion* was written nearly fifteen years after the turn of the nineteenth century, near the height of the Romantic movement, which took as one of its goals, especially as seen in the poetry of Wordsworth, the depiction of the *real lives* of common people—a far cry from the sensibility of the eighteenth century. Alleva also asserts that Austen equals sensibility—that is, her work *belongs* in the eighteenth century. This attempt to put Austen "in her place" in effect brackets Austen's life after the turn of the century and denies her novels a place in history after 1800.

Another interesting point in light of Jameson's argument is Alleva's criticism of the use of Chopin's music in the film. Given the notion of "bracketing the past," Alleva's criticism of the music in the 1995 film version of *Persuasion* has less to do with the fact that it is anachronistic than with the fact that it is by Chopin (1810-49), whose recognizable melodies ground the film in some sort of historical place, in this case the nineteenth century. This idea is also supported by the fact that Alleva does not recognize Patrick Doyle's score for *Sense and Sensibility*, written in the 1990s, as anachronistic. Doyle's score, supposedly modeled after the music of Mozart, apparently is ambiguous enough to both seem appropriate to the film's "sometime in the late eighteenth century" setting and to elude casual attempts to associate it with any particular composer. Rather than create a new text, or simulacrum, like Ang Lee and Emma Thompson did with *Sense and Sensibility*, Roger Michell and Nick Dear did what the postmoderns find unacceptable: they grounded the film *Persuasion* in a specific historical moment. It is connected to the past and to Jane Austen's novel in a way that Emma Thompson's *Sense and Sensibility* is not.

We can see the detachment from historical time in Thompson's screenplay, especially in her characterization of the youngest Dashwood sister, Margaret. In the film version, Margaret is endowed with far more characterization and importance to the plot than she is afforded in Austen's novel. Because *Sense and Sensibility* was first written as an epistolary novel (a very popular format in the eighteenth century), Margaret in the novel was not what E.M. Forster would call a "round character" simply because the letters in the original version were written by Elinor and Marianne, which did not leave much room for the characterization of the youngest sister. In the published novel, the most Austen ever says about Margaret is that she "was a good-humoured well-disposed girl; but as she had already imbibed a good deal of Marianne's romance, without having much of her sense, she did not, at thirteen, bid fair to equal her sisters at a more advanced period of life" (*Sense* 7). This is a far cry from the feisty tomboy Thompson wrote into the story.

In the film, we first see Margaret, or do *not* see her as it turns out, barricaded in a tree house presumably on the grounds of Norland. As Elinor, played by Thompson, calls up to her from the ground that she must come down because John and Fanny, who have inherited Norland as the laws of primogeniture decree, will arrive soon, the disembodied voice of Margaret asks, "Why are they coming to live at Norland? They already have a house in London." Elinor's reply, a brief explanation of the inheritance laws with regard to daughters, seems to place Margaret in the film as a sort of mouthpiece for the questions the presumably historically deficient audience will be expected to have about the customs and practices of the past. While this might seem an attempt to place the Dashwoods in a historical time period, this effort seems overshadowed by the further characterization of Margaret. For it is also in this scene that we first see Margaret associated with the atlas that will figure largely in the development of her character. Richard Blake writes in his review of the film: "The youngest daughter, 11 year old Margaret (Emilie François), has more perspective on life. She climbs into tree houses to observe at a distance the lunacy of English customs. She learns how to fence and pores over atlases to plan the expedition she will lead to China. Margaret is not yet trapped in the web of injustices that may yet destroy her sisters. She still inhabits a child's world of endless possibilities" (21). What I would like to focus on now is the way in which Thompson infuses the character of Margaret with an utterly twentieth-century persona. I would argue that the "world of endless possibilities" that Blake describes is a creation made to soothe the liberated female audience watching the film in what Elayne Rapping calls "the brave new world of postfeminist 'liberation'" (37). Throughout the film, Margaret seems to have more freedom than her sisters, both because she is a child, and because it is she who represents the future generation in the film. And while postmodern audiences might "[savor] the luxury of sinking into a fairy-tale landscape" (Rapping 37), they find in Margaret the character most like themselves, who is free (at least in her mind) to grow up to be whatever she wants to be.

In her review of the film, Lizzie Francke refers to the fact that Thompson adapted *Sense and Sensibility* because she "was keen to do something for women" (43). This seems to place in perspective the characterization of Margaret, for in the film, she has far more common sense than Jane Austen's Margaret could ever boast. This change seems to suggest that Thompson, in her attempt to adapt the novel in a way that would appeal to the filmgoer of the 1990s, rewrote the past in order to meet the postmodern demand for nostalgia.

One of the factors that I believe doomed *Persuasion* to receive such mixed reviews from the critics was Nick Dear's failure to rewrite the past in the way that Emma Thompson did. Thompson's screenplay of *Sense and Sensibility*, despite its single reference to manure in the streets, is shrouded in the rose-colored sheen of nostalgia. Dear's adaptation of *Persuasion*, by contrast, is unstinting in its depiction of both the beautiful and the bleak aspects of life in the nineteenth century. This realism, however, was not met with approbation by critics. In her essay "Jane Austen for the Nineties," Brooke Allen writes of *Persuasion:* "In their attempts to purify the movie of Hollywood sheen and give it an air of naturalism, the producers . . . have too zealously ripped away the romantic gauze: the distressing results are an unappealing Anne Elliot, a pockmarked Captain Wentworth, a greasy necked Benwick, and a slovenly looking Lady Russell" (15). In Allen's essay, we see again a disparaging of historical realism or, as Allen puts it herself, "naturalism." While she seems to be petulantly decrying the lack of polish in *Persuasion,* we can also see a sort of desire for the past to be changed. She has no desire to witness the consequences of living in a world that does not contain tetracycline or skin-smoothing techniques to repair the sun-damaged skin of naval officers like Wentworth. Nor does she want to visit a world in which bathing is not as important as it is today. In short, she wants the film to represent the past without reflecting those aspects she finds "distressing." Allen also reveals a tendency to devalue the film simply because the actors are not physically beautiful. This attitude is ironically close to the philosophy of the superficial Sir Walter Elliot, played by Corin Redgrave in the film, who is given to much the same critique of his fellow characters in *Persuasion.*

In another version of this desire to "bracket the past," Donald Lyons added this comment about Michell's direction of the film to the conclusion of his review: "The glum, made-for-TV *Persuasion* of Roger Michell left me as cold as its characters; it was a pinched (mis)reading of the book that turned Austen into Charlotte Bronte, cod liver oil, and a rainy Sunday afternoon" (41). This statement seems to criticize the film for not being as upbeat and, in his own word, "happy" as *Sense and Sensibility.* Though he does not mention any particular details of the film, the mention of Charlotte Brontë, whose novels are much darker than Austen's, suggests a distaste for interpretations that portray the disturbing elements of Austen's world as well as the happy ones. Part of this could stem from a misunderstanding of the historical backgrounds of these two very different novels: *Sense and Sensibility* was Austen's first novel and its first draft was written before the turn of the eighteenth century; *Persuasion* was written between 1814 and 1815. But such criticism also suggests that Lyons does not *want* to be reminded of either Austen's text or the historical period in which it took place. He wants what Jameson calls "a world transformed into sheer images of itself" (197). Thus both Lyons and Allen privilege the Thompson/Lee rewriting of Austen (which, though adapted to reflect the postmodern awareness of the struggles of women in the eighteenth and nineteenth centuries, still manages to avoid grounding the film in the particular dates of a "real past") over the Dear/Michell project (which made every effort to place Austen's story in a very definite historical time period).

In the writing of such critics as Allen and Lyons, it is possible to see the extent to which nostalgia and the simulacrum have become a factor in the success and failure of films. We can also see now why those who were in charge of marketing *Persuasion* on videocassette chose to resort to the simulacrum as a means of drawing in viewers. Rather than risking more sales by packaging it as a realistic historical film, the marketers presented *Persuasion* as a romance, as evidenced by the clinch cover, pretty people, and pretty scenery. The decision to use a generic "beautiful" couple instead of Ciaran Hinds and Amanda Root on the front of the box, since the video came out nearly a year after the reviews, appears to have been a result of the critical complaints about the stars' unattractiveness—yet another manifestation of the current cultural disdain for the "real."

For years before this boom in Austen films, literary critics have fought long and hard over the interpretation of her novels. Jane Aiken Hodge, in her biography of Austen, avers that the two most prominent camps have posited two very different visions of Austen herself. By one side she is seen as "Aunt Jane," the virtuous, feminine lady who dabbled in writing witty tales of social mishaps in which every ending is a happy one. By the other side, she is thought of as Miss Jane Austen, a woman writing about her time, whose novels reveal a shrewd understanding of the ways in which her society operates and an awareness of the constraints placed on women in her time (Hodge 10-12). Now it seems we are seeing a similar debate being played out in the world of film criticism.

While it should be remembered that films and novels are two very different kinds of texts, this filtering of what was once thought to be an esoteric argument among literary scholars into the realm of popular culture reveals an instability in the way that our culture perceives the past with regard to all sorts of texts. In this admittedly limited set of reviews, there does seem to be a collective need for the past to be nostalgic, a need to value "romanticized" versions of Austen's texts over "realistic" ones. With the advent of Emma Thompson's Oscar-winning screenplay and the appearance of the diaries from the filming of *Sense and Sensibility* on the paperback market, we may see the "hyperreal" Austen of the 1990s become an even more powerful force in this debate, especially with regard to future film versions of her novels. While one cannot say that one is better than the other, it is true that this tendency to privilege the "hyperreal" Austen films over attempts that depict the realities of life in her world is part of a growing trend among postmoderns, as we near the turn of the millennium, to devalue the "realistic." Like the British of the late eighteenth century about whom Austen wrote in *Sense and Sensibility,* we too want to lose ourselves in the realm of the imagination. Like Marianne Dashwood, we would rather abandon ourselves to imagination than deal with the petty annoyances of the real world, whether they be in the present or the past.

These films, of course, must be recognized as products of the culture in which they were made, and as such, they document this contradictory discourse among filmmakers about the degree to which history and the author's text should play a part in the adaptation of novels to the screen. Both of these films take liberties with Austen's text, and both attempt to fulfill the current societal need for romanticism, albeit in vastly different ways. To criticize them for this would be foolish—they are, after all, adaptations. But to ignore the differences in the popular response to these films, to ignore the marked difference in the critical reception of these two films, would be to ignore the records of a conflicting discourse which reveal a great deal about the desires of the contemporary filmgoer.

As a literary critic, I must admit my own tendency to see Jane Austen's novels as records of her responses to the cultural and historical happenings of her lifetime, and I believe it would be a shame to erase her commentary from the adaptations of her works for the screen. Each time one of her novels is brought to the forefront of twentieth-century popular culture, the renewed interest in her work and times seems to reveal a general desire to learn more about the past. But it is a desire to learn about the past as it relates to the present, and as a result the films are judged not on the basis of their historical realism but on their ability to mold history into a form which is reminiscent of the present.

If this appropriation of the past for our own use is to continue, a recognition of the "hyperreality" of these artificial images is crucial to maintaining a sense of the past as past. It is all too easy to fall into the "romantic" trap, as the reviews of the film versions of *Persuasion* and *Sense and Sensibility* reveal, and a healthy respect for the power of this desire for historical romanticism may contribute to a better understanding of the impulses that prompt us to prefer one film to another. If we can learn to value works of art that attempt to make some sense of history as it was as much as we value those works which mold history into images of the present, perhaps we can achieve a fuller understanding of both the past and the present. Until then, our society is quickly moving toward a time in which we really don't know much about history.

Works Cited

Allen, Brooke. "Jane Austen for the Nineties." *The New Criterion* Sept. 1995: 15-22.

Alleva, Richard. "Emma Can Read, Too." Review of *Sense and Sensibility*. *Commonweal* 8 Mar. 1996: 15-18.

Austen, Jane. *Persuasion*. Ed. R.W. Chapman. Rev. Mary Lascelles. 3d ed. Vol. 5 of *The Novels of Jane Austen*. 6 vols. Oxford: Oxford UP, 1966.

———. *Sense and Sensibility*. Ed. R.W. Chapman. Rev. Mary Lascelles. 3d ed. Vol. 1 of *The Novels of Jane Austen*. 6 vols. Oxford: Oxford UP, 1966.

Baudrillard, Jean. From *Simulations*. In Easthope and McGowan. 203-5.

Blake, Richard A. "Plain Jane." Review of *Sense and Sensibility*. *America* 9 Mar. 1996: 20-21.

Easthope, Anthony, and Kate McGowan, eds. *A Critical and Cultural Theory Reader*. Toronto: U of Toronto P, 1992.

Francke, Lizzie. Review of *Sense and Sensibility*. *New Statesman and Society* 23 Feb. 1996: 43.

Hodge, Jane Aiken. *Only a Novel: The Double Life of Jane Austen*. Greenwich: Fawcett, 1973.

Jameson, Fredric. From *Postmodernism*. In Easthope and McGowan. 196-202.

Kauffmann, Stanley. Review of *Persuasion*. *The New Republic* 9 Oct. 1995: 26-27.

———. Review of *Sense and Sensibility*. *The New Republic* 8 Jan. 1996: 34-35.

Lyons, Donald. Review of *Sense and Sensibility*. *Film Comment* Jan.-Feb. 1996: 36-42.

Persuasion. Director Roger Michell. Writer Nick Dear. With Amanda Root and Ciaran Hinds. BBC/WGBH, 1995.

Rapping, Elayne. "The Jane Austen Thing." *The Progressive* July 1996: 37-38.

Sense and Sensibility. Writer Emma Thompson. Director Ang Lee. With Emma Thompson and Hugh Grant. Mirage-Columbia (Sony), 1995.

Simon, John. Review of *Persuasion*. *National Review* 23 Oct. 1995: 58-59.

———. Review of *Sense and Sensibility*. *National Review* 29 Jan. 1996: 67.

6

"A Correct Taste in Landscape"

Pemberley as Fetish and Commodity

H. Elisabeth Ellington

> "He liked the landscape well enough, but the natives, Colonel
> Fitzwilliam, the natives! What boors! What savages! Utterly
> insupportable. Isn't that so, Mr. Darcy?"
> —Elizabeth Bennet to Colonel Fitzwilliam,
> 1940 film of *Pride and Prejudice*

Pride and Prejudice, written in the 1790s and extensively revised before
its publication in 1813, is, arguably, the first of Jane Austen's novels to make
extensive use of what Austen in *Mansfield Park* terms "the influence of place."
According to Ann Banfield, the "influence of place" determines the development of individual characters as physical setting "interacts with and forms
consciousness" (35). In *Pride and Prejudice,* this is best illustrated in what
Roger Sale refers to as the "Pemberley chapters" (42), which describe Elizabeth Bennet's journey to Derbyshire with her aunt and uncle and their tour of
Mr. Darcy's ancestral estate at Pemberley. As Elizabeth interacts with the landscape surrounding Darcy's home, she is, depending upon one's reading, either
inspired for the first time with feelings of love for Darcy or first recognizes the
feelings that she already has for him. In either reading, the physical setting of
Pemberley forms Elizabeth's consciousness of her love for Darcy. As she face-
tiously tells her sister, Jane, who asks when Elizabeth first began to love Darcy,
"I believe I must date it from my first seeing his beautiful grounds at Pemberley"
(Austen 373). As Michael Riffaterre persuasively argues in *Fictional Truth,* Darcy's
grounds and home symbolize their owner; the repetition of adjectives such as
"large," "beautiful," and "handsome" in Austen's description of Pemberley refer
not to the landscape or the house itself, but to its owner, who becomes, through
his landscape and through his role as a landowner, worthy of Elizabeth's love.
Landscape, in *Pride and Prejudice,* becomes the sign of desire.

Austen's use of landscape in *Pride and Prejudice* is, however, much more complex than Sale allows in his examination of the Pemberley chapters. Through landscape, Austen addresses the wider social and economic issues many critics of her fiction claim she ignores. Class issues come to the forefront in *Pride and Prejudice:* we can read the history of land transformation through enclosure and agricultural advances, the vogue for landscape gardening, as well as the growth of middle-class consumerism in the rise of domestic tourism. Austen's was an age of art about nature: connected with the agricultural revolution and the rise of domestic tourism was a new interest in looking at the land and representing landscape in paintings and poetry and in theorizing principles of Beautiful, Sublime, and Picturesque landscape. The ideas about landscape and ways of reading landscape that were current during Austen's lifetime inform all of her works. In reading *Pride and Prejudice,* we become, in effect, consumers of landscape as much as of love story.

Pride and Prejudice, easily the most visual of Austen's six completed novels, is, not coincidentally, the most frequently filmed of her works, lending itself to cinematic adaptation more readily than her other novels through its extensive use of visual imagery and language. Both the 1940 Hollywood version, adapted for the screen by Aldous Huxley and Jane Murfin and directed by Robert Z. Leonard, and the 1995 joint BBC/A&E version, scripted by Andrew Davies and directed by Simon Langton, capitalize on the "visual pleasure" of the text (Mulvey 412) and borrow many of Austen's own devices for setting scenes, such as shots divided by windows which place the spectator on the inside looking out at the scene or on the outside looking in on the scene. Langton and Davies enjoy certain advantages that Leonard and Huxley/ Murfin simply did not have available to them, such as a six-hour running time and the possibility of filming on location. Landscape imagery is thus much more developed in the 1995 version. Both films, however, offer readings of Austen that, through landscape, direct our attention to or away from certain episodes, offer subtle rereadings or (perhaps) misreadings of the novel, and show us what elements of Austen's narrative were ideologically current and thus worth emphasizing in 1940 and what elements are ideologically current in the 1990s.

The films, like Austen's novel, convert the viewer/spectator into a consumer, both of pastoral English landscape and of what constitutes Englishness at a given time period. In this essay, I will focus on the ways in which our consumption of landscape as readers informs and differs from our consumption of landscape as viewers of two filmed versions of *Pride and Prejudice.* One motive behind the Huxley/Murfin production was to capitalize on the success of recent adaptations of English novels, like *Wuthering Heights*

(1939), filmed as an epic of the English landscape, and *Rebecca* (1940), both starring Laurence Olivier. The England of MGM's *Pride and Prejudice,* however, is less pastoral than pugilistic. World War II, which broke out several days after Aldous Huxley began working with Jane Murfin on an adaptation of Helen Jerome's successful play based on *Pride and Prejudice* (Turan 141), colors Huxley and Murfin's conception of Austen's novel. The 1995 adaptation by Davies capitalizes on the recent spate of Austen adaptations, most of which can be read as tributes to the English countryside and nostalgia for a bygone lifestyle.

Film adaptations necessarily convert the active pleasure of reading a text to the passive pleasure of viewing an image. Laura Mulvey argues that the pleasure of cinema is, in part, scopophilic. We find pleasure in looking, and, through our identification with the characters, in being looked at (Mulvey 416). Cinematic codes, she contends, "create a gaze, a world, and an object, thereby producing an illusion cut to the measure of desire" (427). What defines cinema is "the place of the look . . . the possibility of varying it and exposing it" (427). In this essay, I will be tracing "the look" as it is directed toward landscape—the gaze both of the characters within the narrative and of the viewer watching the narrative unfold in Austen and in two film versions of *Pride and Prejudice.* What visual directions does Austen give in the text? Do the filmmakers follow Austen or diverge from her in focusing our gaze on landscape and characters in landscape? What are we looking at and what does it mean for us to look at it? What kind of world and object do these filmmakers create for our gaze? How do they capitalize on British and American nostalgia for Old England? Mulvey's theories about the gaze and spectatorship, which she applies to women and to images of women in film, are equally applicable to the use of landscape and of characters, particularly women, in the landscape for adaptations of *Pride and Prejudice.* In what Mulvey and other film theorists call "Hollywood cinema," women on film are "simultaneously looked at and displayed, with their appearance coded for strong visual and erotic impact so that they can be said to connote *to-be-looked-at-ness*" (Mulvey 418): "Going far beyond highlighting a woman's to-be-looked-at-ness, cinema builds the way she is to be looked at into the spectacle itself" (427). The two versions of *Pride and Prejudice* negotiate the to-be-looked-at-ness of Austen's landscape in different ways: landscape in the Huxley/Murfin production is overshadowed by the to-be-looked-at-ness of Greer Garson as Elizabeth Bennet, while in the Davies adaptation, Jennifer Ehle as Elizabeth Bennet is superseded by the real star of the show, Old England, bucolic and gorgeous.

The Fields

The 1995 version of *Pride and Prejudice* opens, like the 1940 film, with a scene that is not in Austen's novel. Bingley and Darcy, accompanied by the sound of horns signifying the hunt, gallop on horseback across an English field toward Netherfield Park, a large brick building framed in the distance by trees. They stop some distance from the house to discuss its merits and compare it to Pemberley. After Bingley agrees to sign the lease, the camera cuts to Elizabeth Bennet, who watches the two men from her perch at the top of a hill, too far above them to hear their conversation. The two men gallop off, and Elizabeth continues the first of many walks that punctuate the narrative. From our perspective at the top of the hill, we see the English countryside fanning out beneath us, divided into a myriad of lush green fields fenced by dark green hedges. This is the landscape most immediately recognizable as England, timeless and rustic, and exploited to the fullest by the makers of period-piece films such as this, Ang Lee's *Sense and Sensibility* (1995), or even Christopher Hampton's *Carrington* (1995).

The characteristic English fields and hedges did not become characteristic, however, until sometime during Jane Austen's lifetime. The eighteenth century witnessed a series of Enclosure Acts, passed by Parliament in an effort to make the land more productive agriculturally by consolidating it and parceling it out in uniform plots. First, the open fields that then characterized the English landscape were surveyed and assessed; next, the complicated and tortuous road systems were destroyed and new roads, straight and logical, were planned; finally, allotments for the Church and for individual landowners were marked out and distributed "into rectangular fields of more or less uniform size" (Barrell 94). The end product of enclosure was the series of small rectangular fields, bordered by hedges, that we now think of as the most typically English landscape. Enclosure accelerated toward the end of the eighteenth century; only 74,000 acres were enclosed by Parliamentary acts during the first half of the century, compared with 750,000 acres enclosed during the second half (Bermingham, *Landscape* 10). Agricultural production was indeed augmented: by 1800, England had become the world's most agriculturally productive country (9). It was productive, however, at the expense of the small landowners whose land had been consolidated and redistributed. The bucolic English landscape which filmmakers and studios sell to us in period-piece films was made possible only through social and economic upheaval.

The 1940 version of *Pride and Prejudice*, filmed not on location but on MGM's back lot, relies on brief visual cues to set the stage. The film opens with the instruction, "It happened in OLD ENGLAND . . . in the village of

Meryton . . . ," which is followed by drawings of a quaint country village, which represents Meryton, and of a pleasant country house, which represents Longbourn. The filmmakers assume that images of Austen's "OLD ENGLAND" are so fully ingrained in American audiences that real scenes of the English countryside are unnecessary: viewers of the film conjure up the appropriate images solely through verbal suggestion. For budgetary reasons, Austen's numerous outdoor scenes are kept to a minimum, but the filmmakers cleverly suggest the outdoors through the use of windows. For example, when Elizabeth walks the three miles to Netherfield Park to visit Jane, we do not see her on her walk, which is suggested to us, instead, by an interior shot of Caroline Bingley looking out the window at Netherfield and observing Elizabeth's approach.

The camera lingers lovingly over the landscape in the 1995 version, filmed on location in England. The majority of the film, in fact, takes place out of doors, which is perhaps Davies's most radical rewriting of Austen's novel. Several reviewers of the BBC production derided Elizabeth's interminable "languorous walks across meadows" (O'Connor 18); Martin Amis noted "how desperate these filmmakers are to get their characters out-of-doors" (34). More is at stake here than merely adding to an already long film or taking the viewer out for a breath of fresh air. Landscape itself becomes an integral part of the story, a major character. Our understanding of the nuances of the story depends on our ability to read Darcy's and Elizabeth's different reactions to landscape. Nonetheless, there are financial motives for emphasizing landscape; the many shots of the rolling hills and enclosed fields of England's southern counties recreate visually the image of "OLD ENGLAND" and English heritage shared by both British and American viewers. As Fay Weldon cynically, but accurately, remarks in her review of the BBC production, "Experience tells [filmmakers] you can sell English heritage all over the world, and get your money back" (H15). Landscape, in films of *Pride and Prejudice,* is commodified, packaged for our consumption as filmgoers.

The Prospect

The English countryside first became a commodity in the eighteenth century. Enclosure was, ironically, accompanied by a new interest in depicting rustic scenes in painting and a plethora of theories about landscape, countryside, and the Picturesque. As Ann Bermingham explains, "the coincidence of a social transformation of the countryside with the rise of a cultural-aesthetic ideal of the countryside repeats a familiar pattern of actual loss and imaginative recovery" (*Landscape* 9). The loss of contact with the land was recovered through the formulation of an aesthetic of landscape, of views and prospects, that enabled the British imaginatively to recover their "actual loss." People began, for the first time, consciously writing about landscape and the English countryside. As Jane Austen shows, they began making tours of houses and gardens and natural wonders throughout England like the Lake District or the Peaks of Derbyshire. The wealthy collected landscape paintings (Claude, Poussin, Salvator Rosa, and their imitators were especially popular), while the less well-off made do with inexpensive engravings. Landscape became a dominant ideological force culturally, socially, and politically. England itself became a "spectacle to be consumed" (Bermingham, "Picturesque" 86).

A vogue for the Picturesque arose with the new interest in looking at landscape through paintings. Uvedale Price, landowner and agricultural improver, defined the Picturesque as a new aesthetic category, which completed Burke's categories of the Sublime and the Beautiful, descriptions not only of landscape but of a state of mind.[1] Sublime and Beautiful sights inspired the tourist with awe and also the desire to understand and theorize the meaning of nature. The Picturesque, by contrast, was looking for the sake of looking. As defined by Price and other proponents, especially William Gilpin, it appealed "exclusively to the sense of vision" (Bermingham, "Picturesque" 89): "Picturesque theory delighted in details, change, variety, contrast and surprising juxtapositionings. The Picturesque eye comprehended landscape as pure spectacle, a lively surface animated by a melange of ornamental details and decorative effects. . . . Picturesque viewing was 'superficial' in that it was content to examine the appearances of things without necessarily seeking their cause or meaning" (85). The Picturesque was calculated to theorize what was uniquely British about a landscape. For much of the century, wars with France prohibited English travelers from appreciating the Sublime and Beautiful sights of Burke, which were found mostly on the European continent. Picturesque theory evolved as the British began exploring their own island as tourists. Borrowing terminology and theories of spectatorship from landscape painting, it effectively framed and fixed landscape, redefining the viewer's relation to the land, and justifying the exclusion of unpleasant sights like "the habitats and the environs of the poor" from the view (Fabricant, "Aesthetics" 62). Picturesque viewing was curiously unsuited for the newly-enclosed fields and agricultural improvements, however. Archibald Alison, a proponent of the Picturesque, explained that the "sublimest situations are often disfigured by objects that we feel unworthy of them—by traces of cultivation, or attempts toward improvement" (quoted in Barrell 79). The perfect Picturesque landscape was nonproductive, hence aesthetically pure, and best represented not by the enclosed fields and farms of Southern England, the area with which Austen was most familiar, but by what Mrs. Gardiner in the Andrew Davies *Pride and Prejudice* calls "the wild and untamed beauties" of Derbyshire.

The commodification of landscape is nowhere more evident than in the rise of a guidebook industry during the eighteenth century. Before embarking on a tour of the Lake District, or "the celebrated beauties of Matlock, Chatsworth, Dovedale, or the Peak" (Austen 239), the middle-class tourist studied her guidebook and learned the best spots for Picturesque viewing. William Gilpin's illustrated tours of Wales and the Lake District must, indeed, have stimulated the desire to see a particular spot while rendering it all but unnecessary to go, the narrative description superseding the personal experience of the locale. Donald Greene, who claims that Austen had Chatsworth in mind when she created Pemberley, bases his argument on rather tenuous evidence that she traveled to Derbyshire and toured the house. More likely, if she did base Pemberley on Chatsworth, it was because she read an account of it in one of the many eighteenth-century guidebooks to the house and gardens, which would have sparked her imagination and furnished details necessary for a description.

The language of the Picturesque permeates Austen's narrative. She is certainly not unaware of Gilpin's theories, which she subtly pokes fun at, as in the scene at Netherfield when Darcy, Miss Bingley, and Mrs. Hurst are strolling through the shrubbery and come upon Elizabeth. Darcy suggests that they walk "into the avenue" when he realizes that the current path is too narrow to admit a fourth walker. Elizabeth refuses to join them, however, and "laughingly answered, 'No, no; stay where you are. You are charmingly group'd, and appear to uncommon advantage. The picturesque would be spoilt by admitting a fourth'" (Austen 53). The walk might have been spoiled for the Netherfield party if they realized that Elizabeth was comparing them to the picturesque grouping of cows described in William Gilpin's 1792 *Observations Relative Chiefly to the Picturesque Beauty of Cumberland and Westmoreland:* "Cattle are so large, that when they ornament a foreground, a few are sufficient. Two cows will hardly combine. Three make a good group— either united—or when one is a little removed from the other two. If you increase the group beyond three; one, or more, in proportion, must necessarily be a *little detached*" (quoted in Hunt 6). Austen is less subtle in a later speech of Elizabeth's in which she derides the typical tourist who jumbles together the many "scenes" that he or she views:

"Oh! what hours of transport we shall spend [traveling]! And when we *do* return, it shall not be like other travellers, without being able to give one accurate idea of anything. We *will* know where we have gone—we *will* recollect what we have seen. Lakes, mountains, and rivers shall not be jumbled together in our imaginations; nor, when we attempt to describe any particular scene, will we begin quarrelling about its relative situation. Let *our* first effusions be less insupportable than those of the generality of travellers." [Austen 154]

Elizabeth's unpleasant tourist is easily identifiable as the Picturesque tourist who tramps about England, so intent on collecting views, scenes, and spectacles, on visually consuming the landscape, that he can make no sense of what he sees.

In Davies's screenplay of *Pride and Prejudice,* Elizabeth herself becomes the ideal Picturesque tourist, preferring "woods and groves" to any other sight. I have already noted that in this film she is a great walker who dutifully stops to gaze in satisfaction at pretty scenes. The filmmakers apparently take Elizabeth's enthusiasm for a vacation with the Gardiners ("What are men to rocks and mountains?" she "rapturously cried" [Austen 154] when Mrs. Gardiner proposed the trip) as proof of her Picturesque soul and, accordingly, transform her from a young woman who enjoys a fine view to a Picturesque tourist who exults in one during her trip to Derbyshire. Austen's narrator intrudes herself into the narrative at this point in the novel to explain to the reader, in a move possibly calculated once more to undercut the Picturesque (and the Gothic), that it "is not the object of this work to give a description of Derbyshire, nor of any of the remarkable places through which their route thither lay; Oxford, Blenheim, Warwick, Kenelworth, Birmingham, &c., are sufficiently known" (240). In the novel, the viewer's scopophilic pleasure and desire are constantly undercut and thwarted, while the film exploits the scopophilic potential of Austen's text by eroticizing and commodifying a fine view. The filmmakers lift the veil Austen has satirically drawn over travel narrative and include several extended shots of Elizabeth (with or without the Gardiners) viewing scenery. The first scene depicting Elizabeth in Derbyshire is, in fact, a model of Picturesque viewing. The camera is positioned very close behind Elizabeth as she climbs a large rock; the viewer follows her up the rock until she reaches the top, then the camera cuts to a frontal shot of Elizabeth standing at the top of the prospect, looking at the view. We look at her as she looks out at something that we cannot yet see. She murmurs, "Beautiful," and the camera finally cuts to a shot taken from behind Elizabeth. We see what she sees while also seeing her seeing. Our scopophilic pleasure is, thus, doubled as woman and landscape merge into one. What we, viewer and Elizabeth, see are clumps of shrubs and hedges, tall grasses, distant hills, scatterings of trees, all signs of agriculturally nonproductive, indeed uncultivated, land. The limited viewpoint to which we, as spectators, have access in this scene effectively turns us into Picturesque viewers as well. The good Picturesque tourist, according to John Barrell, climbs hills to discover "what can be seen from the top of them; and from the *top,* not from half-way or three quarters of the way up. So Richard Jago, climbing Edgehill, keeps his back scrupulously turned to the landscape below him, and his mind on the difficulty of the ascent, until 'the summit's gained!' and he allows himself to spin round and be overwhelmed by the vastness and the beauty of the prospect under his eye" (21). The 1995 film denies the spectator's desire by prolonging our anticipation of the beautiful view that absorbs Elizabeth. The scene also functions to separate us from Elizabeth, to deny our identification with her, because we climb the rock with her, but are not privileged to see with her. Once the summit is gained, our attention is drawn to different objects—hers to the landscape, ours to her in the landscape. From such a height, Elizabeth, as viewer, commands the landscape spread below; she is distanced from active participation in it by her viewpoint. Carole Fabricant spells out the importance of mountain peaks, hilltops, and promontories to eighteenth-century tourists: "From such heights the eighteenth-century spectator, like a lord overseeing his creation, was able to 'command' a view of the country stretching out beneath him and thereby exert control over it in much the same way that the aristocratic class (at least through the seventeenth century) ruled over those on the lower ranges of the social hierarchy" ("Aesthetics" 56). Commanding a prospect was a way of expressing ownership over the land, of taming and possessing what was "raw, hostile, discomforting, dangerous" (Hunt 4). The Picturesque viewing of landscape, which involved the visual consumption of land, was a decidedly middle-class phenomenon: it allowed the middle classes imaginatively to own land and thus to express their desire for an alliance with the landed aristocracy. Moreover, through looking at land, they could make it, in a sense, their own. An understanding of the figurative conquering that took place as the Picturesque spectator consumed a view gives the scene of Elizabeth's looking out over the prospect added meaning, which the filmmakers underscore by juxtaposing an invented scene of Darcy's fencing while muttering to himself as he holds his phallic sword, "I shall conquer this, I shall!" His mutterings refer to his undesired love for Elizabeth and are contrasted with the image of Elizabeth metaphorically conquering the landscape of Derbyshire, his home county. Conquering nature is a prelude to overcoming Darcy himself.

The Grounds

In the scene after Elizabeth views the Derbyshire landscape, Mrs. Gardiner persuades her to make a side trip to Pemberley, the pivotal moment in both the novel and the 1995 film. Viewing Darcy's personal environment enables Elizabeth to see through the arrogant facade he presents to Hertfordshire and to appreciate his merit and worth, which are revealed "in his aesthetic practice" of house- and groundskeeping (Duckworth 403). Austen's physical description of Pemberley is deceptively vague:

> The park was very large, and contained great variety of ground. They entered it in one of its lowest points, and drove for some time through a beautiful wood, stretching over a wide extent.
>
> Elizabeth's mind was too full for conversation, but she saw and admired every remarkable spot and point of view. They gradually ascended for half a mile, and then found themselves at the top of a considerable eminence, where the wood ceased, and the eye was instantly caught by Pemberley House, situated on the opposite side of a valley, into which the road with some abruptness wound. It was a large, handsome, stone building, standing well on rising ground, and backed by a ridge of high woody hills;— and in front, a stream of some natural importance was swelled into greater, but without any artificial appearance. Its banks were neither formal, nor falsely adorned. Elizabeth was delighted. She had never seen a place for which nature had done more, or where natural beauty had been so little counteracted by an awkward taste. They were all of them warm in their admiration; and at that moment she felt, that to be mistress of Pemberley might be something! [Austen 245]

What seems nonspecific in Austen—the "large, handsome" house, the "high woody hills," the informal banks of the stream—is, in fact, a highly detailed description of the perfect late eighteenth-century landscape garden. Influenced by theories of the Picturesque and the rise of landscape painting, landowners went to great pains to conceal their houses along the approach until a "considerable eminence" was reached which would afford a commanding view of the property, transforming the land and house into a picture: "This method of landscaping inevitably demanded that the pictures thus created be seen from ordained and fixed points of view, connected with each other by walks thickly wooded enough to prevent the pictures being glimpsed from anywhere except the right place" (Barrell 47). The setting of Pemberley in the Davies production conforms in all particulars to Barrell's description. Situated among what Mr. Gardiner in the film calls "woods and groves enough to satisfy even your enthusiasm for them, Lizzy," Pemberley is reached from a long drive that conceals all views of the house itself until the visitor is nearly there. At this point, trees have been cleared to open a view across the stream to the house itself, a Palladian-style mansion. Mr. Gardiner, recognizing that this view has been created especially for him and other tourists, commands the carriage to stop so that its occupants can consume the spectacle of Pemberley, presented like a painting between the frame of trees.

Elizabeth continues her Picturesque touring even on entering the house, which does not, however, interest either her or Austen overly much; its rooms, like its exterior, are merely handsome and large.[2] Austen and Elizabeth save their attention for Darcy's "beautiful grounds" (373). Even when Elizabeth is inside the house, her attention turns to the outdoors:

> Elizabeth, after slightly surveying it [the dining-parlor], went to a window to enjoy its prospect. The hill, crowned with wood, from which they had descended, receiving increased abruptness from the distance, was a beautiful object. Every disposition of the ground was good; and she looked on the whole scene, the river, the trees scattered on its banks, and the winding of the valley, as far as she could trace it, with delight. As they passed into other rooms, these objects were taking different positions; but from every window there were beauties to be seen. [Austen 246]

The windows frame the landscape for Elizabeth, presenting her with shifting perspectives on the same scene. As she watches through windows, Pemberley's grounds become the spectacle to be consumed, a model of the Picturesque prospect. The grounds give the impression of naturalness, which Austen does not correct, but clearly the hand of man was at work to create the spectacle that is Pemberley. As Austen implies in her description of Elizabeth's first view of Pemberley, obvious artifice was unseemly; the goal of late eighteenth-century garden design was to take into account the natural characteristics of the land, in the case of Pemberley, woods and a stream, and "improve upon them by art, make [them] more beautiful by art, so that the garden would look like nature untouched by man" (Hall 108). The goal, in other words, was to swell the natural importance of the house and grounds into greater eminence, through precise prunings, plantings, and subtle ornamentation.

The most indispensable element in this kind of landscaping is land—"not simply as the raw material to be worked but as its own ornament and aesthetic effect as well" (Bermingham, *Landscape* 13)—of which Darcy has abundance. His gardener proudly informs the Gardiners that Darcy's property is "ten miles round" (Austen 253), which means that Darcy owns somewhere between four and five thousand acres (Greene 16). As Austen's description makes clear, Pemberley's gardens do not consist of ornamental trees, topiary, or flower beds, but rather of lawn sweeping up to the building itself, a fine wood, and a stream. The Davies production follows Austen in focusing on land, trees, and water in its shots of Pemberley; there is one brief scene of Elizabeth strolling through a more formal garden, laid out beside the house behind a high brick wall, but the garden consists of grasses, shrubs, and trees rather than flowers. The land itself provides the visual interest at Pemberley. Pemberley's grounds bear the unmistakable imprint of Capability Brown, whose improvements at Chatsworth bear a remarkable similarity to Darcy's improvements at Pemberley: "[Brown] widened the river and contrived so to raise its level as to bring it into his picture. . . . He planted the trees on the rising ground above the cascade and across the river, and laid out a new drive" (Hyams 219). Austen was clearly familiar with his work when she wrote *Pride and Prejudice,* since she mentions by name three of the houses whose gardens he improved: Chatsworth, Blenheim, and Warwick Castle. Brown was famous for using elements such as "serpentine waters, belts and clumps of trees, [and] smooth lawns right up to the house walls" (Hunt 151) in his designs; Brown's trademark touches in using the land itself as orna-ment aptly describe Darcy's improvements at Pemberley.

Simon Langton, the director of the 1995 version of *Pride and Prejudice,* chooses, not surprisingly, to linger lovingly at Pemberley. We see Pemberley from a distance and up close; we walk along its stream and through its trees; we go inside to gaze in awe at the Great Staircase and the Picture Gallery; we see its inner courtyards and outer staircases. As if this were not enough, Langton improvises an ornamental pond, some distance from the stream, beside which a hot and sweaty Darcy, just arrived on horseback from Lon-don, strips off most of his clothing to take a swim. How could Elizabeth, the model middle-class Picturesque tourist, help falling in love with all this? As she says rapturously when she and her uncle and aunt first spy Pemberley through the trees, "I don't think I've ever seen a place so happily situated. I like it very well indeed."

According to Carole Fabricant, great houses and grounds like Pemberley were calculated to inspire desire in their spectators. Landscape painting, tourist guides, and domestic tourism worked in conjunction to render "pieces of privately owned land accessible—and in a vicarious sense possessable—by their often middle-class audience" (Fabricant, "Literature" 259). The visual consumption of the houses and lands of the aristocracy in which the middle classes indulged themselves was akin to symbolic ownership; while the vast riches of Blenheim or Chatsworth would never (except in novels) be theirs, the middle classes could enjoy the pleasure grounds, tour the house, talk to the housekeeper, and take home a little piece of the great house in the form of a guidebook or engraving. Domestic tourism and the opening of great houses to the public coincide with the rise of the middle class as an economic and political force in British society; ideologically, domestic tourism bolstered the power of the aristocracy by calling attention to the disparity between the classes through the display of ancestral riches. Fabricant theorizes domestic tourism did, however, possess subversive potential "by virtue of exposing these creations to the hungry, perhaps covetous or resentful gaze of others, thereby possibly fostering, in spite of its official agenda, feelings of dispossession and alienation" (Fabricant, "Literature," 271-72).

Elizabeth herself is not unaware of the class tensions that underscore her visit to Pemberley. Darcy's class consciousness prevented him from dancing with her, a gentleman's daughter, at the Assembly Ball in Hertfordshire; how can she help believing that he will shun an acquaintance with her uncle, a tradesman with an unfashionable London address? At Pemberley, however, Darcy has an opportunity to shine as landlord, brother, master, to display his good taste and breeding, to show Elizabeth that her rejection of his proposal has influenced him to change, to become more open and less arrogant. Austen demonstrates Darcy's willingness to please through his treatment of the Gardiners. The makers of the 1995 film show him, instead, asking Elizabeth eagerly if she approves of his house. They downplay Elizabeth's attraction to his possessions by giving most of Austen's lines about the beauty of Pemberley's surroundings to the Gardiners. The filmmakers shy away from presenting Elizabeth at Pemberley as Austen presents her, consuming the view from Darcy's window with "something like regret" (Austen 246) for having rejected his proposal. The bond between Elizabeth and Darcy is forged not through her admiration for his possessions but through their mutual love of the wild and untamed landscape surrounding Pemberley. The filmmakers' focus throughout the film on landscape and fine views and, particularly, on depicting Elizabeth as part of the landscape, reaches its culmination in the Pemberley episodes, which are filmed as the apotheosis of landscape imagery. Depicting Elizabeth so exclusively within the landscape makes it seem natural for her to become mistress of what is, in the film, the most beautiful of many landscapes. The filmmakers reinscribe Elizabeth's desire for Pemberley into the viewer's desire to see Elizabeth at Pemberley.

The Davies production follows Austen in using the Pemberley episodes to focus Elizabeth's attention on a different side of Darcy, to correct her prejudice, and to counteract her dislike of Darcy. Elizabeth's appreciation of Pemberley's landscape is crucial to the development of her love for its owner: closure depends on Elizabeth's mental absorption in Darcy's landscape, which prefigures her physical absorption as mistress of the estate. Because the Pemberley chapters provide such richly suggestive visual material for filmmakers, especially for filmmakers trying to sell us a version of "OLD ENGLAND," it comes as a surprise that the makers of the 1940 film choose to dispense with Elizabeth's domestic tour and her visit to Pemberley. The financial exigencies of Hollywood filmmaking are partly to blame for this: unlike the 1995 film, Huxley/Murfin's *Pride and Prejudice* was filmed inside a studio with backdrops representing gardens and houses. More important, however, is Huxley and Murfin's conception of Austen's novel, which differs significantly from Davies's conception in the BBC production. The 1940 *Pride and Prejudice,* more than the 1995 television film, reduces the novel to the pure "linear narrative" (Axelrod 205) of the love story between Darcy and Elizabeth. In Huxley and Murfin's rewrite of Austen's story, the Pemberley episodes are not necessary for closure. Elizabeth's prejudice against Darcy has been overcome long before the Pemberley chapters, as we realize shortly after the proposal scene, when Darcy arrives at Longbourn in person to acquaint her with Wickham's true character. After he leaves, she gazes out the window and wonders aloud, "Will he ever ride back?" The melodrama and sentimentality inherent in such a line indicate the nature of many of Huxley and Murfin's revisions.

Huxley and Murfin do follow Austen, however, in setting the scene of Elizabeth's change of heart toward Darcy outdoors. They choose to replace Bingley's ball with a garden party at Netherfield Park in celebration of May Day. At Bingley's garden party, Darcy and Elizabeth become friends. He protects her from the officious Mr. Collins who pursues her through the shrubbery. They stroll together over a bridge and watch couples boating. She beats him at a game of archery. He comforts her on the terrace after Miss Bingley snubs her. They have effectively kissed and made up and are on their way indoors to dance together when they overhear Mrs. Bennet through an open window loudly predicting wedding bells for Jane and Bingley. Mrs. Bennet's impropriety necessarily separates Darcy and Elizabeth, but their final rapprochement has already been foreshadowed. Netherfield's garden, with its terrace, vast shrubs, sweeping lawns, ornamental lake, and giant flower pots, serves as the scene of their first reconciliation. The Pemberley scenes are unnecessary for the plot of the 1940 film because Elizabeth has fallen in love with Darcy long before she visits her friend Mrs. Collins in Kent, where she meets Darcy at his aunt's house, or travels to Derbyshire with her aunt and uncle. She does not need to see his estate or listen to his laudatory housekeeper to realize she has been prejudiced against him; Darcy persuades her of that himself.

Adapting Austen for the screen necessarily entails a considerable revision and rereading of her text because events must be dramatized and much must be cut, as Huxley was well aware:

In any picture or play, the story is essential and primary. In Jane

Austen's books, it is a matter of secondary importance (every dramatic event in *Pride and Prejudice* is recorded in a couple of lines, generally in a letter). . . . The insistence upon the story as opposed to the diffuse irony which the story is designed to contain is a major falsification of Miss Austen. [quoted in Clark 41-42]

If Huxley and Murfin had retained Austen's landscape imagery, they might have retained more of the complexities of Austen's writing. Landscape, however, as we have seen, was not essential to the "primary" focus of the film, the plot; had Elizabeth spent much time gazing at hills and woods, she might have lost the interest and attention of the audience. I want to suggest one other reason why Huxley may have chosen to downplay Austen's pastoral elements. The 1940 *Pride and Prejudice* is, on one level, an adaptation in response to World War II. Austen, like Shakespeare and the Brontës, was shorthand for English heritage, "green fields and cream teas," as Fay Weldon puts it (H24). The decision to adapt *Pride and Prejudice* was made long before World War II broke out, but the screenplay was written in the early days of war and the film released in America and Britain during the war's first year. Allusions to Britain's wartime status pepper the screenplay. Mrs. Bennet, for instance, claims that Bingley's £5,000 are "the most heartening piece of news since the Battle of Waterloo," which actually took place two years after *Pride and Prejudice* was published. This reference to the most glorious moment in Britain's military past serves as subtle propaganda for the Allied cause. Darcy's praise of Elizabeth's fine eyes is exchanged for praise of her skills with a bow and arrow, which she demonstrates at Bingley's garden party. More significantly, Darcy offers to protect Elizabeth from Mr. Collins with the inscrutable comment, "If the dragon returns, Saint George will know how to deal with it." The dragon, Germany, has returned, but St. George, England's patron saint, will deal with it, Darcy assures the viewer. Associating himself with St. George bolsters Darcy's status, although surely Mr. Collins does not deserve to bear the symbolic burden of Nazi Germany. Huxley wants to present an image of England, first, as an ideal worth fighting for and, second, as certain to win the battle: references to the Battle of Waterloo and St. George accomplish both purposes. In the 1940 film, England is transformed from Austen's pastoral green fields to martial Britannia, leading her country to war. Huxley and Murfin's interpretation of Austen remains problematic, however, because they jettison the novel's images of bucolic England that reinforce an American sense of what is at stake in the war and what is worth preserving about the English lifestyle. In following Helen Jerome's play too closely, which minimized outdoor scenes in order to create a stageable play, Huxley and Murfin exclude scenes that could be remarkably effective as wartime propaganda.

The Window

Jane Austen often depicts her characters peering through windows, but with nothing like the frequency of the 1940 film. The suspense of Huxley/Murfin's adaptation centers around the window: around who is inside looking out or who is outside looking in, around who sees or overhears what he or she is not supposed to see or overhear. The opening scene, for example, takes place in a milliner's shop where the Bennets and the Lucases, shopping for new dresses for the upcoming Assembly Ball, watch the arrival of a carriage through the window. Mrs. Phillips enters to fill her sister in on the good news: Mr. Bingley and Mr. Darcy, the men they observe through the window, are single men of good fortune, with annual incomes of £5,000 and £10,000 respectively. The window functions as a screen enabling the women to look at the objects of all their desires while remaining hidden from the men. Our gaze as spectators is drawn in these early moments not to the young women but to the young men. As we follow the eyes of the women, we, too, consume the spectacle of two wealthy young men in their carriage. The 1940 film, at least in its opening scenes, follows Jane Austen in fetishizing men and their wealth rather than women and their beauty.

The filmmakers also use windows as framing devices that limit and contain individual scenes much as frames are used to set off paintings. Darcy himself becomes a picture after he abruptly leaves Elizabeth during the garden party at Netherfield. As a humiliated Elizabeth proceeds indoors, Darcy remains outdoors, but his relation to indoor space is complicated by his position in front of an open window. The window frame separates him from the indoor action but enables him to watch and overhear as Jane and Bingley dance together and talk. Coupled with the expectations he has just heard from Mrs. Bennet through another open window, Jane's and Bingley's evident happiness in each other's company is decisive: Darcy resolves to entice his friend away from Netherfield, as we learn in the next scene, which opens with a repetition of the framing device. Darcy's and Elizabeth's positions are now reversed: she is framed by the window, looking out toward the garden as she waters a window box filled with flowers, but she is identified with outdoor space in a way that Darcy is not: unlike Darcy, Elizabeth is leaning through the window, bridging the gap between indoor and outdoor space. The reversal of images within the window frame serves to link Darcy and Elizabeth and reinforces their similarities and, thus, foreshadows the film's conclusion.

An analysis of an earlier scene introducing Mr. Bennet to the audience teases out the meaning behind the trope of the window as both an intradiegetic and extradiegetic structuring device. A shot of Mrs. Bennet's carriage competition with Mrs. Lucas cuts to an interior shot of Mr. Bennet's library, in which the viewer is positioned in Mr. Bennet's chair, sharing his perspective from the picture window of the family carriage approaching. The perspective utilized by the filmmakers turns the sight of the Bennets' garden into a landscape painting, with Mrs. Bennet and her daughters serving as the distant human interest. Gina Crandell claims that English landowners throughout the eighteenth century learned to frame their gardens into living paintings through the careful placement of scenes outside large windows: "When English landowners had learned to see the way painters saw, they wanted the views from the windows of their estates to look like pictures" (112). The view through Mr. Bennet's window works on one level as a historically accurate interpretation of the way eighteenth-century landowners saw their land, but it works on a second level to swell the importance of the spectator: "Linear perspective creates the illusion of seeing spatial relationships from a single vantage point. It glorifies the spectator by organizing everything in the picture in relation to the location of the beholder. It takes absolute control of the subject and submits it as an object for view" (Crandell 8). Our perspective as viewers in this scene causes us to identify with Mr. Bennet because we are seated in his chair and to objectify, for the first time in the film, the women as objects of our gaze. This brief scene, like most of the scenes involving the spectator's view through a window, both reinforces and subverts the convention of film, which demands that it "portray a hermetically sealed world that unwinds magically, indifferent to the presence of the audience, producing for them a sense of separation and playing on their voyeuristic fantasy" (Mulvey 416). The window functions in the MGM production as a film within a film. Viewing scenes through an onscreen window produces a doubling effect: the audience is separated extradiegetically from the film by the physical screen on which it is projected and intradiegetically by the onscreen window which separates inside from outside, spectator from spectacle. Our impression of watching "a hermetically sealed world that unwinds magically" is intensified because we are, in effect, watching two hermetically sealed worlds unfold before our eyes: the world seen by the film character through the window and the world of the film character looking through the window. Film itself becomes reified through the doubling of the cinematic metaphor.

The 1995 *Pride and Prejudice* pays homage to its predecessor by building on its window metaphors, with one significant distinction: in the 1940 film, Elizabeth is the character most often depicted looking out the window, while in the 1995 version, Darcy is most often depicted gazing outside. In literally every scene of the film up to the Pemberley episodes, Darcy is initially shown looking out a window or moving toward a window in the course of the dialogue. A curious reversal occurs in the 1995 film between expected gender roles because Darcy is most often inside looking out, while Elizabeth is most often outside. Her innumerable tramps through the countryside contrast her relative freedom with his apparent imprisonment. The metaphor works well for actor Colin Firth's interpretation of Darcy: smoldering, passionate, but repressed. Darcy turns his back on the sumptuous settings of Netherfield and Rosings and flees to the window, as Elizabeth does in his dining room at Pemberley. Elizabeth, however, simply admires the view. Darcy's move toward the window signifies his entrapment in his own pride and arrogance. The clear glass of the window gives him the illusion of escape, but freedom is possible only by conquering his pride. In one invented scene, for example, Darcy, who has just finished a bath, slips on his robe and moves toward the window to look outside. He sees Elizabeth down below, frolicking in the grass with a very large dog. The sexual symbolism of this scene is almost too obvious, but it works on another level to suggest a communion with nature on Elizabeth's part that Darcy, overcome by pride, cannot yet share. The changes wrought in Darcy by Elizabeth's example (and her rejection of him) enable him to progress from the emotional confinements of indoor space to the freedom of outdoor space in the Pemberley episode. His move outdoors during the scenes at Pemberley indicates his emotional transformation as much as does his kindness to the Gardiners. Darcy's participation in the English landscape is the sign of his redemption.

The 1995 production uses the window much more consistently than the earlier version of *Pride and Prejudice* to mirror intradiegetically the experience of the extradiegetic spectator. Instead of sitting in Mr. Bennet's chair looking out at an approaching carriage, we follow Darcy from window to window looking out at Elizabeth. As Laura Mulvey explains, the "conditions of screening and narrative conventions give the spectator an illusion of looking in on a private world" (416). As we watch Darcy, he watches Elizabeth through the window. Our action mimics his: we are both in effect spying on another's privacy, or we enjoy the illusion that we are spying. The window functions as Darcy's movie screen, projecting the actions of another character for his, and our, visual consumption. The power of Darcy's gaze is undercut by his vulnerability: his bird's-eye view of the action imprisons him within doors and separates him from Elizabeth. The viewer of the 1995 film is more sympathetic toward Darcy's pride than the reader of Austen's novel because our views—his and the spectator's—are so often aligned. Closure becomes possible only when Darcy relinquishes the gaze to participate in landscape and distance himself from the spectator.

Conclusion

The Huxley/Murfin and the Davies adaptations of *Pride and Prejudice* expand Austen's metaphor about the influence of place by including the spectator among those influenced. Not only is our understanding of character dynamics within the films dependent upon our understanding of the dynamics of landscape, but the English landscape and ideas of England presented in both films subtly alter our concept of England and Englishness. The 1940 film's image of wartime England as Britannia reflects its contemporary audience's concerns about World War II, while the bucolic, peaceful English countryside of the 1995 film (and of other recent Austen adaptations) expresses the new conservatism of both Britain and America. Both films were remarkably successful, so clearly audiences are eager to consume the ideas about England these films propound.

The conventions of Hollywood cinema, which directs our gaze to a world and object seemingly created solely for our consumption, reinforce the influence of place. The makers of both films reproduce the visual pleasure of traditional Hollywood cinema by focusing our attention on the woman "as erotic object for the characters within the screen story, and as erotic object for the spectator within the auditorium" (Mulvey 419), but they complicate the to-be-looked-at-ness of woman by placing her in a lush, lavish landscape. We are buying not only an image of woman but an image of England. I am unsure, finally, how to read our willing consumption of English landscape. On the one hand, these films argue for a British heritage of art, people, and, especially, landscape that is worth preserving; productions of Jane Austen (and other classic British authors from Shakespeare to the Brontës, who continue to be adapted and re-adapted for the cinema) benefit from an ecocritical reading which can place filmmakers' use of nature and landscape in the context of the current nature conservancy movement. Nevertheless, visions of "OLD ENGLAND" are conservative and attempt to sell a lifestyle—and a landscape—that no longer exist (if they ever did). Adaptations of *Pride and Prejudice* draw our attention to landscape instead of to people or social problems and thus strip Austen of her social awareness; they are powerful assuagements for the middle classes because they reinforce the centrality of a middle-class perspective and exclude any elements, such as visual images of the poor, that might unsettle a middle-class viewer. Becoming aware of the ideological purposes of these films does not mitigate the danger, however, because the two *Pride and Prejudices* and other recent adaptations of Austen are simply too beautiful to resist. As Emma Thompson, who acted in and won a Best Screenplay Oscar for the gorgeous *Sense and Sensibility,* claims, these films are "too pretty. . . . That's what's wrong with the television versions of Jane Austen. They're just—Well, I find them so offensive. They're so *cozy*—there's no sense at all that they're satire" ("Emma Thompson" 56). The beauty of these films, the visual pleasure of lavish costumes and interiors, lush gardens and landscapes, beautiful and beautifully-lit actors and actresses, is what is so seductive about them. We are seduced by the prettiness of the film and overlook its questionable subtexts for the scopophilic pleasures we find in the cinematic experience of England's landscapes.

Notes

1. Austen's subtext was not lost on Aldous Huxley and Jane Murfin, who include a scene in the 1940 film of the pedantic Mary exiting a bookshop where, she informs her family, she has just purchased Burke's *Essay on the Sublime and Beautiful*.
2. Donald Greene argues in his provocative article, "The Original of Pemberley," for an identification of Pemberley as Chatsworth, ancestral home of the dukes of Devonshire. He compares Austen's description of Pemberley's grounds with a contemporary guidebook describing the grounds of Chatsworth and finds remarkable similarities. Comparison of the houses is complicated by Austen's minimalist description: both have great staircases, impressive libraries, and picture galleries, as do many other great houses. It would be useful to compare Austen's description with eighteenth-century guidebooks to which she would have had access.

Works Cited

Amis, Martin. "Jane's World." *The New Yorker* 8 Jan. 1996: 31-35.

Austen, Jane. *Pride and Prejudice*. Ed. R.W. Chapman. Rev. Mary Lascelles. 3rd ed. Vol. 2 of *The Novels of Jane Austen*. 6 vols. Oxford: Oxford UP, 1966.

Axelrod, Mark. "Once upon a Time in Hollywood: or, The Commodification of Form in the Adaptation of Fictional Texts to the Hollywood Cinema." *Literature/Film Quarterly* 24 (1996): 201-8.

Banfield, Ann. "The Influence of Place: Jane Austen and the Novel of Social Consciousness." In *Jane Austen in a Social Context*. Ed. David Monaghan. Totowa, N.J.: Barnes & Noble, 1981. 28-48.

Barrell, John. *The Idea of Landscape and the Sense of Place, 1730-1840: An Approach to the Poetry of John Clare*. Cambridge: Cambridge UP, 1972.

Bermingham, Ann. "The Picturesque and Ready-to-Wear Femininity." In *The Politics of the Picturesque: Literature, Landscape, and Aesthetics Since 1770*. Eds. Stephen Copley and Peter Garside. Cambridge: Cambridge UP, 1994. 81-119.

———. *Landscape and Ideology: The English Rustic Tradition, 1740-1860*. Berkeley: U of California P, 1986.

Clark, Virginia M. *Aldous Huxley and Film*. Metuchen, N.J.: Scarecrow, 1987.

Crandell, Gina. *Nature Pictorialized: "The View" in Landscape History.* Baltimore: Johns Hopkins UP, 1993.

Duckworth, Alistair. "Gardens, House, and the Rhetoric of Description in the English Novel." In *The Fashioning and Functioning of the British Country House.* Hanover, N.H.: UP of New England, 1989. 395-413.

"Emma Thompson: A Close Reading." *The New Yorker* 21-28 Aug. 1995: 55-56.

Fabricant, Carole. "The Aesthetics and Politics of Landscape in the Eighteenth Century." In *Studies in Eighteenth-Century British Art and Aesthetics.* Ed. Ralph Cohen. Berkeley: U of California P, 1985. 49-81.

———. "The Literature of Domestic Tourism and the Public Consumption of Private Property." In *The New Eighteenth Century: Theory, Politics, English Literature.* Ed. Felicity Nussbaum and Laura Brown. New York: Methuen, 1987. 254-75.

Ferguson, Otis. "Class-A Paint Jobs." Review of Huxley and Murfin's *Pride and Prejudice. The New Republic* 19 Aug. 1940: 246.

Greene, Donald. "The Original of Pemberley." *Eighteenth-Century Fiction* 1 (1988): 1-23.

Hall, Collette, et al. "Paradox in Paradise: Nature and Art in the Eighteenth-Century Landscape Garden." In *Man, God, and Nature in the Enlightenment.* Eds. Donald C. Mell, Jr., Theodore E.D. Braun, and Lucia M. Palmer. East Lansing, Mich.: Colleagues, 1988. 107-19.

Hunt, John Dixon. *Gardens and the Picturesque: Studies in the History of Landscape Architecture.* Cambridge: MIT P, 1992.

Hyams, Edward. *Capability Brown and Humphry Repton.* New York: Scribner, 1971.

Mulvey, Laura. "Visual Pleasure and Narrative Cinema." In *Women and the Cinema: A Critical Anthology.* Ed. Karyn Kay and Gerald Peary. New York: Dutton, 1977. 412-28.

O'Connor, John. "An England Where the Heart and Purse Are Romantically United." Review of *Pride and Prejudice. New York Times* 13 Jan. 1996: 13, 18.

Pride and Prejudice. Writer Andrew Davies. Director Simon Langton. With Jennifer Ehle and Colin Firth. BBC/A&E, 1995.

Pride and Prejudice. Writers Aldous Huxley and Jane Murfin. Director Robert Z. Leonard. With Greer Garson and Laurence Olivier. MGM, 1940.

Riffaterre, Michael. *Fictional Truth.* Baltimore: Johns Hopkins UP, 1990.

Sale, Roger. *Closer to Home: Writers and Places in England: 1780-1830.* Cambridge: Harvard UP, 1986.

Turan, Kenneth. "*Pride and Prejudice:* An Informal History of the Garson-Olivier Motion Picture." *Persuasions: Journal of the Jane Austen Society of North America* 11 (1989): 140-43.

Weldon, Fay. "Jane Austen and the Pride of Purists." *New York Times* 8 Oct. 1995: H15, H24.

7

Mr. Darcy's Body

Privileging the Female Gaze

Lisa Hopkins

When I first had the idea of writing on Andrew Davies's 1995 adaptation of *Pride and Prejudice,* a year and a quarter after it had been shown on BBC Television, I at once lamented the fact that I had not thought to keep any cuttings of the numerous articles in the British press which had focused on it, and, in particular, on the appeal of Colin Firth's portrayal of Mr. Darcy. However, I need not have worried. Sixteen months on, the impact of the series was still so great in England that two of the newspapers I have delivered featured images of Firth as Mr. Darcy on successive days. On Friday, 24 January 1997, the *Sheffield Star*'s Lifestyle section ran a feature about a craft fair, entitled "Ideas to Have You in Stitches," illustrated by a picture of Mr. Darcy and Elizabeth captioned, "Mr. Darcy's outfit, worn by actor Colin Firth in Pride and Prejudice will be on show."[1] Next day, the Saturday *Guardian* included an article titled "The Life of brain" by the architect (and recently elevated Labour peer) Richard Rogers, calling for "all of us to think less of heritage and engage more in real culture." The article did not mention *Pride and Prejudice* at all but was illustrated by a picture of Firth as Mr. Darcy—this time on his own, though the shot had originally been of the wedding, with Elizabeth at his side—with the caption "Heritage masquerading as culture . . . Colin Firth as Mr. Darcy (right) won't do, whereas going to the opera (above), will." Two days after that, Firth was in the *Sheffield Star* again (28 Jan. 1997), this time dressed for his role in *Nostromo;* the article was headed "Drama Firth and Foremost." Potential viewers of the series were coaxed with the information that "The actor who changed the fortunes of period romance when he played Jane Austen's dashing Mr. Darcy is back in the past once more for his latest small screen role," while the *Guardian* writer Maggie Brown rhapsodized that "Mr. Darcy—sorry, Colin Firth—looks great in jodhpurs" (1 Feb. 1997). The next day, *The Observer* used a shot of the Darcy-Elizabeth wedding to discuss whether costume drama was played out (2 Feb. 1997).

The phenomenal success of *Pride and Prejudice,* thus reflected in the continued prevalence of images from it so long after the original screening, is undoubtedly attributable in large part to the intense enthusiasm with which Firth's portrayal of Mr. Darcy was received. Ironically, in view of the effect it was to have on Firth's life, A&E Television's official website for the series begins its profile of Firth with his admission that, before he took the part, he "didn't have the slightest clue on earth [who] Darcy was." For the producer Sue Birtwistle, however, quoted on the same website, Firth became "the definitive Darcy. He's just perfect in every regard." She views *Pride and Prejudice* as "simply the sexiest book ever written . . . Darcy staring at Elizabeth across a room is exciting, and Darcy and Elizabeth touching hands the first time they dance is erotic. I don't mean naked bedroom scenes." Moreover, while Colin Firth had never previously read Jane Austen because he thought her books would be "sissy," Sue Birtwistle had been a fan of the novel since she was fifteen.

The markedly different perspectives of the star and the producer are, I think, interestingly manifested in the finished product. In Laura Mulvey's influential proposition, it is, traditionally, men who are possessors of the gaze in viewing on screen and film (Mulvey 25-26; Kaplan 30ff; Kuhn 63-64). *Pride and Prejudice,* however, is unashamed about appealing to women—and in particular about fetishizing and framing Darcy and offering him up to the female gaze.

The process starts early. The title sequences are displayed over a piece of embroidered material, with its fringe, the details of the cloth, and the details of the needlework all closely and lingeringly observed (the "femaleness" of this image is emphasized when, after the Meryton assembly, Mr. Bennet exclaims, "No lace, Mrs. Bennet, I beg you!"). The fabric gives way to the first shot: Bingley and Darcy, on horseback, galloping toward a viewpoint of Netherfield. Apparently masters of all they survey, they decide the estate will do for Bingley. Meanwhile, Elizabeth, quiet and unseen on a hilltop, is watching them. This offers an understated but still powerful prefiguration of the extent to which women's views, both literally and figuratively, will be privileged throughout, and one that is still further underlined when Elizabeth herself, shortly afterwards, is given that most celebrated of lines, "[For] it is a truth universally acknowledged that a single man in possession of a good fortune must be in want of a wife."

The emphasis on point of view is, of course, complemented by the novel's own pervasive concern with the power of appearances, and the extent to which they are always partial and perhaps misleading—not for nothing was it originally entitled *First Impressions.*[1] In the film, though much of the dialogue has of necessity been cut, the passages which relate to appearances, impressions, and viewpoints have, on the whole, been kept: told that if she walks to see Jane she will not be fit to be seen, Elizabeth duly retorts that she will, at any rate, be fit to see Jane; Maria Lucas invites Elizabeth to come and marvel at the sight of Lady Catherine; and Mr. Darcy retains his remark that Miss Bingley and Elizabeth are presumably walking about the room expressly in order to be looked at. But though the language may thus focus on what *women* look like, what the camerawork picks out, apart from one brief scene in which Elizabeth assesses herself in her bedroom mirror, is primarily how *men* are seen.

This is unashamedly the case for Kitty and Lydia: going on to Meryton, they giggle appreciatively, "Let's call on Denny early, before he's dressed— mmm!" When Mr. Collins enters the narrative, it is less his language than his appearance which is allowed to condemn him. With his face invariably fixed into a rictus of self-satisfaction, the voice-over of his letter is supplemented by a sequence of him attending to Lady Catherine de Bourgh. When Collins proposes to Elizabeth, he is even more obviously presented as an object of the gaze because his head is neatly framed by a painting on the wall behind him, which presents a suitable contrast with his fatuousness by representing a glamorous young couple of romance.

The technique, however, is used most extensively—predictably enough—when it comes to Mr. Darcy. The video adaptation of the novel currently available is divided into two slightly unequal halves, part one cul- minating in Darcy's first, unsuccessful proposal of marriage to Elizabeth. Throughout the first half, Darcy is presented carefully and consistently in two specific ways: either in profile by a fireplace (usually with a mirror above) or looking out of a window. When Mr. Bingley, his sisters, and Darcy make their initial appearance at the Meryton assembly, the scene is structured pri- marily around the interaction of their party with that of the Bennets. Each presents a line of people, with the static nature of the grouping emphasized by the dancing already taking place at one side. Though the Bingley sisters are for the most part shot frontally, Darcy, whenever he is discussed, is seen in profile. When Bingley moves forward to speak to Jane, Darcy hangs back, standing at an angle to his friend, which again presents his profile. Finally, after the ball is over, he stands in profile by the fireplace at Netherfield, dis- cussing the event with Bingley and his sisters.

At the dance at Lucas Lodge, the same emphasis is maintained. Darcy stands in profile by a mirror and is also seen reflected in another directly opposite it. While Elizabeth and Charlotte discuss him, his head is seen in profile between them. When Elizabeth visits Jane at Netherfield, Darcy en- ters the shot from one side. When the Bingley sisters discuss her unexpected appearance, he first stands in profile by the window and then turns to gaze out of it. Not until after the discussion of accomplishments is Darcy shown full-face, center-screen, with his eyes fixed meditatively on something or someone whom we cannot see, but whom we may well presume to be Elizabeth. The moment is significant not only in the development of the narrative but also in the representation of Darcy, for even as Elizabeth becomes the object of *his* gaze, he himself is clearly offered as the object of *ours*.

This is even more obvious in the scene which shortly follows, one of the most famous of Andrew Davies's additions to the original novel: Darcy is seen in the bath. Chastely, we are shown only his back and shoulders before a servant covers him with a robe, and he then gazes down from the window to where Elizabeth plays with a Great Dane. Once again, he looks at her, and we look at him. The extent to which we are markedly more interested in Darcy than in Elizabeth is suggested by the fact that while Darcy's dress—and undress—attracted much press comment and is obviously deployed to carefully calculated effect, Jennifer Ehle, as Elizabeth, was allowed to wear whatever she liked: she was simply given a wardrobe of dresses and left to her own devices (A&E, "Jennifer Ehle").

From the bath scene onwards, Darcy looking at Elizabeth becomes a recurrent and compelling image, used both to provide a crucial insight into his character and to build up a powerful erotic charge, of which he is clearly the center. When Elizabeth and Jane leave Netherfield, Darcy watches their departure from a window. The moment recapitulates his earlier gazing out of windows, as for instance when he is bored by Mrs. Bennet on her visit to Netherfield, but with a significant difference: this time, we know what he is looking at and are invited to decode the meaning of his gaze. When she returns to Netherfield for the ball, Elizabeth looks around for Wickham. Heads part to show Mr. Darcy in profile—and he then turns to look at her. However, the fact that we are by no means drawing toward the end of the story is clearly signaled by the persistence of some of the earlier iconography. When he and Colonel Fitzwilliam visit Hunsford parsonage, Darcy looks out of the window, and on his first trip alone there, he sits sideways on, revealing only his profile. Most crucially, for the first proposal scene he is again, as at Lucas Lodge, standing at first by a mirror; when rejected, he immediately moves into profile, walks agitatedly, and then returns to the mirror, standing sideways on. Though his propensity to look out of windows as well as into mirrors may acquit him of simple vanity, the iconography nevertheless insistently suggests that he has, as yet, not looked fully either at what lies within him or at the woman who sits in front of him.

After the first proposal—the moment when, in the video version, the first part comes to an end—the presentation of Darcy shifts: from being a figure of side-shots and glances away, he becomes one of iconic centrality for both visual and narrative imperatives. The opening shot shows the immediate aftermath of the rejection, but it focuses, notably, not on Elizabeth, but on Darcy. The first thing we see is him striding away from the parsonage, with Elizabeth's dismissal of him heard in voice-over, obviously still ringing in his ears. When her accusations reach the subject of Wickham, he says aloud, "Well at least in *that* I may defend myself." Returning to his aunt's house, he immediately rushes upstairs, excusing himself to Colonel Fitzwilliam. We follow him into his bedroom and see him at once begin to write the letter, which we hear him reading in voice-over. As the voice-over continues, he moves away from the desk and looks out of the window, through which we see a flashback to his Cambridge days. Darcy, in cap and gown, is walking down a college cloister; he opens a door and finds Wickham *in flagrante* with a young woman. Looking disgusted, Darcy closes the door, and we revert to the present, with the older Darcy, his shirt now open, throwing back his head in his chair. The light picks out his throat, so vulnerable in this position. Next, with his shirt still further thrust open, he plunges his face into a basin of water.

The whole sequence is highly suggestive in a variety of ways. In general, Andrew Davies's adaptation is extremely faithful to the novel, even when to be so may not be in the interests of clarity. For example, we are first told that Elizabeth and the Gardiners will be going to the lakes and then have to go through the ins and outs of the change of plans. Later, the phrase "they are certainly not gone to Scotland" is never explained and would, I think, remain utterly opaque to a viewer unacquainted with the historic function of Gretna Green as a place where marriages could be solemnized without the usual preliminaries required by English law. It is really only with Mr. Darcy that changes have been made, and as a general rule, they all tend in the same direction: to focus on his feelings, his desires, and his emotional and social development.

It is, perhaps, not coincidental that the implicit focus on Darcy is made explicit in Janet Aylmer's 1996 novel *Darcy's Story,* which shows clear signs of having been influenced by the Andrew Davies film version of *Pride and Prejudice.* The cover picture shows a house with a lake in front of it, strongly reminiscent of the "Pemberley" of the series (and certainly bearing little resemblance to the topography of Chatsworth, the house more usually identified with Pemberley and featured on the cover of Emma Tennant's sequel *Pemberley,* but which is twice mentioned in contradistinction to Pemberley in the Davies adaptation). The lake is also mentioned in the text (Aylmer 129), and another detail in the novel that might seem to derive from the televised version is that Darcy departs in search of Lydia and Wickham "in his coach" (152)—a reasonable inference, undoubtedly, but something not explicitly stated in the Austen original. Given these similarities, it may well be instructive to notice the stated agenda of *Darcy's Story,* as given on its back cover:

> Millions of readers over the years have been intrigued by Mr. Darcy, the handsome, proud hero of Jane Austen's most famous and popular novel. *Pride and Prejudice* has little to say about how Mr. Darcy is changed from a "haughty, reserved and fastidious" young man to the ardent and humble suitor for the hand of Miss Elizabeth Bennet. Now, at last, Darcy's own story is told for you to enjoy.

Viewers of the Andrew Davies adaptation may well feel that his changes to the text, slight though they are, have worked in the direction of making the miniseries, too, into Darcy's Story.

During Darcy's writing of the letter, the visual imagery is structured by a heady mingling of two *leitmotifs:* heat and sex. There is a particularly telling counterpoint between the heated contemporary Darcy and the buttoned-up younger self who bursts in on Wickham: Wickham's animalistic copulation may be deplored, but a subtler eroticism is not. The episode also inflects the next section of the letter, in which we cut from Darcy writing to Elizabeth reading, as we hear of his comments on the Bingley episode and particularly on Jane's apparent lack of response. Not only is our awareness of Darcy's qualifications to judge responsiveness heightened, but the whole question of sexual attraction and female desire is thus sharply highlighted.

After Elizabeth's departure from Kent, Darcy temporarily disappears from the narrative. In the novel, he does not reenter it until Elizabeth unexpectedly encounters him on his grounds at Pemberley. In his adaptation, however, Andrew Davies has added another interpolation: just as Elizabeth and the Gardiners make their trip north, Mr. Darcy is seen fencing—and scoring a hit against the professional with whom he is fighting. As he leaves, Darcy mutters between his teeth, "I shall conquer this—I shall!" Whereas the reader is left first to guess at and later to infer Darcy's feelings, the television viewer is thus reminded of their continuing force. However, the scene also suggests something else. Charles Wenz comments that "Darcy is seen fencing, and at Pemberley he is dripping wet in shirtsleeves, after an energetic dip in the lake, when he meets Elizabeth. These scenes, and others of Lydia and Wickham in London, are added to show the modern viewer that gentlemen did more than just dance, pose in drawing rooms and shoot wildlife." I think it is pretty obvious what other activity is being symbolized here, and the suggestion is directly underlined by a visual echo of an earlier BBC classic serial, *Clarissa,* in which Lovelace, too, is seen fencing. Briefly, but powerfully, Darcy's appeal is further enhanced by this borrowing from the iconography of the eighteenth-century rake.

The comparison with *Clarissa* is instructive for its differences as well as its similarities, though. In the BBC *Clarissa* (1991), as I have argued at greater length elsewhere, it was, in effect, only the female characters for whom psychologies and motives were established. In Richardson's novel, Lovelace, who dreams so blatantly of good and bad mother figures and who fantasizes about Clarissa breastfeeding twin miniature versions of himself, is a man ripe for psychoanalysis. The televised adaptation omits all of this: the only dream is Clarissa's, and it clearly represents a fantasy of being penetrated by Lovelace, so that she is seen not as the virtuous victim of the novel but as an eagerly aware sexual creature. In particular, the camera lovingly traces every detail of her large and frequently heaving bosom. The generous cleavages of the female characters in *Pride and Prejudice* also attracted attention—there was much snide press comment on the surprising prevalence of Wonderbras in Regency England, and one of the articles illustrated with a picture of Elizabeth and Darcy bore the heading "Cut the bosoms, back to the grit" (*Observer* 2 Feb. 1997). The difference of focus of the two series can, however, be clearly seen in the fact that while it was Colin Firth's Mr. Darcy who became the abiding memory of *Pride and Prejudice,* much of the press coverage of *Clarissa* focused on the female star, Saskia Wickham.

It is, perhaps, particularly important that the fencing episode should occur where it does because it immediately precedes our first sight of Pemberley. In Davies's adaptation, as in the novel, Elizabeth will eventually say that she dates her change of heart toward Darcy from her first sight of his beautiful grounds at Pemberley, but both she and Jane laugh, and the viewer is never tempted to believe her. For here, far more than in the book, the emphasis is never on what Darcy *has,* only on what he *is.* Though Mrs. Bennet, after Bingley's proposal to Jane, gloats over his £5000 a year, her reaction in the book to Elizabeth's engagement—"how rich and how great you will be! What pin-money, what jewels, what carriages you will have!" (Austen 378)— is cut from the adaptation, and we hear virtually nothing of Darcy's £10,000 a year. As their carriage pulls in sight of Darcy's Derbyshire house, Mrs. Gardiner remarks, "One would be willing to put up with a good deal to be mistress of Pemberley," and her husband replies that one would have to. Elizabeth, however, merely gasps at her first sight of the house and stares in silence. Not until she is looking out of the window of the music room does she say quietly to herself, "Of all this I might have been mistress," but she smiles as she does so.

If interest in the glories of Pemberley is thus muted, interest in Darcy himself is vigorously sustained. A shot of Elizabeth looking up at his portrait cuts abruptly to one of the man himself in the grounds, newly arrived from London on horseback and stripping down to his shirt. We cut back to Elizabeth, still looking, and then immediately revert to Darcy plunging into a pond, with an underwater camera to show him swimming. The fever-heat of his passion, it seems, is still in need of cooling. The technique of cutting backwards and forwards continues to be used, clearly building up the tension, and just as Elizabeth walks along the lawn, we see Mr. Darcy, wearing only his breeches and a loose shirt, still dripping, walking toward the house. His surprise at seeing her renders his speech barely comprehensible, but then it hardly needs to be: the visual imagery is clear enough.

The focus continues on Darcy during the evening at Pemberley. As Elizabeth sings a love song, Darcy watches her in mute but speaking appeal, a look which, finally, wins a response from her. Afterwards, he walks alone with candles along a long corridor, imagining Elizabeth's face. Even when Elizabeth and the Gardiners have returned to Longbourn, Mr. Darcy is kept firmly in the eye of the viewer in a way that does not happen in the novel. We first see him in his coach—heading, we may guess, for London—then searching through London, and finally virtually forcing his way into the house of Mrs. Younge. At Lydia's wedding, Wickham stands up in the front pew, and then beside him, a thunderous Darcy also rises. We see him negotiating with the Gardiners, and, a little later, revealing to Bingley that Jane had been in town all winter. Throughout this final part of the story, then, we never lose sight of Darcy.

Our perspective in this regard is notably different from Elizabeth's. She knows nothing of these events, and although she does indeed imagine a Darcy, it is not the one that we see. Waiting for news of Lydia after her elopement, Elizabeth gazes into her mirror and sees Darcy uttering the words with which he parted from her in the inn at Lambton: "I have stayed too long. I shall leave you now." When the dream-Darcy does indeed leave the mirror, he does so by stepping to one side, thus echoing the emphasis on profiles and side-shots of the first part of the adaptation. Later, still unhappy about Lydia, Elizabeth imagines Darcy looking at her sternly and unsmilingly, as he did during the balls and parties of the early part of their acquaintance.

When the real Mr. Darcy returns, he does indeed revert, however briefly, to that earlier body language. When he and Bingley visit Longbourn, Darcy stands in profile, before turning to look out of the window. This may well be seen as part of what appears to be the primary aim of this final section of the adaptation—to tease out as much suspense as possible. In the early part of the story, balls and parties have been depicted with so leisurely a narrative pace that they seem virtually to represent real time, a device that contributes powerfully to our sense of the excruciating embarrassment inflicted on Elizabeth by her family. That same technique is repeated for the scene of Mr. Bingley's proposal, to which there is a buildup of brilliant slowness and horror as Mrs. Bennet calls each of her daughters out of the room in turn. We are not, however, offered the closure of actually witnessing Bingley's proposal, and even Mr. Darcy's own proposal is, in some respects, anticlimactic: when he asks if her feelings are still what they were last April, Elizabeth says simply, "Just the opposite," a declaration rather lacking in the language of passionate feeling. There is no kiss, no touch, and Mr. Darcy does not even smile; they merely walk on down the lane, side by side. This is, of course, true to the novel, but Andrew Davies's treatment of the closing moments suggests that he was concerned not so much about that as with teasingly keeping back full resolution for as long as possible. At the double wedding of the two Bennet sisters with Mr. Bingley and Mr. Darcy, the words of the marriage ceremony are pointedly illustrated by close-ups of the various already existing couples present: first Mr. and Mrs. Bennet, then the Collinses, then the Gardiners—the only ones to exchange an affectionate glance—and finally Lydia and Wickham, seen in flashback when they were living in sin. It is not until we have been thus reminded of the essential meanings of marriage and the couples have left the church that we finally see Darcy smile; then at last, as their carriage drives away, he and Elizabeth kiss, and the credits immediately roll over that frozen image.

It has been something of a trend in the most recent Austen adaptations, particularly British ones, both to fetishize the looks of the heroes and also to foreground that fetishization by a variety of devices. In Davies's screenplay for the ITV/A&E *Emma*, for instance, Kate Beckinsale's Emma habitually imagines the men she knows playing out their parts in the little scenarios she mentally scripts for them. In one of the most extreme instances of this, she gazes on a framed portrait of Frank Churchill which, as she looks at it, appears to come alive, with a pliant Frank smilingly signaling his amenability to her plans. The moment is telling in two respects. Emma has not even met Frank yet, so it is particularly ludicrous that she should have formed such elaborate plans for him. At the same time, though, it would be too simple to say that the image simply critiques her: it also celebrates her power. Framing and containing the male, *Emma*, too, privileges the female gaze.

There is arguably a similar attitude visible in Ang Lee's *Sense and Sensibility*, for which the British actress Emma Thompson was both scriptwriter and star. Thompson is celebrated for her wit and her acting ability, but not, in particular, for her looks; by contrast, all the male stars—Greg Wise, Alan Rickman, and Hugh Grant—are widely regarded as attractive. Of course,

Jane Austen's heroines, with the possible exception of Emma Woodhouse, are never particularly distinguished for beauty. Laura Miller comments that "*Persuasion*'s heroine, Anne Elliot, has lost her looks, which ought to disqualify her as the subject of any Hollywood movie (and perhaps it does; the film is a British production)." (Ciaran Hinds's Captain Wentworth was also the subject of some appreciative press comment, though not on the same scale as the Darcy phenomenon.) But while the women in these adaptations may have lost their looks or may not have become celebrated for them, they, and those watching, are given every opportunity and encouragement to exercise the pleasures of looking.

It is, however, not a simple act of ogling that is solicited by the visual emphases of the Davies adaptation of *Pride and Prejudice,* nor would such a strategy have been likely to succeed. Colin Firth might be thought to add to the visual appeal of *Nostromo;* nevertheless, the *Observer*'s media editor, Richard Brooks, wondered whether it "might suffer from the *Rhodes* syndrome—lack of women. Firth's character, Charles Gould, cares more for his gold mine than his gorgeous wife" (*Observer* 2 Feb. 1997). This comment actually implies more than it states: not only do there need to be women on-screen, it seems, but the men must be interested in them. In the fantasies of Kate Beckinsale's Emma, Frank Churchill and Mr. Elton gaze adoringly at women—not necessarily, suggestively enough, at Emma herself—in ways that they stubbornly refuse to do in the waking world. Emma's pleasure—perhaps all women's pleasure, in the *Observer*'s theory—appears to consist simply in seeing a man as a suitor.

This is, in fact, little more than a variant on one of the oldest answers given to that resonant question, "What do women want?" In Chaucer's Wife of Bath's tale, the Loathly Lady supplies the answer that women want control over men. In the world of romance in general, women authors have delighted in creating male characters who crave the love of the heroines with an intensity which, we may fear, real men rarely experience. Perhaps the deepest appeal of *Pride and Prejudice* lies in the extent to which it has exploited the medium of television to lend physical actuality to that fantasy. What we want to see, I think, is not just Darcy in the abstract: it is Darcy looking—particularly at Elizabeth but also, on other occasions, at images which have been contextualized as being poignantly redolent of her absence. These looks too can signify his need. And we look back in a silent collusion, because it is in that need that we most want to believe.

Notes

This essay first appeared in *Topic: A Journal of the Liberal Arts* 48 (1997): 1-10.
1. On the importance of the gaze in *Pride and Prejudice,* see Murray (44-46).

Works Cited

A&E Television. "Behind the Scenes: Colin Firth as Mr. Darcy." Online at http://www.aetv.com/scenes/pride/pride3b.html (20 July 1997).
———. "Behind the Scenes: Sue Birtwistle." Online at http://www.aetv.com/scenes/pride/pride3f.html (20 July 1997).
———. "Behind the Scenes: Jennifer Ehle." Online at http://www.aetv.com/scenes/pride/pride3a.html (28 March 1998).
Austen, Jane. *Pride and Prejudice.* Ed. R.W. Chapman. Rev. Mary Lascelles. 3d ed. Vol. 2 of *The Novels of Jane Austen.* 6 vols. Oxford: Oxford UP, 1966.
Aylmer, Janet. *Darcy's Story from Pride and Prejudice.* Bath: Copperfield Books, 1996.
Clarissa. Writers David Nokes and Janet Barron. Director Robert Bierman. With Saskia Wickham and Sean Bean. BBC, 1991.
Emma. Writer Andrew Davies. Director Diarmuid Lawrence. With Kate Beckinsale and Mark Strong. Meridian (ITV)/A&E, 1996.
Hopkins, Lisa. "The Transference of *Clarissa:* Psychoanalysis and the Realm of the Feminine." *Critical Survey* 6:2 (1994): 218-25.
Kaplan, E. Ann. *Woman and Film: Both Sides of the Camera.* London: Methuen, 1983.
Kuhn, Annette. *Women's Pictures: Feminism and the Cinema.* London: Routledge, 1982.
Miller, Laura. "Austen-Mania." Online at http://www.salon1999.com/02dec1995/features/austen.html (25 Apr. 1997).
Mulvey, Laura. *Visual and Other Pleasures.* Bloomington: Indiana UP, 1989.
Murray, Douglas. "Gazing and Avoiding the Gaze." In *Jane Austen's Business: Her World and Her Profession.* Ed. Juliet McMaster and Bruce Stovel. London: Macmillan, 1996. 42-53.
Pride and Prejudice. Writer Andrew Davies. Director Simon Langton. With Jennifer Ehle and Colin Firth. BBC/A&E, 1995.
Sense and Sensibility. Writer Emma Thompson. Director Ang Lee. With Emma Thompson and Hugh Grant. Mirage-Columbia (Sony), 1995.
Wenz, Charles. "BBC Videos." Reprinted in *Jane Austen's Novels: BBC and Other Film/Video Adaptations.* Online at http://www.pemberley.com/janeinfo/jabbcvid.html (20 July 1997).

8

Emma Becomes Clueless

Suzanne Ferriss

Ranked among the top ten entertainers by *Entertainment Weekly* (Ascher-Walsh), Jane Austen is "the posthumous queen of genteel cinema" (Maslin). Recent film versions of *Emma* invite speculation about the novel's appeal in the 1990s. Written in 1816, *Emma* traces a classic comic arc: a misguided matchmaker, overconfident in her abilities, learns the error of her perceptions and discovers love in the process. As in other Austen novels, the female protagonist's success comes through marriage, a clear reflection of the text's comic roots and also an indication of its essential conservatism. Apart from the outspokenness of its protagonist, the novel bears few signs of the nascent feminism introduced in Britain by Mary Wollstonecraft's *A Vindication of the Rights of Women* (1792), published decades earlier. What accounts, then, for the novel's current vogue in the popular media? Three cinematic versions of *Emma* have appeared since 1995. Two of the three, Douglas McGrath's *Emma,* featuring Gwyneth Paltrow, and Diarmuid Lawrence and Andrew Davies's *Emma,* with Kate Beckinsale, go to great lengths to evoke the Regency period. In the Merchant-Ivory school of filmmaking, they lure audiences with the traditional promise of escape into a cinematic reconstruction of the past. Plunged into an ornately costumed, socially stratified society characterized by lavish, but tasteful, displays of wealth, inordinate amounts of leisure, and strong family values, moviegoers may leave behind the burdens of contemporary existence: economic uncertainty, family conflict, racial strife. As faithful adaptations, both productions succeeded owing to their remoteness from our day.

Amy Heckerling's inspired update, *Clueless,* brings the novel into our own era, successfully translating *Emma* into the California high school culture of the 1990s. Heckerling offers a series of suggestive parallels between Austen's heroine and her cinematic counterpart, Cher (Alicia Silverstone), despite their surface differences. *Clueless* features the same key themes relating to the roles of women (the fallibility of matchmaking and flirtation; the danger, in the words of the novel, of a girl "having rather too much her own way" and thinking "too well of herself" [Austen 1]). In fact, Heckerling's version presents women of the 1990s as less empowered or enlightened than women in the original novel. Ironically, the more faithful adaptations are more modern in their re-presentations of *Emma* than the "modernized" *Clueless*.

In Heckerling's hands, Austen's novel proves itself to be surprisingly malleable and readily adaptable to the contemporary period. Some updating is only minor: photography substitutes for portraiture, convertibles for carriages, parties in the Valley for fancy dress balls. Others are less obvious: Mr. Woodhouse's preoccupation with his digestion and Emma's concerns about his health undergo a contemporary twist in Cher's imposition of a low-cholesterol diet on her father. Even Emma's mother's death receives the 1990s treatment: Cher's mother died undergoing liposuction. More significant changes challenge the rigidity of time boundaries: class differences in the novel are complicated as the film adds racial and sexual diversity to the mix (the orphaned Harriet Smith becomes a Hispanic transfer student, Frank Churchill is revealed to be gay, and Emma's best friend becomes a moneyed African American).

Heckerling exploits the contemporary medium of film to create an Emma for our time. This, in itself, is a significant achievement, for Austen's works cannot be described as intensely visual. Austen was, after all, writing well before the invention of photography. She was also, as Martin Amis has noted, "notoriously cerebral—a resolute niggard in her descriptive dealings with food, clothes, animals, children, weather, and landscape" (34). Rather than simply filling in the visual gaps in the plot—clothing Austen's characters in period costume and placing them against the sumptuous settings of drawing rooms and English landscapes—Heckerling employs cinematic techniques to capture the satiric dimension of the novel. She reveals the glaring gap between the heroine's perceptions of events and the events themselves.

While written in the third person, the novel is told from Emma's point of view. The reader perceives events as Emma does, and thus is deliberately misguided. The chief delight of the novel comes through revelation, through the comic recognition of Emma's lack of insight. Swayed by Emma's own confidence in her perceptions of events, the reader is equally startled when her views are found to be wildly in error.

Cinema inevitably transforms narrative point of view. Since the photographic medium represents exterior states, film can only suggest interior states through subjective point-of-view shots, visually rendering the protagonist's perceptions.[1] The cinematic convention of rendering subjectivity can be seen in *Emma:* as Emma gazes on a portrait of Frank Churchill, the image metamorphoses into the real man, an embodiment of Emma's fantasy. This, however, suggests but cannot reveal Emma's thoughts.

To gain insight into her heroine's thinking, Heckerling employs the alternative technique of voice-over for Cher. Cher's first-person voice-over neatly captures the contradiction between actual events and her perceptions. As a commentary on events, a voice-over is always temporally distinct from the visually realized events, occurring in narrative time necessarily after the events pictured have unfolded. Simultaneously, the voice-over illustrates the disjunction between Cher's perceptions and reality, and her confidence in her own misguided views for it emphasizes her outspokenness. The film is intensely verbal. As one of the film's reviewers noted, "almost all the humor in *Clueless* is verbal—a patter of quotable epigrams, asides, and ironic by-play" (Doherty).

Emma is an "imaginist" (Austen 335). The term neatly captures Emma's tendency to view events from her own perspective—as imagined, not real—as well as her predilection for scheming. As a matchmaker, Emma plots her moves like a novelist, and critics have viewed the novel as a commentary on the act of writing itself. Heckerling represents this self-referential dimension cinematically. The film's opening montage, set to the tune of "Kids in America," offers images of Cher and her contemporaries at play, shopping, and relaxing poolside. Cher intrudes to comment that their lives look like "a Noxema commercial." Named after famous infomercial stars, Cher and her best friend, Dionne, inhabit and control a superficial world governed by fashion and makeup. As such, Heckerling stresses the "image" in "imaginist."

Matchmaking is still central to the story of the film but more clearly allied with the heroine's "imaginist" tendencies. Cher's two matchmaking efforts center on "making over" women: Miss Geist, the spinster teacher, and Tai, the transfer student. Cher and Dionne strip Miss Geist of her glasses and dowdy sweater. Tai undergoes a more rigorous regimen to change her hair color, her body (through exercise), her accent, and her vocabulary. In a fitting comment on the 1990s, image is everything. To Cher, makeovers offer "control in a world of chaos."

The film's emphasis on the superficial is at once a commentary on the contemporary media's dominance and a reflection of the novel's emphasis on signs, particularly on their misinterpretation. For this reason, *Clueless* is most faithful to *Emma* in its recreation of the plot involving Mr. Elton, Harriet Smith, and Emma. Determined to find a match for the clergyman, Mr. Elton, Emma fixes on Harriet Smith. To orchestrate their involvement, Emma sketches a portrait of Harriet, intending the exercise as a ruse to draw Mr. Elton's attention to Harriet's beauty. Instead, Mr. Elton's praise of the portrait is not meant for its subject, but for Emma's artistry, a fact that Emma discovers, to her horror, only after he reveals his passion for her during an intimate carriage ride. This scene is exactly duplicated, though modernized, in *Clueless*.

Cher takes Tai's photograph and mistakes Elton's request for a copy as evidence of his attraction to her protégée. As in the novel, Elton arranges to drive Cher home alone, and shocks her with his attempt to kiss her. Significantly, both Eltons object to the protégée's class. Mr. Elton exclaims, "I need not so totally despair of an equal alliance as to be addressing myself to Miss Smith!" (Austen 132). His cinematic counterpart asks incredulously, "Don't you know who my father is?"

Cher, like Emma, misreads the intentions of three men. The novel's Frank Churchill, the second source of Emma's errors, appears in the film version as Christian, the handsome boy who makes a sudden appearance at midterm. Emma's gossip and wordplay with Frank become games of a different sort on film. Cher sends herself flowers and love letters to attract Christian's attention. Despite her ability to manipulate images and appearances, she fails to read the images offered to her critically. Christian's clothes and fondness for the film *Spartacus* clearly signal his sexual preference, but Cher does not see it. Emma, blind to the signs of Frank Churchill's engagement to Jane Fairfax, mistakes the object of his attraction; Cher misreads the nature of the attraction itself.

The fact of Christian's gayness is, along with the film's ethnic diversity, a clear sign of its contemporaneity, not to mention Heckerling's remarkably flexible updating of the plot. In the sexually savvy 1990s, Cher's naïveté fully reveals her cluelessness. It also points out the film's social conservatism, despite its nod to alternative sexual orientation and behaviors. Worldly appearance aside, Cher (like Emma and other respectable nineteenth-century women) remains "hymenally challenged"—a virgin. The fact that she is saving herself for Luke Perry makes her chastity a joke, but does little to diminish the essentially conservative image of relationships presented in the film. Marriage remains the goal, and father (or his substitute) knows best.

Both the film and novel stress paternal wealth as the key to the heroine's sense of self-worth and confidence. The novel's famous opening line makes this clear from the outset: "Emma Woodhouse, handsome, clever, and rich, with a comfortable home and happy disposition, seemed to unite some of the best blessings of existence; and had lived nearly twenty-one years in the world with very little to distress or vex her" (Austen 1). In the absence of her mother, Emma is mistress of Hartfield, secure enough in her own right to dismiss marriage as an option. Cher, too, is mistress of her father's house, possessed of all the modern trappings of excess: designer clothes, sport utility vehicle, cellular phone, and so on. To a great extent, Cher, like Emma, is a spoiled daughter, used to getting her own way and indulged in her penchant for manipulation.

The novel presents Emma as a member of the leisured and monied gentry. In the nineteenth century, the social structure was highly stratified, based on lineage and inherited wealth. Claudia Johnson has argued, however, that "*Emma* is a world apart from conservative fiction in accepting a hierarchical social structure not because it is a sacred dictate of patriarchy . . . but rather because within its parameters class can actually supersede sex" (127). Emma's wealth relieves her of the problems of being a single woman: she will never become an impoverished spinster like Miss Bates or another Jane Fairfax, who must marry to escape work as a governess. Cher's situation is similar in that she does not need to marry or to work. Though, unlike Emma, Cher, as a woman of the 1990s, is clearly afforded the option of pursuing a career, Heckerling sidesteps the issue, focusing instead on Cher's need for "direction." Like Emma, her "occupation," apart from matchmaking, is charitable: she organizes the Pismo Beach Disaster Relief.

Both women owe their economic stability to their fathers. This fact, in itself, makes the novel and its cinematic counterpart inherently conservative and traditional. In the novel, however, this is undercut to some extent by the representation of the father. Mr. Woodhouse, with his frail health and constant fussing over drafts and diet, appears more like the stereotypical "old woman" than the patriarch of the family. According to Johnson, "the intellectual, physical, and even moral frailty of this paternal figure necessitates a dependence upon female strength, activity, and good judgment" (124). Emma, not her father, rules at Hartfield. The same can be said of Cher only to the extent that she controls her father's diet. As a successful litigator, pictured throughout the film at work on an "important case," Cher's father is clearly the patriarch. He barks orders and controls her behavior, grounding her for unpaid speeding tickets. Ironically, then, *Clueless* offers a far less "modern" image of female power than *Emma*.

This is not to say that Emma can be taken as a fully empowered woman. Her father does not criticize her, but Knightley does, often scolding her as though she were a child. In fact, he assumes the paternal role in several instances in the novel, most notably after she has heartlessly mocked Miss Bates. He chastises her: "How could you be so unfeeling to Miss Bates? How could you be so insolent in your wit to a woman of her character, age, and situation?—Emma, I had not thought it possible" (Austen 374). Knightley's criticism forces Emma to realize that she has been "clueless," that she has misread the motives of Mr. Elton, Frank Churchill, and Knightley himself. She thus capitulates on two levels: to the man and to his perceptions. Their difference in age—sixteen years—reinforces Knightley's paternal position, yet Austen pictures him more often in the role of an older brother. To pave the way for their relationship, both must agree "we are not really so much brother and sister as to make it at all improper" (331).

Clueless sustains this family connection: Josh is Cher's step-brother. The film skates over the significant age difference of the novel, however: Josh is in college, while Cher is on the verge of sixteen. Nonetheless, Josh, true to character, is critical of Cher's behavior. He upbraids her for referring generically to the family maid as "Mexican," when, in fact, she is from El Salvador. And it is Josh who tells Cher, "use your popularity for a good cause." As in the novel, romance necessitates a denial of family ties. Bristling at his criticism, Cher objects: "Josh, you are not my brother." Still, in the film as in the novel, love arises out of the female character's recognition that she is wrong and he is right.

Again, the novel's conservatism is tempered to some extent. Generic constraints make a conservative ending inevitable: as a comedy, the novel must end with a marriage. Nonetheless, Austen tweaks the ending to give it a more feminist turn. Knightley's agreement to move into Hartfield, Emma's home, can be taken as a recognition of her power. Johnson argues, "The conclusion which seemed tamely and placidly conservative thus takes an unexpected turn, as the guarantor of order himself cedes a considerable portion of the power which custom has allowed him to expect. In moving to Hartfield, Knightley is sharing *her* home, and in placing himself within her domain, Knightley gives his blessing to her rule" (143). Both of the *Emma* adaptations replicate this scene and underscore Emma's rule. However, *Clueless* offers no comparable scene. Instead, the film ends with 16-year-old Cher catching the bouquet at Mr. Hall and Miss Geist's wedding, anticipating her own.

Ironically, the more "faithful" cinematic adaptations of the novel may offer a more modern Emma than the "modern" *Clueless*. Austen purists objected to Gwyneth Paltrow's Emma as vociferously as they rejected the sexualized Darcy in the 1995 BBC/A&E adaptation of *Pride and Prejudice*. In Douglas McGrath's version, Emma was pictured engaging in target archery and driving her own carriage, actions that have no source in the novel. Such actions do, however, capture Emma's daring and reflect the emerging feminism of the era. McGrath has done his homework. Archery, for instance, was a newly popular sport among the upper classes, with women competing directly against the men (Troost 11). The image of Emma engaging simultaneously in athletic and verbal competition with Knightley has a particular resonance for contemporary women, who are regularly exhorted to "Just Do It" like their male counterparts. McGrath's version thus offers an active, competitive heroine, whose physical daring mirrors her outspokenness and verbal self-confidence. In the film, Emma accuses men of "preferring superficial qualities," such as physical beauty, a charge that clearly invokes contemporary feminist objections to the over-emphasis on the female body characteristic of consumer culture.

Contemporary social commentary is more muted but equally evident in the most recent *Emma*. Lawrence's directing and Davies's screenplay highlight class differences, stressing Emma's class biases in particular. Scenes of sumptuous dinners contrast jarringly with images of servants carrying furniture and supplies for picnics on the lawn.[2] The juxtaposition serves as a visual critique of monied excess. The film's ending offers a telling contrast to *Clueless* in its democratic leveling. Overtones of late eighteenth-century revolutionary tendencies can be glimpsed in the invented final scene of a harvest feast at Donwell Abbey. In a speech to his workers, Knightley emphasizes stability and continuity at the abbey but admits that he personally will change. Emma is shown breaking the class barrier by directly approaching the farmer, Mr. Martin, and his new wife, Harriet, to invite them to Hartfield.

Davies's script also daringly flirts with incest in its repetition of the "we are not really so much brother and sister" line. Knightley's attraction to Emma first becomes evident to viewers as he looks lovingly on her as she holds her sister's and his brother's young son. In a marked departure from Austen's text, Knightley reminds Emma that he held her at a similar age. As Knightley recognizes Emma, with babe in arms, as a potential wife and mother, he highlights their quasi-incestuous relationship. Throughout the film, he is pictured alternately as brotherly in his affections and patriarchal in his disapproval. Emma's later dream reinforces these incestuous overtones. Emma's fears that Knightley's affections lie elsewhere are unconsciously revealed in a dream about his marriage to Jane Fairfax. Standing at the door of the church, Emma, with her nephew in tow, asks, "But what about little Henry?" In her distraught appearance, she appears more like a spurned single mother than a concerned aunt. Davies has unearthed the titillating associations generally evaded in Austen's works. As Glenda A. Hudson has argued, "Austen's novels present incestuous alliances that preserve order and reestablish domestic harmony" (105). Davies, by contrast, shows Emma's visions, at least, as disturbing.

In fact, Davies's adaptation exploits cinematic innovations to probe Emma's psyche in typical twentieth-century psychoanalytic style, and Lawrence's directing employs contemporary cinematic techniques to stress the heroine's inner states and longing. Emma identifies Harriet Smith as a possible mate for Mr. Elton when a beam of light "miraculously" illuminates her. A similar "miracle" of cinema occurs as Emma gazes dreamily on a portrait of Frank Churchill. The painted image morphs into the real man, who leans forward to kiss her gloved hand. Emma's imaginist tendencies are presented more as unconscious processes than as willed creations.

Ultimately, however, the cinematic versions capture the same contradictions of the novel. The outspoken, intelligent heroine is revealed to be "clueless" about herself. The stalwart pseudo-brother is the agent of her re-

Pride and Prejudice (BBC/A&E). Elizabeth Bennet (Jennifer Ehle) and Mr. Darcy (Colin Firth), dressed for the Netherfield Ball. Ehle's *embonpoint* provoked witticism in the press about the existence of Wonderbras in the Regency; Firth's snug trousers and repressed smoldering ignited Darcymania in the United Kingdom. Photo: Joss Barratt.

Pride and Prejudice (BBC/A&E). Sensible Charlotte Lucas Collins (Lucy Scott) and the oleaginous Mr. Collins (David Bamber) visit Darcy's aunt, Lady Catherine de Bourgh (Barbara Leigh-Hunt), at Rosings Park in Kent. Like Elizabeth, Darcy has embarrassing relatives. Photo: Joss Barratt.

Pride and Prejudice (BBC/ A&E). Darcy on the staircase at Rosings, just after being rejected by Elizabeth. The camerawork often frames him with architectural details and serves him up as the object of the gaze, a visual treatment usually accorded to women in film. Belton House in Lincolnshire served as Rosings. Photo: Michael Birt.

Pride and Prejudice (BBC/A&E). Visitors at Pemberley: the amiable Mr. Bingley (Crispin Bonham-Carter), flanked by his two elegant but snobbish sisters, Caroline Bingley (Anna Chancellor) and Louisa Hurst (Lucy Robinson). The interior scenes for Pemberley were filmed at Sudbury Hall, Derbyshire, the exteriors at Lyme Park. Photo: Joss Barratt.

Pride and Prejudice (BBC/A&E). "It is a truth universally acknowledged, that a single man in possession of a good fortune, must be in want of a wife." Jane Bennet (Susannah Harker) and Mr. Bingley (Crispin Bonham-Carter) leave for their honeymoon. Many of the Austen adaptations end with interpolated wedding scenes to provide closure. Photo: Joss Barratt.

Emma (Miramax). Camerawork reinforces Emma Woodhouse's socially egalitarian views: Harriet Smith (Toni Collette), a parlor-boarder at the local school, and Emma (Gwyneth Paltrow), the highest-ranking woman in Highbury, are often captured in symmetrical two-shots that allow neither figure to be dominant. Photo: David Appleby.

Emma (Miramax). McGrath's interpolated archery scene between Emma and Mr. Knightley (Jeremy Northam) evokes a similar scene in the 1940 film *Pride and Prejudice*, but it is also historically correct. Mixed-sex archery matches were popular among the gentry in Austen's time. Photo: David Appleby.

Emma (Miramax). The nouveau-riche, busy-body bride Augusta Hawkins Elton (Juliet Stevenson) is a moral and visual foil to the elegant Emma and serves as both reward and punishment for the ambitious Mr. Elton (Alan Cumming). Photo: David Appleby.

Emma (Miramax). In a conflation of the Donwell Abbey strawberry-picking scene and the Box Hill picnic, Mr. and Mrs. Elton, Jane Fairfax (Polly Walker), and Frank Churchill (Ewan McGregor) play at being rustics, with unfortunate consequences. Photo: David Appleby.

Emma (Miramax). Mr. Knightley and Emma, finally understanding their love for each other, embrace. Austen's novel gives us only a cagey proposal scene: "What did [Emma] say?—Just what she ought, of course. A lady always does." McGrath's American vision swells this skimpy material into a romantic Hollywood finale of heart-stopping proportion. Photo: David Appleby.

Emma (Meridian/A&E). Kate Beckinsale poses as the "handsome, clever, and rich" title character in the British adaptation of *Emma*. Andrew Davies's screenplay underscores Emma Woodhouse's "imaginist" tendencies by interpolating several fantasy sequences. This British production also plays up the class system of Austen's world by showing the large number of servants the gentry required to maintain their lives of leisure. Photo: Neil Genower.

Emma (Meridian/A&E). Emma and her protégée Harriet Smith (Samantha Morton) in the garden of Donwell Abbey, Mr. Knightley's estate (filmed at Sudley Castle, Gloucestershire). Blonde Harriet's delicacy and sweetness contrast with brunette Emma's confidence and energy. Photo: Neil Genower.

Emma (Meridian/A&E). Mr. Knightley (Mark Strong) is Highbury's only possible match, both socially and intellectually, for Emma. The telefilm does not downplay the sixteen-year age difference between the characters. Photo: Neil Genower.

Emma (Meridian/A&E). Davies concludes with an invented harvest supper at Donwell Abbey (filmed in the Great Hall of Broughton Castle, Oxfordshire), which emphasizes the cohesion of the British agrarian community in the early nineteenth century and displays the sense of duty of the neighborhood's major landowner. Mr. Knightley speaks to his assembled tenants and neighbors about "stability" and "continuation," even though his "life is to change." He promises that, even after his marriage to Emma and his relocation to Hartfield, he will continue farming his estate and "looking after" his tenants. Photo: Neil Genower.

Clueless (Paramount). Cher Horowitz (Alicia Silverstone), the Emma character transferred to present-day California, shows "a little skin" to attract the attention of Christian, the Frank Churchill character (Justin Walker), unaware that he is not an eligible bachelor. Amy Heckerling's update of *Emma* presents a modern equivalent to Frank's ineligibility by making Christian gay instead of secretly engaged. Photo: Elliot Marks.

Clueless (Paramount). Dionne (Stacey Dash), a character with no parallel in Austen, helps Cher "makeover" Tai (Brittany Murphy) by raiding Cher's extensive wardrobe for chic outfits. The plan to match Tai (the Harriet character) with the tall snob Elton (the Mr. Elton character) nonetheless fails. Photo: Elliot Marks.

Clueless (Paramount). The students of Bronson Alcott High School are multiculturally harmonious because race is not a class marker in this film. A public high school, with its cliques, provides a modern equivalent to Austen's Highbury, but intelligence and fashion sense replace lineage and inheritance as indicators of status. Pictured from left to right: Christian, Amber (Elisa Donovan), Dionne (Stacey Dash), Cher, Elton (Jeremy Sisto), Tai, Murray (Donald Faison), Travis (Breckin Meyer), and Josh (Paul Rudd). Photo: Elliot Marks.

Sense and Sensibility (Mirage). Screenwriter Emma Thompson invents parallel scenes to contrast Marianne's two suitors. Here, Willoughby (Greg Wise) presents Marianne Dashwood (Kate Winslet) with a bouquet of wildflowers as her sisters, Margaret (Emilie François) and Elinor (Emma Thompson) watch. Willoughby is equated with the flowers he has brought—his spontaneous affection and natural blossoms get an eager reception. Col. Brandon's hothouse flowers, presented in the previous scene, face neglect, as does Brandon himself. Photo: Clive Coote.

Sense and Sensibility (Mirage). In another scene invented by Thompson (perhaps borrowed from *Emma*), Marianne's enthusiastic acceptance of Brandon's gift of a pianoforte and some sheet music symbolizes her ultimate romantic acceptance of its giver. Left to right: Margaret, Marianne, Mrs. Dashwood (Gemma Jones), and Elinor (Emma Thompson). Photo: Clive Coote.

Sense and Sensibility (Mirage). Alan Rickman as Colonel Brandon cuts a Byronic figure in the film, exuding danger, mystery, and barely controlled passion—a very different figure from the stolid character Austen created. In the novel, Marianne sees the error of her passionate ways and marries the dull Brandon; in the film, however, Brandon's emotions are enhanced to make him a worthy husband for Marianne. Photo: Clive Coote.

Sense and Sensibility (Mirage). Hugh Grant's handsome and gentle Edward Ferrars is unlike Austen's diffident and not especially attractive suitor. Although he has trouble expressing himself verbally, Edward reveals his goodness through his kindness to little Margaret, another character extensively reworked from the novel. We see him coax her from under a table, teach her to fence, and consent to swab the decks of her ship. Photo: Clive Coote.

Persuasion (BBC/WBGH). Anne Elliot (Amanda Root), during a visit to her married younger sister Mary Musgrove, displays a downtrodden demeanor and limp hair. Her homely appearance, in keeping with Austen's description of a woman whose "bloom had vanished early," annoyed many viewers and critics, who expected a pretty costume drama with pretty characters. Photo: BBC.

Persuasion (BBC/WBGH). Henrietta Musgrove (Victoria Hamilton), Louisa Musgrove (Emma Roberts), and Mary Musgrove (Sophie Thompson) applaud as Mary's husband and Captain Wentworth shoot pheasants that have been flushed by beaters. This telefilm went out of its way to present the texture of gentry life in Regency England. Photo: BBC.

Persuasion (BBC/WBGH). Henrietta, Charles (Simon Russell Beale), Louisa, Mary, and Captain Wentworth walk through the southern seacoast town of Lyme on their way to the Harvilles' home. The local women in the scene remind us that most women did not have the leisure of the gentry, and the visual details of coastal life are more gritty and realistic than romantic. Photo: BBC.

Persuasion (BBC/WBGH). "Fetch a surgeon!" Anne (Amanda Root) takes command after Louisa's leap from the sea-wall in Lyme, while Captain Benwick (Richard McCabe) looks hapless and Captain Wentworth (Ciaran Hinds) is desperate. The trip to Lyme proves a turning point for all concerned. Anne's confidence and beauty begin to revive, and Wentworth learns to appreciate the advantage of Anne's quiet steadiness over Louisa's lively obstinacy. Photo: BBC.

Persuasion (BBC/WBGH). At the Octagon Room in Bath, Anne tries her best to encourage Captain Wentworth after she learns that he is not engaged to Louisa. Her hair is now stylishly arranged, reflecting her improved self-image. Of all the Austen heroes, the dashing and outspoken Went-worth needed almost no alteration to suit the tastes of 1990s audiences. Photos: BBC.

education, revealing this most "liberated" of Austen's heroines to be, in fact, dependent on a masculine figure. By perpetuating this ambiguity, the films suggest that contemporary women are no more independent or empowered than women of the early nineteenth century. If Cher, as the most "modern" of all the cinematic Emmas, is any indication, contemporary consumer culture has sold women a distorted image of feminine achievement.

Notes

1. In film, we thus experience a curious admixture of subjective and objective point-of-view shots, one following on the heels of the other. Were this to happen in, for example, the same paragraph of a novel, the reader would be hopelessly confused.
2. Maaja Stewart has noted that Austen's novels represent the increasing poverty of the underclass and women resulting from British imperialism and industrialization. Emma particularly identifies poverty with women, as in the cases of Miss Bates and Jane Fairfax.

Works Cited

Amis, Martin. "Jane's World." *The New Yorker* 8 Jan. 1996: 31-35.

Ascher-Walsh, Rebecca. "EW Entertainers of the Year: Jane Austen." *Entertainment Weekly* 22 Dec. 1995. Online at http://pathfinder.com /ew/960105/features/eoty/307-308-EOTY10.html.

Austen, Jane. *Emma*. Ed. R.W. Chapman. Rev. Mary Lascelles. 3d ed. Vol. 4 of *The Novels of Jane Austen*. 6 vols. Oxford: Oxford UP, 1966.

Clueless. Writer and director Amy Heckerling. With Alicia Silverstone and Paul Rudd. Paramount, 1995.

Doherty, Tom. "Clueless Kids." *Cineaste* 21 (Fall 1995): 14-17. Online edition.

Emma. Writer and director Douglas McGrath. With Gwyneth Paltrow and Jeremy Northam. Miramax, 1996.

Emma. Writer Andrew Davies. Director Diarmuid Lawrence. With Kate Beckinsale and Mark Strong. Meridian (ITV)/A&E, 1996.

Hudson, Glenda A. "Consolidated Communities: Masculine and Feminine Values in Jane Austen's Fiction." In *Jane Austen and Discourses of Feminism*. Ed. Devoney Looser. New York: St. Martin's, 1995. 101-14.

Johnson, Claudia L. *Jane Austen: Women, Politics, and the Novel*. Chicago: U of Chicago P, 1988.

Maslin, Janet. "So Genteel, So Scheming, So Austen." Review of *Emma*. *New York Times* 2 Aug. 1996: C1.

Stewart, Maaja. *Domestic Realities and Imperial Fictions: Jane Austen's Novels in Eighteenth-Century Contexts*. Athens: U of Georgia P, 1993. 137-68.

Troost, Linda V. "Diana's Votaries; or, the Fair Toxophilites." *The East-Central Intelligencer* 10.1 (1996): 9-15.

9

"As If!"

Translating Austen's Ironic Narrator to Film

Nora Nachumi

It is a truth, universally acknowledged, that each of Austen's novels ought to make a good movie. Four of them already have. Between 1995 and 1997 versions of *Sense and Sensibility, Emma* and *Persuasion* were released as feature-length films, and on television, the BBC/A&E *Pride and Prejudice* was watched by over eleven million viewers in England alone (Randle). Despite mixed reviews from its viewers, the Meridian/A&E version of *Emma* nevertheless earned a great deal of critical respect. As Caryn James writes, "its charms are those Austen herself might have valued. It is understated and sly, loaded with a sense that even a society as well-ordered as Emma's leaves plenty of room for comic misjudgments and happy endings" (21).

Granted that a movie need not be "just like the book" in order to be good, there is a crucial problem in translating Austen's novels to film: what happens to the ironic, third-person narrative voice when Austen's novels are made into movies? As this look at the three large-budget, non-BBC movies illustrates, the loss of the ironic third-person narrator requires some form of compensation. Although Emma Thompson's adaptation of *Sense and Sensibility* (1995), Douglas McGrath's *Emma* (1996), and Amy Heckerling's updated *Emma,* entitled *Clueless* (1995) employ strategies that make the movies "work" in and for themselves, the solution achieved by *Clueless*—a solution which foregrounds the incongruity between the film's visual and verbal elements— is the solution that comes closest to replicating Austen's ironic narrator. Consequently *Clueless,* a film that its own heroine compares to a Noxema commercial, is the film that remains most faithful to Austen's spirit of pop-cultural critique.

In the context of Austen, irony is best understood as a mode of expression that calls into question the way things appear. As Marvin Mudrick remarks, "irony . . . consists in the discrimination between impulse and pretension, between being and seeming, between . . . man as he is and man as he aspires to be" (3). Irony, he adds, is not always comic: "it becomes comic when its very neutrality is exploited as a kind of relief from man's conventional response of outrage and involvement toward delusion and error" (3). Austen, however, used irony for satiric as well as comic effect. Often, then, the ironic comments in her novels do more than expose her characters' misguided assumptions; irony helps her condemn the social norms that help foster such beliefs.

In Austen's novels, irony can appear in innumerable ways. It can occur during a verbal exchange. For instance, in *Sense and Sensibility,* this is how Elinor defends Colonel Brandon's use of a flannel waistcoat: "Had he been only in a violent fever, you would not have despised him half so much. Confess, Marianne, is not there something interesting to you in the flushed cheek, hollow eye, and quick pulse of a fever?" (Austen, *Sense* 38). Obviously, the real object of Elinor's remark is to reveal the absurdity of Marianne's romantic sensibilities. Sometimes Austen's irony is visual. For example, in *Emma,* the fact that Emma blithely idealizes a portrait of Harriet Smith underscores the fact that Emma imagines much that is not true about her new friend. Austen's irony may also depend upon a disparity between what can be seen and what is invisible. Willoughby's "person and air" are "equal to what [Marianne's] fancy had ever drawn for the hero of a favourite story" (Austen, *Sense* 43); however, he *behaves* like a cad. The disparity between Willoughby's appearance and character calls into question readers' assumptions about what heroes ought to look like and casts doubt onto novels that glorify excessive sensibility.

I am not, however, suggesting that Austen does anything as straightforward as condemn novels of sensibility. The structural irony in *Sense and Sensibility* makes this quite clear. After all, Elinor's refusal to succumb to romantic assumptions fails to protect her from the same kind of heartbreak that grieves Marianne. To make a large claim, and to echo Claudia Johnson, I believe that Austen's irony exposes social structures that make women dependents and fools and that weaken and corrupt men.[1]

Integral to this campaign is her witty deflation of literary tropes that train readers to reproduce romantic clichés. In *Sense and Sensibility,* for instance, the narrator ridicules silly ideals of romance by remarking upon Willoughby's "incivility in surviving [the] loss" of Marianne (Austen, *Sense* 379). Romantic convention, asserts the narrator, requires that he at least "[flee] from society or [contract] an habitual gloom of temper, or [die] of a broken heart" (379). In *Emma,* the heroine's ignorance of her own heart is suggested thus:

Emma continued to entertain no doubt of her being in love [with

Frank Churchill]. Her ideas only varied as to the how much. At first, she thought it was a good deal; and afterwards, but little. She had great pleasure in hearing Frank Churchill talked of . . . she was very often thinking of him, and quite impatient for a letter. . . . But, on the other hand, she could not admit herself to be unhappy, nor, after the first morning, to be less disposed for employment than usual; she was still busy and cheerful; and, pleasing as he was, she could yet imagine him to have faults. [Austen, *Emma* 264]

By the end of this passage, the only thing more apparent than Emma's indifference to Frank Churchill is the absurdity of her criteria for judging the extent of her own affections. As Rachel Brownstein points out, the danger facing Emma, and all of Austen's heroines, is that they may "let the right man and the chance for action pass them by" (90). Consequently, she adds, the happy conclusions of the novels depend upon the heroines' ability to know their own hearts and to interpret the world around them correctly (91). Often, as in *Sense and Sensibility* or *Emma,* this requires that the heroines reject romantic conventions. Despite her earlier prejudice against them, Marianne finally realizes that second attachments may actually work while Emma eventually accepts the difference between her real and imagined worlds.

Written by Emma Thompson and directed by Ang Lee, the 1995 movie version of *Sense and Sensibility* actually celebrates the conventions of romance the novel condemns. The book ends as it begins, by foregrounding the relationship of Elinor and Marianne. The movie concludes with the marriage of Colonel Brandon and Marianne and—in direct opposition to the novel—emphasizes Willoughby's sorrow. The book tells us that Willoughby "lived to exert, and frequently to enjoy himself" (Austen, *Sense* 379). The screenplay, however, ends with Willoughby on a white horse, "*on the far edge of [the] frame,*" watching as Brandon tosses coins into the air. "*As we draw back further still,*" the screenplay concludes, "*he slowly pulls the horse around and moves off in the opposite direction*" (Thompson 202).

Willoughby's white horse, and horses in general, are a key to the movie version of *Sense and Sensibility.* That Willoughby rides the white horse of a hero suggests that Emma Thompson clearly understands Austen's intentions regarding the disparity between the way Willoughby looks and behaves (a stage direction when Willoughby leaves Barton Cottage describes him as "*looking about as virile as his horse*" [Thompson 100]). However, the fact that Brandon's black charger is equally, if more subtly, virile points to a crucial difference between the novel and the film. Despite a few reservations, Thompson's screenplay intentionally glorifies the romantic conventions that

Austen deflates. In her published diary, Thompson remarks that "making the male characters effective was one of the biggest problems" in translating the novel to film (269). "In the novel," she remarks, "Edward and Brandon are quite shadowy and absent for long periods" (269). In a movie that ends up celebrating romance, this is a serious problem.

Thompson's solution was to "keep [the men] present even when they're off screen" (269). One way this was accomplished was in the casting. Austen's Edward Ferrars is not a hunk. He "was not recommended to [the Dashwoods] by any peculiar graces of person or address" remarks the narrator. "He was not handsome, and his manners required intimacy to make them pleasing" (Austen, *Sense* 15). In the movie, Edward is played by Hugh Grant, a man Thompson describes as "Repellently gorgeous . . . much prettier than I am" (212). Although he is not precisely pretty, Alan Rickman as Brandon is definitely more macho than someone who is described as wearing flannel waistcoats has a right to be. He frequently is filmed with a gun or a horse, and his disheveled appearance as Marianne lies ill out-Byrons Willoughby. "Give me an occupation," he murmurs to Elinor, "or I shall run mad" (Thompson 181). After this, the screenplay asserts, he is *"dangerously quiet"* (181). This is much more exciting than Austen's description of a man who, "with a readiness that seemed to speak the occasion, and the service pre-arranged in his mind . . . offered himself as the messenger who should fetch Mrs. Dashwood" (Austen, *Sense* 311). Clearly Brandon, as played by Rickman, is far sexier than Austen intended him to be.

Indeed, the movie works hard to create the impression that Brandon is the perfect romantic hero for Marianne. Specifically, Thompson's screenplay revises the novel so that Brandon's later actions mirror Willoughby's earlier behavior. In the movie, both carry an incapacitated Marianne through the rain. Both ride powerful chargers, and both recite poetry to her with heartfelt conviction. Brandon even concludes his poetry reading with what the screenplay describes as a *"soul-breathing glance"* (Thompson 187). Austen, in contrast, is notoriously reluctant to describe love scenes of any kind. In the novel, the courtship of Marianne and Colonel Brandon is described thus: "With such a confederacy against her—with a knowledge so intimate of his goodness—with a conviction of his fond attachment to herself, which at last, though long after it was observable to everybody else—burst on her—what could she do?" (Austen, *Sense* 378). Thompson's movie works, but, ironically, it works by celebrating the very tropes Austen destabilizes.

Like Austen's *Sense and Sensibility*, *Emma* is also not really about romance. *Emma* is a story about how a girl learns to be kind. Set on a pedestal by virtue of her social position, spoiled by her father, Emma "dangerously imagines herself a splendid free young goddess whose connection to most people is an amused puppeteer's" (Brownstein 104). Throughout the novel, Emma gradually learns that she is like everyone else. However, until she learns to value and join a community, the third-person narration mercilessly exposes Emma's delusions and satirizes the social conventions that nurture them.

Viewed in this light, Douglas McGrath's *Emma* is a vexed piece of work. Although the film ultimately refuses to knock Emma off her perch, it occasionally succeeds in exposing the delusions of its principal characters. One illustration of Emma's ignorance of her own heart, for instance, is accomplished through the casting. Gwyneth Paltrow's Emma and Jeremy Northam's Mr. Knightley are extremely good-looking. Moreover, the sixteen-year age gap that exists between Emma and Mr. Knightley is, here, invisible. Their union is so aesthetically pleasing that Emma's inability to see Knightley as anything other than a brother-in-law is called into question within the movie's first five minutes. The camera also insists that the two be viewed as a pair. Whenever the two share a scene, the camera either frames them within a single shot or shows us that they are aware of each other. We see Mr. Knightley watch Emma with more than brotherly interest at a piano recital. Later, at a ball, we observe Mr. Knightley rescue Harriet Smith from Emma's point of view. When their eyes meet, Emma and Mr. Knightley are inevitably drawn to each other. At the recital, Knightley joins Emma on the sofa and a close-up shuts out the rest of the room. At the ball, the two turn away from the camera and the camera pulls back, dramatizing their intimacy by shutting us out. Subtly, the casting, the blocking, and the camera work all expose Emma's lack of self-knowledge. This dramatic irony is what helps us see Emma's mistakes. We are aware of Emma's delusions and suspect the plot's outcome before she has a clue.

McGrath's movie is a comedy, and his use of visual irony occasionally reveals the characters' misconceptions in broad strokes. Knightley's sense of entitlement is lampooned, for example, when he complains about leaving his home for a ball. "I just want to stay here, where it's cozy," he mutters to Emma as the camera swings around to reveal the enormous proportions of Donwell Abbey. In a longer scene, an archery game turns ugly when the two disagree about Harriet Smith's rejection of Robert Martin. Dressed in pink and equipped with bow and quiver, Emma resembles nothing so much as a peculiar combination of Diana and Cupid. Although her sense of herself as a virginal goddess remains relatively intact, her incompetence as Cupid quickly becomes apparent. As Emma defends her actions, her shots grow wilder. "He is not Harriet's equal," she says and her arrow bounces off the target. "It would be a degradation for [Harriet] to marry a man I could not admit as my own acquaintance," she huffs, and her arrow sinks into the target's outer edge. "Upon my word, Emma," says Knightley, "better be without sense than misapply it as you do." Emma misses the target entirely and almost kills Knightley's dog. The incongruity between what Emma says and what we see on the screen clearly points out that Emma is wrong. As when Knightley insists upon the comforts of home, this juxtaposition of visual image and verbal display provides the most obvious and effective way of exposing and commenting on a character's point of view. As the arrows bounce off the target, Emma's snobbery and her ill-judgment are not only made apparent but are also condemned.

So why, with her faults, is Paltrow's Emma so appealing? Austen herself wrote that Emma was a heroine that "no one but myself will much like" (quoted in Austen-Leigh 157), and to all intents, she should have been right. In her review of the movie, Janet Maslin remarks "what makes the hauteur of *Emma* so forgivable are the facts that the heroine will know better by the time the story is over and that her instincts are so reliably wrong" (C1). The movie's ability to depict Emma ironically, Maslin suggests, releases us from the burden of judging Emma for ourselves. We can like Emma (both the movie and the character) because we are certain that the movie, which espouses our values, will chastise Emma for us.

Or will it? Another aspect of McGrath's *Emma* substantially undermines the movie's efforts to portray its heroine in an ironic light. This movie banked on its ability to make Paltrow a star. Timed to coincide with the movie's release, countless articles were written lauding Paltrow's beauty and charm.[2] Almost all of them mentioned her romantic relationship with the actor Brad Pitt. So prevalent was this deification that Paltrow's public persona seriously interferes with our view of the character she portrays. Despite her credible performance, Paltrow cannot avoid her reputation as the golden girl who landed the best-looking guy in the movies. With Paltrow as Emma, Emma's union with Knightley is a foregone conclusion. Moreover, as a star, Paltrow's apparent perfection works against the notion that Emma must get off her pedestal and rejoin the human race. Despite her faults, this Emma ends the movie where she begins it, firmly fixed upon Mount Olympus.

Indeed, the movie works hard to deify Paltrow. She is lit to perfection. In interior scenes, she always seems to be in a little more light than the rest of the cast. The camera, notes Maslin, loves to linger on her "fine-boned beauty," often to the detriment of the supporting players (C1). As befits an Olympian, Paltrow is often dressed and posed like a Greek goddess. While her empire waists correctly recall the period's obsession with ancient Greece, other details are somewhat anachronistic. Unless she is at church or visiting the poor, Emma tends to show a substantial amount of bosom and neck. She frequently wears only one color, a device that reinforces the sense that she is a complete entity unto herself. Her upswept hair is never allowed to curl near her face, and she is often bareheaded. Dressed thus, she resembles a statue brought to life or a girl on a pedestal.

Emma's poses reinforce the impression. As Emma awaits the Coles' invitation, she is shown on a settee built to resemble the double scrolls that top Ionic columns. The white curtain behind her and the two potted orange trees that frame the scene emphasize the neoclassical aesthetic organizing the tableau. At another point, Emma's superiority to Mrs. Elton is dramatized by her appearance and pose as they sit drinking tea. Dressed in a dark red long-sleeved dress, Mrs. Elton sits on a couch at least four inches lower than Emma's chair. Her curls hang to her shoulders. Clad in pale green, Emma sits perfectly upright on the edge of her seat. Her hair is pulled back and orna-mented with a green and white ribbon. Considered together, Mrs. Elton's appearance amounts to an ostentatious display of self while Emma's reflects a fondness for understatement and simple, pure lines. In a movie so besotted by the physical beauty of its hero and heroine, Emma's good looks thus be-come an indication of her moral worth. This Emma, the film tells us, *deserves* to be on a pedestal because she truly is a young goddess. She may make mistakes, but she is never really in need of any serious improvement. Thus, what could have been a *Bildungsroman*—a story of a young woman's educa-tion—ends up as a simple comedy of manners.

While McGrath's worship of Paltrow ultimately undermines the movie's original project, Amy Heckerling's *Clueless* faithfully replicates the ironic spirit of Austen's fifth novel. The protagonist Cher's skewed perspective and the role her environment plays in her misconceptions are dramatized by the con-trast between her oh-so-literal narration and what we see on the screen. Her insistence, for example, that she is a normal teenager who gets dressed in the morning accompanies a vision of Cher in her dressing room coordinating outfits on a computer. Her matter-of-fact description of her mother's acci-dental death during a "routine liposuction" identifies a terrifically tacky por-trait of a woman with feathered hair. Later, Cher's need for a quiet place to relax introduces a shot of the shopping mall. In this manner, the film makes the relationship between the realities of Cher's environment and her self-absorbed image hilariously clear.

Although Heckerling's *Clueless* has been dismissed as a charming but "light" version of Austen, *Clueless* is the only one of the three non-BBC films to recognize and replicate the most profound of *Emma*'s ironies. The genius of *Emma* is that it forces its readers to question the values and expectations they bring to the book. As Terry Castle points out, "we enjoy Emma because she is smart and she is good; but we positively dote on her mistakes because they allow *us* to feel superior" (xv). Upon reflection, however, we have to admit that we are not so superior, nor Emma so wrong, as we originally thought. Many first-time readers, for example, are surprised to learn about the secret engagement between Frank Churchill and Jane Fairfax.[3] Indeed, without the narrator's help, many of us are no more perceptive than Emma herself. Emma, moreover, is not so misguided as she initially appears: "Emma's wish to improve Harriet's situation is not intrinsically wrong," remarks Claudia Johnson (132). Indeed, Mr. Knightley points out that Emma chose better for Mr. Elton than he did himself: "Harriet Smith has some first-rate qualities, which Mrs. Elton is totally without" (Austen, *Emma* 331). Emma is also correct in suspecting Jane Fairfax's involvement in a secret romance. Austen's irony thus functions on multiple levels. While Emma's "mistakes" expose her own arrogance, they also open the door for a critique of those social conventions that deem a Harriet or Jane less of a "catch" than a woman like Mrs. Elton. Austen's irony, I think, encourages her readers to call into question those things we take for granted. If the fact that we misread the evidence suggests that we, like Emma, are shaped by the shape of our worlds, then Emma's awakening suggests that we also are able to consciously improve how we think and behave.

Although it tries, *Clueless,* does not go this far. Unlike Frank's love for Jane, Christian's homosexuality is probably clear to most viewers long before it is apparent to Cher. As in McGrath's *Emma,* Cher's union with Josh is also obvious from the start. However, Cher's moral growth and her genuinely likable nature pose a challenge to those of us who harbor stereotypes about spoiled teenagers who live in Beverly Hills. More seriously, the film goes to great lengths to reinforce an image of Cher that it eventually dismantles. The first-person narration is extremely important to this endeavor because it makes Cher immensely appealing. It lets us know that a good heart beats within that shell of self-involved ignorance. The fact that Cher finally understands her own heart is—importantly—signaled by a newfound harmony between what she says and what we see on the screen. Like a giant cartoon lightbulb, a huge glowing fountain erupts in the background to signify the truth of Cher's revelation. Cher's new perspective is more than a realization about her feelings for Josh. She sees her old behavior as shallow, and this gives her the power to alter her world. There is no question that *Sense and Sensibility* is a less "silly" book than *Clueless* a movie. But, in its own charming way, *Clueless* encourages its viewers to "makeover their souls."

Notes

1. According to Claudia Johnson, Austen employs "strategies of subversion and indirection" to create novels of social criticism (19). Throughout the book, Johnson demonstrates that irony is one of those strategies of indirection.
2. Hendricks's "The Lovely Gwyneth Paltrow" webpage lists over twenty-five articles on Paltrow in magazines such as *Vogue, Time,* and *New York Magazine.* See especially Corliss's profile, where he calls her "that cheerfully ravishing wraith on the arm of Hollywood dream supreme Brad Pitt" (74), and Rochlin's discussion of Paltrow and her celebrity status.
3. Here I disagree with Castle who, in her introduction to *Sense and Sensibility,* remarks that "it must be a colossally incompetent reader who misses . . . that Frank Churchill and Jane Fairfax are in some manner romantically involved" (xiv). As Johnson observes, "Such is the consummate mastery of Austen's plotting . . . that Emma's misapprehensions seem utterly plausible when we read the novel for the first time, and she appears willfully to 'mis-read' the sunny clarity of truth only when our own repeated readings of this romance, the stuff of literary criticism, have laid her misconstructions bare" (133).

Works Cited

Austen, Jane. *Emma.* Ed. R.W. Chapman. Rev. Mary Lascelles. 3d ed. Vol. 4 of *The Novels of Jane Austen.* 6 vols. Oxford: Oxford UP, 1966.

————. *Sense and Sensibility.* Ed. R.W. Chapman. Rev. Mary Lascelles. 3d ed. Vol. 1 of *The Novels of Jane Austen.* 6 vols. Oxford: Oxford UP, 1966.

Austen-Leigh, James Edward. *Memoir of Jane Austen.* 1870; rev. 1871. Ed. R.W. Chapman. Oxford: Clarendon P, 1926; rpt. 1951.

Brownstein, Rachel. *Becoming a Heroine: Reading about Women in Novels.* New York: Viking, 1982.

Castle, Terry. Introduction to *Emma.* By Jane Austen. Ed. James Kinsley. Oxford: Oxford UP, 1995.

Clueless. Writer and director Amy Heckerling. With Alicia Silverstone and Paul Rudd. Paramount, 1995.

Corliss, Richard. "A Touch of Class." *Time* 29 July 1996: 74-75.

Emma. Writer and director Douglas McGrath. With Gwyneth Paltrow and Jeremy Northam. Miramax, 1996.

Hendricks, Ben. "The Lovely Gwyneth Paltrow." Online at http://www.ugcs.caltech.edu/ ~bh/gp/GPreal.html (20 July 1997).

James, Caryn. "An *Emma* Both Darker and Funnier." Review of *Emma. New York Times* 15 Feb. 1997: 28.

Johnson, Claudia L. *Jane Austen: Women, Politics, and the Novel.* Chicago: U of Chicago P, 1988.

Maslin, Janet. "So Genteel, So Scheming, So Austen." Review of *Emma. New York Times* 2 Aug. 1996: C1.

Mudrick, Marvin. *Jane Austen: Irony as Defense and Discovery.* Princeton: Princeton UP, 1952.

Randle, Nancy Jalasca. "Austen—A Woman for All Seasons." *Standard-Times,* 16 Feb. 1997. Online at http://www.s-t.com/daily/02-97/02-16-97/e07ae311.htm (1 April 1998).

Rochlin, Margy. "Like Emma, Setting Her World All Astir." *New York Times* 28 July 1996: sec. 2, p. 11.

Sense and Sensibility. Writer Emma Thompson. Director Ang Lee. With Emma Thompson and Hugh Grant. Mirage-Columbia (Sony), 1995.

Thompson, Emma. *The Sense and Sensibility Screenplay and Diaries.* Rev. ed. New York: Newmarket, 1996.

10

Emma Thompson's *Sense and Sensibility* as Gateway to Austen's Novel

M. Casey Diana

Many English instructors use film clips in an effort to help students visually "connect" with a text. Sometimes, let us say in the case of Kafka's *The Trial,* the entire Orson Welles film (1962) can be particularly helpful in allowing students to navigate Kafka's labyrinth. The recent spate of literary film adaptations and the amount of video equipment utilized by English department media centers support the idea of an increasing dependence upon this pedagogical methodology. However, are we doing students a disservice by allowing them access to film, especially before they have had a chance to experience the literary text? By showing them film clips, or an entire film, do we curtail their imaginative capacities? Do we make them dependent upon another's interpretation and imagination? For instance, will Emma Thompson's version of Elinor (Emma Thompson) and Marianne (Kate Winslet) in the 1995 film of *Sense and Sensibility* live within students' minds instead of their own carefully crafted mental blueprints of the dueling Dashwood sisters?

In an attempt to answer these questions, I divided my section of English 103, "Introduction to Fiction," a class of thirty-two University of Illinois undergraduates, into two groups. Group A viewed the Academy Award-winning motion picture *Sense and Sensibility* in its entirety, and Group B read Austen's complete novel. The film viewers were advised not to read the text before viewing the movie; those who had already seen the movie were placed in the film group. The groups were then reversed, with the film viewers now reading, and the reading group now viewing. Immediately following each stage, the students took a comprehension quiz, wrote a 250-word essay, and filled out a questionnaire designed to ascertain which medium, film or novel, engaged them more. In addition to pedagogical concerns, additional questions were designed to determine why Austen herself is today so appealing—what timely need her work fills.

The questionnaires revealed that students who viewed the film followed the plot far more closely, had a deeper involvement with and readily differentiated between characters, and remembered a greater amount of detail than did the readers. For the most part, the film viewers enjoyed a positive experience and—most important, in my estimation—genuinely anticipated reading the book. On the other hand, the book readers (with one or two exceptions) were frustrated. Many missed major plot developments, displayed confusion over characters, recalled minimal (if any) detail, and either dreaded viewing the film or desired to see it merely for clarification: "I'm hoping to understand the book better by watching the movie. The writing style in the book was hard to follow. Perhaps if I 'see' it, I'll get a better understanding"; and "after seeing the movie I probably could have followed the novel much better." Conclusively, Thompson's film version of *Sense and Sensibility,* and probably other film versions of Austen's classics, instills a desire for—and provides a gateway to—a positive, in-depth reading experience for college students. In other words, the film unlocks the mind, cultivates the intellect, and implants the desire to pick up and read the novel. In fact, 90 percent of the film viewers expressed a desire to read the book. By providing an entertaining, positive learning experience, the film equips college students to read and understand the novel by transmitting to them a greater historical, social, and cultural sense of the period. Also, the film cultivates a deeper feeling for and attraction to the characters.

In both classroom groups, gender seemed to account for various responses. Female students comprehended and enjoyed both Austen's and Thompson's versions of *Sense and Sensibility* more than males. On a scale of one to ten, ten being the highest score, female students rated the film at 8.75 while male students ranked it at 6.37. The women scored the book (on the same scale) two points lower at 6.75, and the men ranked it 4.2. Quiz scores provided additional evidence for greater comprehension among viewers over readers, and contributed additional evidence for gender variance. The film viewers averaged 6.35 out of ten points; females averaging 7.4 and males 5.6. The book readers did not perform as well, averaging 4.78, with males at 4.4, and females at 5.0.

Questionnaires revealed that students who viewed the movie comprehended plot developments better than those who had only read the novel. To get an idea of their understanding of plot formation, I asked both groups to explain why the Dashwood family had to move from Norland to Barton Cottage and also to describe events immediately preceding, during, and after the scene in which Marianne first encounters Willoughby. Although the book readers understood that the Dashwood family had to move, many were not sure why. They hesitated in their assertions: "the father of Marianne and

Elinor passes away and the family is left without money. As a result they move homes to avoid the problems which would occur if they had stayed." The film viewers, on the other hand, demonstrated greater insights into the socioeconomic mores of the historical period and exhibited a deeper realization of how certain characters force the issue:

> First of all, I don't think they should have to move. The only reason they leave is because that witch of a sister-in-law doesn't want them there. And Fanny has her husband wrapped around her little finger so he'll do anything she says. I think another reason they leave is because of the way society was in that day. Properties and money always went to the next male descendant. And since Norland was rightfully John's, I think Mrs. Dashwood thought it was the "proper" thing to move out.

Clearly, this film viewer writes with confidence, naming not only the major characters but minor characters as well as the properties at issue. The student has grasped the timely concept of male primogeniture as well as the period's imperative to "do the right thing." Also, film viewers more precisely remembered the chronology of events. For example, they used elaborate detail in their descriptions of Marianne and Willoughby's first encounter:

> Marianne and Margaret go for a walk in the meadow. Marianne falls, sprains her ankle, and is helped by Willoughby. She is dazzled by him. He returns the next day with flowers as does Col. Brandon. Brandon's flowers are ignored and he is hurried out with Willoughby's arrival. Willoughby reads poetry with Marianne and the love affair begins. He captures her passions.

Some film viewers even prefaced the encounter with additional information:

> at the cottage, Mrs. Dashwood, Elinor, Marianne and Margaret received a package from Edward. It was the atlas that Margaret played with from the old house. Emotional feelings arise for Elinor. Marianne and Margaret go for a walk to stop Margaret from asking questions about Elinor and Edward.

On the other hand, the book readers, for the most part, were befuddled about plot details. Some could not even recall Marianne and Willoughby's meeting. Although one or two students remembered the events, most wrote vague responses: "I don't remember the first time they met really except that they talked and talked about every subject and would only have one or two more meetings until they were out of accepted topics to discuss." And, "I can recall that the instant Marianne and Willoughby met there was a spark. They spent a lot of time together. Elinor was quite aware of her sister's behavior (jealous?)."

Both groups exhibited disparate responses to the characters. Those characters most favored by the film viewers included Elinor Dashwood by the women and Edward Ferrars (Hugh Grant) by the men. Fanny Dashwood (Harriet Walter) was the least favorite among both male and female film viewers. Conversely, the younger sister Marianne was voted the most popular novel character by women students, with Edward again favored by book-reading males. Edward and Fanny tied for least preferred character among the reading women, with Willoughby selected by the men. Interestingly, not one woman designated the cad, Willoughby, as their least-favorite character.

Most film viewers distinguished the screen characters as well rounded, and they easily discerned Austen's thematic expertise in defining the differences between Elinor's rational Enlightenment values and Marianne's passionate Romantic impulses. Primarily, they demonstrated a greater sense of personal involvement with the characters than the readers:

> Each one seems very round. Austen draws you into each one—helping you identify with each character. I identify with both Elinor and Marianne. I used to be exactly like Marianne—impulsive, emotional, etc. But like Marianne got hurt, so did I, and have since identified myself more like Elinor (—silently emotional, thinks with her head first.)

Undoubtedly, this student strongly connects with Thompson's filmic version of the Dashwood sisters and uses the film as a tool for self-analysis.

Conversely, most book readers considered Austen's characters inaccessible and flat: "something separates me from the two sisters. The flowery language, the propriety of their culture leaves me at a loss for total comprehension. . . . I cannot follow many of their responses because I cannot understand what they are saying." Another student responded: "the characters are flat because they tend to each have a specific quality, or trademark, and that is all there is to them. Never much more development than that." Primarily, the readers got confused when they had to distinguish among characters, and they also exhibited very little personal involvement with them: "I can't remember who is who, so I have real trouble trying to identify with them. A visual image (from movie maybe) would certainly help me to remember who was who."

Questionnaires also revealed that students who viewed the film version of *Sense and Sensibility* came away with a much richer idea of setting. Both groups were asked what they remembered of Barton Cottage, the new home of the Dashwood ladies after they are forced to leave Norland. The film viewers had Thompson's bucolic vision to recollect: "It was a two-story house placed up-hill on a grassy covered ground. It looked old, but comfortable. Wilouby [*sic*] favored the cottage and gave it high praise. It was surrounded by grass and trees. It had a gravel pathway at the foot of the hill." Another student also described the screen version accurately: "Barton Cottage was actually a pretty large house. The inside was white/off white, without much adornment. It sat on a large amount of land." These students have integrated Thompson's vision of Barton Cottage and made it their own.

For students who did not initially view the film, one would conclude that they would construct their own versions of Barton Cottage, but among the book readers, instead of varied imaginings of idyllic country bungalows, there was hardly any discernment of setting at all: "I honestly do not remember much about Barton Cottage. This is where the family moved to upon leaving Norland. It was not as attractive or as expensively decorated as their previous home and I remember it being significantly smaller." Another book reader wrote, "If Barton Cottage was where the four women move to (not from) then it was tiny. It was in a valley, or plains." The question about setting, without exception, garnered such vague, wishy-washy responses from this group.

In summary, the film version of *Sense and Sensibility* engaged students and left a stronger, far more lasting impression upon them. The film viewers demonstrated a greater understanding of plot, a stronger identification with characters, and a clearer concept of setting. Ninety percent of the students who viewed the film first maintained that they looked forward to reading the novel: "I want to see the characters put into words"; and "after seeing the movie, I can't wait to read it."

Students who read the book after seeing the movie voiced appreciation. Many realized that without the movie as a gateway, they would have had a more difficult reading experience:

> Because of the language, I could not relate as well to the characters as I did when I watched the movie. An example of the language used is, "and to aim at the restraint of sentiments which were not in themselves illaudable, appeared to her not merely an unnecessary effort, but a disgraceful subjection of reason to common-place and mistaken notions" [Austen 53]. I absolutely love this story. But if I would of [*sic*] read the book first I believe my

opinion would be different. I probably would have become very bored with the book and never read anything by Jane Austen again.

Another student comes to the point more quickly: "I found the book hard to read, and I definitely would have put it down within the first few pages had I not seen the movie first."

At this point, we have to wonder just what the catalyst is that converts today's college student from film to literary text. Although it may seem simply to be a case of curiosity—"I'm interested to see how the characters are portrayed" or "I own the movie and have seen it a few times; now it's interesting to read the book and compare both similarities and differences between the novel and film"—they want something more complex. While they naturally wish to continue an enjoyable experience, in a manner analogous to today's popular movie sequels—"I want to see the characters put into words. I heard it's a wonderful book"—they also strongly yearn to expand upon the delight the movie induced: "I hope I will be able by reading to get into a character and see through their eyes."

In addition to pedagogical concerns, my investigation also sought to gain understanding of Austen's appeal today. Her books continue on bestseller lists (Penguin reports a 40 percent increase in sales) and film adaptations (including *Sense and Sensibility,* which earned $42 million at the box office) have hit theaters in successful financial wave after wave (Brennan). Austen has been applauded in *People* magazine and profiled on CNN. *Entertainment Weekly* even featured a "photograph" of her beside the exclusive Beverly Hills Hotel pool (Westenberg). She is worshipped at electronic shrines (see Churchyard, Riches), and Home Pages have sprung up in Spanish, Polish, Swedish, and German (Brennan). So, we have to question, why is the author, who has been dead for 180 years, so popular? What timely itch does the author scratch? I asked both of my groups to write a paragraph addressing this question. In addition, I asked whether they felt they would have enjoyed living during this period.

Although the student responses to this assignment at first seemed scattered and vague, I eventually catalogued their responses into three groups: strong identification with characters, a longing to return to a simpler era, and a desire for love and romance. In responding to the question on Austen's popularity, many students revealed that they identified with the characters and assumed that others did, too: "the characters exemplify such varied personalities that most viewers probably relate personally to at least one of them"; and, "Elinor reminds me of myself in that I think very logically and I try not to let my emotions affect me" and:

[Marianne's sentiments] could be a page out of my autobiography or any woman's autobiography. It shows how heartbreak makes women do the same senseless rituals of playing "our song" over and over again just like women were doing two hundred years ago. The technology may have changed but the emotions certainly have not.

Although most students were adamant about the eighteenth not being their century of choice—"are you kidding? I love the twentieth century," and "I need a computer, a car, medicine. I don't want to be bled, and I like good shoes"—many students, males and females both, wistfully mused about a kinder, gentler era: "I think their everyday lives are fascinating. Although courting is very strict and structured, men treated women with total respect (and vice versa)"; and "things were a lot simpler"; and "men respected women more in a dating situation. Today's expectations for dating are way too high."

At this point, we have to wonder at time's swinging pendulum. One young male student wrote with particular poignancy:

I also truly enjoy the respect and manners which the characters displayed, especially from the men towards the ladies. The way in which the men bowed their heads to greet the ladies and the ladies responded back by bending at the knees and bowing their heads, added to the romance and charm. Today this sense of romance and chivalry has died. On campus, for example, the closest thing to romance is going to [a local bar], getting drunk, and trying to shack up with someone even drunker than yourself.

Finally, students referred to the overriding reason for Austen's popularity as the timeless desire for love and romance:

our generation is unfortunately one full of thoughtless, meaningless sex. The idea of true love, true companionship between a man and a woman is practically ridiculed in our culture. Austen's sensibility touches a chord—a reminder of the God-given beauty of true love and romanticism.

Another succinctly stated that "the game of love has always been a struggle between the heart and mind."

Clearly, *Sense and Sensibility* in both forms, film and novel, affected these students. However, they would not—or perhaps could not—have delved as deeply into their analysis had they not seen the movie. Most of the students who read the text first could not get beyond Austen's prose—the "flowery language," as they put it. However, the film enabled students to grasp the plot more fully, to engage on a deeper level with the characters, and to remember a greater amount of detail. While we still could argue that passively watching film constructs a literary text for students and deactivates their imagination, this particular literary film-adaptation, in my estimation, provides a gateway to a positive reading experience. One may hope the interest kindled by Thompson's film version of *Sense and Sensibility* will ignite in young scholars a greater desire for Austen that only the literary text can quench.

Note

This essay first appeared in a shorter form in *Topic: A Journal of the Liberal Arts* 48 (1997): 49-55.

Works Cited

Austen, Jane. *Sense and Sensibility*. Ed. R.W. Chapman. Rev. Mary Lascelles. 3d ed. Vol. 1 of *The Novels of Jane Austen*. 6 vols. Oxford: Oxford UP, 1966.

Brennan, Mary. "See Jane Surf: Surf, Jane, Surf!" MSNBC circa 15 Aug. 1996. Online at http://www.biddeford.com/~gwallace/surf.html (17 Mar. 1997).

Churchyard, Henry. "Jane Austen Information Page." Online at http://www.pemberley.com/janeinfo/janeinfo.html (20 July 1997).

Magill's Cinema Annual. New York: Magill P, 1996. 458-59.

Riches, Hester Lee. "Movie Links." 31 July 1996. Online at http://www.canoe.com:80/JamMoviesHester/hester_july31.html (17 Mar. 1997).

Sense and Sensibility. Writer Emma Thompson. Director Ang Lee. With Emma Thompson and Hugh Grant. Mirage-Columbia (Sony), 1996.

The Trial. Writer and director Orson Welles. With Anthony Perkins. Paris-Europa Productions, 1962.

Westenberg, Theo. Photo of "Jane Austen" beside the swimming pool. *Entertainment Weekly* 22 Dec. 1995. Online at http://pathfinder.com/ew/960105/features/eoty/CT161.jpg (20 July 1997).

11

"Piracy Is Our Only Option"

Postfeminist Intervention in *Sense and Sensibility*

Kristin Flieger Samuelian

Early in Emma Thompson's 1995 screen adaptation of *Sense and Sensibility*, Elinor Dashwood and Edward Ferrars are riding together in the fields near Norland, the Dashwood family estate—soon to be relinquished to Elinor's half brother. Picking up the thread of a conversation begun earlier and continued over several scenes, Elinor remarks, "You talk of feeling idle and useless—imagine how that is compounded when one has no choice and no hope whatsoever of any occupation" (Thompson 49). When Edward comments, "Our circumstances are therefore precisely the same," she retorts, "Except that you will inherit your fortune. We cannot even earn ours."

This reference to a patriarchal system in which men inherit property while women of Elinor's class have no financial resource outside the demonstrably unreliable benevolence of male relatives is one means by which Thompson injects what appears an explicit feminist rhetoric into the work of an author more often celebrated for the implicitness of her critiques of the customs and institutions that support patriarchy. Feminist criticism of Austen usually focuses on what Claudia Johnson has called her ability "to expose and explore," without appearing to challenge, "those aspects of traditional institutions—marriage, primogeniture, patriarchy—which patently do not serve her heroines well" (xxiv).[1] In contrast, Thompson registers protest through the speeches of her female characters and then quiets it by means of a courtship plot that obviates the conditions protested against. This pattern, I will argue, while seeming to legitimize feminist discourse, is more in line with postfeminism and effectively erases the implicit feminism of Austen's novel.

My use of the term postfeminism is drawn from Tania Modleski's *Feminism without Women: Culture and Criticism in a "Postfeminist" Age*. According to Modleski, contemporary mass culture and cultural criticism, "in proclaiming or assuming the advent of postfeminism," discredits current feminist critique (3). Because this trend purports not to discount the goals of feminism but simply to argue for their redundancy in a postfeminist era, it is often carried out "not *against* feminism but in its very name" (x). Thompson's film reflects this postfeminist consciousness in that it first posits and then rejects the possibility that its heroines' lives are governed by patriarchy. In demonstrating that feminist protest is both tolerated and satisfactorily answered by courtship, Thompson links such protest to the institutions—marriage, the family, compulsory heterosexuality—that feminism is engaged in critiquing. Hence, although appearing sympathetic to the goals of feminism, her film ends by undermining them.[2]

Explicit protest is most thoroughly articulated in the film through the youngest Dashwood sister, Margaret. Transformed by Thompson from a plot device to an integral character, Margaret serves both to voice reasonable dissent and to exhort unpalatable truths from the mouths of her more restrained and practical-minded elders. When she refuses to leave her tree house to meet her half brother and sister-in-law, questioning their right to Norland when "they already have a house in London," Elinor explains to her that "houses go from father to son, dearest—not from father to daughter. It is the law" (Thompson 34). Elinor's closing emphasis on "law" simplifies to the point of obliterating the complicated history of the disposition of the Norland estate given in the first two pages of Austen's novel.[3] At the same time, it reiterates both the inescapable nature of the conditions under which the Dashwood women live—vestigial primogeniture—and Elinor's awareness of these conditions. Her statement to her preadolescent sister can be read as a first step in Margaret's education into eighteenth-century womanhood.

Margaret's recalcitrance, on the other hand, voices a resentment that her mother and sisters clearly feel but will not allow themselves to express openly, and it is one of the ways in which she is constructed in the film as a figure, by virtue of her youth, for healthy nonconformity. The tree house in which she hides reinforces this image: unlike Norland, it is movable; it can be put up anywhere there is a sturdy tree. Instead of going from father to son, Margaret's house remains with her and becomes a symbol, not of patriarchal law, but of female mobility and independence. Her habit of mounting the ladder of the tree house to look through a spyglass reminds viewers that her current ambition is to be a pirate. Presumably, Margaret has not yet learned that she has no choice and no hope of any occupation, but Elinor and Edward's support of her ambitions, however tongue-in-cheek, suggests that she may never need to learn it, that the world she inherits will be far more tolerant than the one her sisters find themselves in after the death of their father.

Conversations like these constitute interventions in Austen's project, revisions that seem designed to "bring out" its buried feminism—to make explicit what Austen, as a single woman and writer at the dawn of the nineteenth century, must have felt but did not dare to say aloud. In doing so, Thompson's screenplay voices an antipatriarchal protest to which few in her audience are likely to object. In the long run, however, because the explicitness of her critique works in concert with her courtship plot, it engenders a complacency that Austen resists. When Elinor explains the principles of primogeniture to her sister, she—or Thompson through her—claims as law what was, in fact, only custom.[4] In doing so, Thompson in effect reclaims Austen's text for a late twentieth-century audience. Elinor's comment, inaccurate though it is, works with her comment to Edward to reassure viewers that the distribution of gender power—figured, appropriately, as the distribution of property—is no longer what it was at the turn of the nineteenth century. Such unfair laws are no longer in place; women today have more choices and more hope.

At the same time, the invocation of an unreasonable law sanctions a kind of lawlessness that, I suggest, characterizes Thompson's response to those aspects of Austen's narrative that are irreconcilable with current notions of courtship but that serve, for Austen's audience, as the site of feminist critique. When Elinor remarks, "you will inherit your fortune. We cannot even earn ours," Edward's response, "Piracy is our only option" (Thompson 50)—an allusion to Margaret's ambition—is a way of deflecting what is unanswerable in Elinor's complaint: her reference to the same law that she has explained to her sister. This deflection is repeated at the level of plot when the courtship between Elinor and Edward obviates the conditions against which she protests and to which he listens with such sympathy.

In a larger sense, then, piracy—the appropriation and adaptation for profit of Austen's courtship novel—is for Thompson a way of deflecting what is unanswerable in the eighteenth-century ideology the novel depicts. Adaptation would seem to be the ethical and practical opposite of piracy in that, while the latter means claiming the work—or the proceeds from the work—of another as one's own, the former usually means an implicit claim that one's own production is a true reproduction of an earlier work belonging to someone else. This claim is perhaps best illustrated, as Patrice Hannon has pointed out, in the television ads that called *Sense and Sensibility* "Jane Austen's most impassioned love story" (quoted in Hannon 27)—referring to a passion largely inserted by Thompson in her reworking of a novel in which Austen, as many critics have noted, condemns passion as at best specious, at worst dangerous.[5]

In fact, however, the distinction between piracy and adaptation is rarely so clear-cut, opening to multiple interpretations not only what constitutes ownership of a text but what constitutes a text itself. The pirating of print texts, especially in the eighteenth and early nineteenth centuries, often involved much the same kind of ideological adjustments and revisions that Thompson makes in her film adaptation.[6] The radical publisher William Hone, for example, printed in 1817 a prose adaptation of Byron's *The Corsair* marketed to and largely rewritten for a working-class audience. Hone's ideologically motivated appropriation and redistribution of Byron's tale, as Peter Manning has pointed out, illustrates "the ways in which a text, once written, separates from its author and enters an economy of production and distribution, to be acted upon by forces beyond the writer's prevision or control" (233). In inserting and authorizing both protest and passion into Austen's courtship plot, Thompson, like Hone, resituates that plot in a cultural context radically different from the one in which Austen was writing. Late twentieth-century postfeminist consciousness demands a reconciliation between female independence and marriage. In Thompson's project, courtship serves both. In Austen's, economic conditions set them at odds.

Austen, as recent feminist criticism has noted, represents the marriages of Elinor and, even more, Marianne Dashwood as fortunate rather than idyllic, thus demonstrating the precarious position of the sisters, throughout most of the novel, as unmarried women of the gentry with no property or expectations.[7] Thompson's screenplay, although it articulates this position early on, ultimately reverses Austen's implicit argument by doing away with what readers have found unexciting in the novel's approved lovers, Edward and Colonel Brandon, and by rewriting their courtships to foreground the very passion and romance Austen condemns.

Both Deborah Kaplan and Devoney Looser have remarked on the sympathy and understanding added to Edward's character in the translation from novel to film—the energy devoted to making him not simply suitable, but ideal: the perfect match for the levelheaded but strong-minded Elinor.[8] In addition to devoting extra attention to the development of his character, Thompson tracks, in detail and with a sympathy that Austen avoids, the progress of Brandon's courtship of Marianne. We see the *"expression of pained surprise"* in his *"melancholy, brooding eyes"* as he watches her playing the pianoforte and singing, unseen by any but Elinor, *"with an unfathomable look of grief and longing"* (Thompson 71). In contrast, Austen's Brandon listens to Marianne "without being in raptures" paying her only "the compliment of attention" (Austen 35). The scene in the novel is one of the few presented through Marianne's (at this stage) extremely limited point of view and gives little insight into the feelings of any of the other characters, Brandon included.

Thompson's Brandon, like Edward, knows instinctively how to ingratiate himself with Margaret Dashwood as well, fascinating her by telling her "*mysteriously*" that the air in the East Indies "is full of spices" (Thompson 72). And he exhibits a tension-creating sexual energy that his counterpart in the novel (whose desire for the narcissistic Marianne is entirely one-sided) lacks. Brandon makes Marianne "*Oddly nervous*" when he "*materialises at her side and wordlessly offers her his hunting knife*" while she is cutting bulrushes (Thompson 75).[9] His courtship of Marianne, after her abandonment by Willoughby, occupies a substantial part of the film's denouement, from the moment of her recovery from illness, through his replacement of Willoughby as literary confidant and his recognition as acknowledged lover when he gives her a pianoforte,[10] to the joyous wedding that closes the film. In contrast, Austen devotes little more than a page to the "confederacy" (Austen 378) of Dashwood women who work to unite a diffident Brandon and an unthinking Marianne.

What Thompson has done, in the characterization of both Brandon and Edward, is to endow them with a substantial portion of the life and attractiveness Austen originally located in Willoughby. In keeping with this effort to redistribute the attractiveness of the male characters, she eliminates Elinor's emotionally charged scene with Willoughby during Marianne's illness. This episode is Austen's first real indicator that Elinor is capable of strong passions and that sensibility is not exclusively the province of the dangerously vulnerable Marianne. Violent emotion seeps into the narrative in advance of Willoughby's entrance, as if to prepare readers for the passions that will be alluded to and generated in his scene. As her sister's illness reaches its crisis, the habitually balanced Elinor suffers an "excess" of "apprehensions" (Austen 312). She finds it "difficult to be calm" (316) in anticipation of her mother's arrival during a violent storm. And when the visitor who comes in out of the storm turns out against all expectation, almost against credibility, to be Willoughby, she reacts "with a look of horror" and tries to leave the room, obeying "the first impulse of her heart" (317), like her sister in an earlier scene. In the ensuing conversation, she finds herself swayed by Willoughby against her reason. When she tries to reprove him, "her voice, in spite of herself, betrayed her compassionate emotion" (329).

The scene illustrates not only Elinor's share of sensibility but her response to Willoughby's sexual power and, consequently, the extent of that power. After he leaves, having explained part of his culpability in abandoning Marianne, she thinks of him

> with a tenderness, a regret, rather in proportion, as she soon acknowledged within herself—to his wishes than to his merits. She felt that his influence over her mind was heightened by circum-

stances which ought not in reason to have weight; by that person
of uncommon attraction, that open, affectionate, and lively manner which it was no merit to possess; and by that still ardent love
for Marianne, which it was not even innocent to indulge. [Austen
333]

Mary Poovey has pointed out that Elinor in this scene is "aroused" by
Willoughby "to a pitch of complex emotion we never see Edward inspire in
anyone" (185). I would suggest that it is for this reason that Thompson, in
adapting the novel, chose to shift much of the passion and complex emotions generated in and by this encounter to a pair of scenes between Elinor
and Edward—reassigning the power to arouse and influence Elinor to the
man she is destined to marry.

In the first of these, Edward calls on Elinor in London, in response to a
message from her. She has been commissioned by Colonel Brandon to offer
Edward a living in Delaford, after the discovery of his engagement to Lucy
Steele results in his disinheritance. This scene follows essentially the one in
the novel, the principal difference being Edward's behavior. With an impetu-
osity far more characteristic of Willoughby in the deleted scene than of Edward as he appears in the novel, he does not at first allow Elinor to begin the
subject that has brought him to her and comes very close to making a declaration of illicit love. Referring immediately to his betrayal of her, he blurts
out, "Miss Dashwood, God knows what you must think of me" (Thompson
169), an anxiety that echoes Willoughby's: "Tell me honestly . . . do you
think me most a knave or a fool?" (Austen 318). When Elinor tries to stop
him from entering on forbidden ground, Edward "*interrupts her, desperate to
explain,*" saying "I have no right to speak, I know—" (Thompson 169).

Both film and novel manage to convey Edward's jealousy of Brandon
and his conviction that Brandon's having trusted Elinor with this message
indicates a growing intimacy between them that will end in marriage. This
knowledge all but silences Austen's Edward, however, whereas it prompts
Thompson's Edward to make a final declaration, if not of love, then of its
only licit substitute. In the novel:

> they parted, with a very earnest assurance on *her* side of unceas-
> ing good wishes for his happiness in every change of situation
> that might befal him; on *his,* with rather an attempt to return the
> same good will, than the power of expressing it. [Austen 290]

In Thompson's screenplay, "EDWARD *looks at* ELINOR, *his eyes full of sad-
ness,*" and tells her, "Your friendship has been the most important of my life"

(171). When she assures him that "You will always have it," his response—"Forgive me"—again echoes Willoughby's desire in his scene "to obtain something like forgiveness" (Austen 319) from Marianne through Elinor.

The second and more passionate of the two scenes depicts the reconciliation between Edward and Elinor, most of which Austen chose not to narrate at all, or to put off to a point after their engagement has been declared, thereby removing it from any significant participation in the narrative tension of the courtship plot. In both novel and film, the knowledge that Edward is not married to Lucy causes Elinor once again to give way to sensibility by weeping uncontrollably. In the novel, however, these tears are wept in private, and she and Edward spend their first moments of freedom as physically removed from each other as they can be within the small space surrounding Barton cottage. Elinor runs further into the house while Edward, after a moment of "reverie," walks "towards the village" (Austen 360). "How soon he had walked himself into the proper resolution, however," Austen continues, "how soon an opportunity of exercising it occurred, in what manner he expressed himself, and how he was received, need not be particularly told" (361). All that need be told is that within the space of three hours "he had secured his lady" and become "one of the happiest of men" (361).

In the film, Elinor bursts into tears in front of Edward. It is her mother and sisters who leave the room, not she. And we are shown precisely the manner in which he expresses himself and how he is received. After a short speech (condensed from a much longer explanatory speech that in the novel he makes only after they have become acknowledged lovers), Edward assures Elinor "that my heart is and always will be yours" (Thompson 198). This declaration so resembles Willoughby's in his scene with Elinor—"tell her that my heart was never inconstant to her, and if you will, that at this moment she is dearer to me than ever" (Austen 330)—that Thompson seems once again to have taken the passionate speeches of one lover and put them, slightly altered, into the mouth of another to render him more interesting than Austen deemed necessary.

This need to make courtship allied with rather than opposed to romance prompts Thompson not only to redistribute the erotic tension of the novel but also to fill in some of its more uncomfortable gaps—as for instance, where Marianne is translated into a married woman and the mistress of an estate virtually overnight, the narration of which focuses almost exclusively on her husband's desire. After Elinor's marriage, she and her mother turn their attention to Brandon's "sorrows, and their own obligations" and agree that "Marianne . . . was to be the reward of all" (Austen 378).[11] "With such a confederacy against her," Austen asks rhetorically, "what could she do?" (378). Marianne, in fact, does very little, seeming to pass almost unconscious through the two years that intervene between her abandonment by Willoughby and her marriage to Brandon, when "she found herself at nineteen, submitting to new attachments, entering on new duties, placed in a new home, a wife, the mistress of a family, and the patroness of a village" (Austen 379). As a result of which change, "Colonel Brandon was now as happy, as all those who best loved him, believed he deserved to be," while Marianne "found her own happiness in forming his" (379). Thompson's rendering of the gradual softening of Marianne toward Brandon, culminating in her radiant happiness at the wedding that closes the film, not only distributes the happiness evenly between both lovers but locates its origins in the courtship rather than in the institution that courtship traditionally supports.

Thompson's interventions in Austen's plot, her need to provide narrative coherence and render it more compatible with contemporary notions of courtship, eliminate a space for feminist critique by eliminating the discomfort generated by such examples of the novel's drive toward closure, a drive that makes us uncomfortable because it highlights what Thompson is at pains to erase: the woman's relative unimportance in the courtship plot. Austen's ending illustrates the unwieldy if not untenable alliance between traditional institutions and the companionate marriage so dear to middle-class hearts, potentiating a critique of these institutions far more resounding than any that Thompson's characters make in the film.

Thompson's pirating of Willoughby's character, moreover, redistributing much of the erotic force Austen has given him, ignores what the novel makes clear: that Elinor's erotic identity is established through romantic linkings with more than one man. D.A. Miller points out that "both sisters are erotically involved with all three men, whatever safeguards are imposed by the categories . . . that differentiate the involvement" (67). What this multiplicity of connections suggests is that no single one of the novel's male characters has the substance to adequately partner either of its heroines, and that both end up marrying men whose combined integrity and passionlessness demonstrate the limited choices available to middle-class women much more effectively than Thompson's Elinor can in speech.

The explicit, if restrained, dissent of Thompson's Elinor Dashwood, the largely unreproved rebelliousness of Margaret, the heightened attractiveness of Edward Ferrars and Colonel Brandon, and the general redistribution of passion and passionate encounters in the transition from novel to film require Thompson to eliminate or explain away much of what is unsettling in Austen's courtship plot. Her adaptation thus highlights not the hidden truth of Austen's novel but the extent to which all adaptations are governed by the consciousness and expectations of their intended audiences, rather than by an adapter's commitment to the author's original aims. To smooth over what is dissatisfying in Austen's narrative is to ignore, and to invite viewers to ignore, what she appears to have known very well: that even for women as beautiful as Marianne, as intelligent as Elinor, the institutions, the customs— more powerful than law because less explicit—that governed their lives offered few choices and little hope.

Perhaps one defining characteristic of a postfeminist consciousness is its conviction that custom can have no material role in governing women's lives—that, for instance, there is no meaningful connection between the custom of assuming a husband's patronym upon marriage, which many women still follow, and the eighteenth-century common law of coverture. Piracy works as a metaphor in Thompson's film because custom is redefined as law. As a fantasy of rebellion or escape, it provides a kind of safety valve for hero and heroine while, because the fantasy is most fully realized in the film's youngest character, it hints at the possibility of a new generation of women whose range of choices, like the imagined range of Margaret's expeditions, will be wider. As a strategy for Thompson, piracy becomes a way of negotiating between prefeminist and postfeminist discourses. If Austen was writing at a time when debate on the condition of women was just beginning and concerted agitation for women's rights still decades in the future, Thompson is writing at a time of disenchantment with the terms of that debate, in particular with feminism's critique of the heterosexual courtship model. Her adaptation responds to that critique (and its implicit working out in Austen's plot) by linking courtship with female passion and independence in a way not only inconceivable in Austen's era but counter to the aims—and the feminism—of her novel.

Notes

This essay first appeared in *Topic: A Journal of the Liberal Arts* 48 (1997): 39-48.

1. For a recent discussion of Austen's critique of traditional institutions and the paternalism that purportedly upholds them, see Smith.
2. Susan Faludi identifies this pattern of advance and retreat as one form of anti-feminist backlash. She cites examples from the film *Crossing Delancey* (1988), which "mouths sympathy for feminist aspirations, then promptly eats its words" (127), and the television series *thirtysomething,* whose characters "mounted a feeble mock struggle against the domestic images of '50s television, then gladly surrendered to them" (161). If this is backlash, however, it is a particularly subtle form, in that it markets itself as a marriage of progressivism and traditionalism. In seeming to adopt an accommodationist stance, paying lip service to one view while endorsing its opposite, it accomplishes what amounts to the patriarchalization of feminism.
3. It is a will made by Henry Dashwood's uncle that effectively disinherits the

sisters and not, as Elinor's remark suggests, an entail on the Norland estate or, as it might appear to twentieth-century filmgoers, an actual law—primogeniture—that bound every Englishman in the eighteenth century.

4. The law of primogeniture was abolished in the late seventeenth century under Charles II, in the sense that a given property owner could thereafter direct his property as he desired, although the principle continued to exert itself as a customary procedure reinforced by legal habits. Primogeniture and the preference of male heirs persisted in inheritance at law (that is, in those cases where no device, such as a will, directed the property otherwise) and in cases of ambiguities within wills, reinforcing the habit of mind in which, in thinking about inheritance, the father images the son. In claiming that the law barred the ability of women to inherit, therefore, Thompson's Elinor is imagining, with some justification, the common law of feudal descent operating. Austen makes it clear, however, that old Mr. Dashwood could have chosen to dispose his property differently than he did. He was not bound by either law or custom. And, in the event, the estate does not go from father to son but from great-uncle to grandnephew, bypassing the father altogether. Henry Dashwood has only a life interest in the property, and he dies before he can make that yield any income for his daughters. For a contemporary discussion of primogeniture's transmutation from law to custom, see Powell.

5. Perhaps the best known discussions of Austen's distrust of passion are by Marilyn Butler and Mary Poovey.

6. For a comprehensive study of copyright law and piracy in Britain, see Feather.

7. See Kirkham (87). Phoebe Smith argues that "the reader's unease at the tidy marital arrangements . . . points to the unequal provisions of the marriage contract under English law at the beginning of the nineteenth century. Without legal changes enabling married women to achieve a measure of economic independence . . . the companionate marriage of mutual choice would continue to rely on the protection of benevolent males, with female autonomy possible only in the domestic sphere" (20).

8. Looser suggests that Thompson renders Edward more "feminist-friendly" (167), "more in keeping with today's model 'new man'" (166). Kaplan argues, as I do, that the film employs an economy of compensation, making up for the defects of both men in Austen's rendition of the courtships (174).

9. See Kaplan's discussion of Alan Rickman's romanticized portrayal of Brandon during Marianne's illness (175).

10. I am indebted to Mark Schoenfield for pointing out that this episode constitutes another act of piracy on Thompson's part: importing into her film a scene from *Emma*, when Frank Churchill (like Willoughby, a dangerously attractive man in contrast to the somewhat staid Knightley) secretly gives a pianoforte to Jane Fairfax.

11. Maaja Stewart accurately identifies this transaction as a "sentimental gift exchange" (85).

Works Cited

Austen, Jane. *Sense and Sensibility.* Ed. R.W. Chapman. Rev. Mary Lascelles. 3d ed. Vol. 1 of *The Novels of Jane Austen.* 6 vols. Oxford: Oxford UP, 1966.

Butler, Marilyn. *Jane Austen and the War of Ideas.* Oxford: Oxford UP, 1975.

Faludi, Susan. *Backlash: The Undeclared War against American Women.* New York: Crown, 1991.

Feather, John. *Publishing, Piracy, and Politics: An Historical Study of Copyright in Britain.* London: Cassell, 1994.

Hannon, Patrice. "Austen Novels and Austen Films: Incompatible Worlds?" *Persuasions: The Journal of the Jane Austen Society of North America* 18 (1996): 24-32.

Johnson, Claudia L. *Jane Austen: Women, Politics, and the Novel.* Chicago: U of Chicago P, 1988.

Kaplan, Deborah. "Mass Marketing Jane Austen: Men, Women, and Courtship in Two of the Recent Films." *Persuasions: The Journal of the Jane Austen Society of North America* 18 (1996): 171-81.

Kirkham, Margaret. *Jane Austen, Feminism, and Fiction.* Sussex: Harvester; Totowa, N.J.: Barnes and Noble, 1983.

Looser, Devoney. "Jane Austen 'Responds' to the Men's Movement." *Persuasions: The Journal of the Jane Austen Society of North America* 18 (1996): 159-70.

Manning, Peter. *Reading Romantics: Texts and Contexts.* New York: Oxford UP, 1990.

Miller, D.A. *Narrative and Its Discontents: Problems of Closure in the Traditional Novel.* Princeton: Princeton UP, 1981.

Modleski, Tania. *Feminism without Women: Culture and Criticism in a "Postfeminist" Age.* New York: Routledge, 1991.

Poovey, Mary. *The Proper Lady and the Woman Writer: Ideology as Style in the Works of Mary Wollstonecraft, Mary Shelley, and Jane Austen.* Chicago: U of Chicago P, 1984.

Powell, John Joseph. *An Essay upon the Learning of Devises from Their Inception by Writing to Their Consummation by the Death of the Devisor.* New York: Brisban and Brannan, 1807.

Sense and Sensibility. Writer Emma Thompson. Director Ang Lee. With Emma Thompson and Hugh Grant. Mirage-Columbia (Sony), 1995.

Smith, Phoebe A. "*Sense and Sensibility* and 'The Lady's Law': The Failure of Benevolent Paternalism." *CEA Critic* 55:3 (1993): 3-25.

Stewart, Maaja A. *Domestic Realities and Imperial Fictions: Jane Austen's Novels in Eighteenth-Century Contexts.* Athens: U of Georgia P, 1993.

Thompson, Emma. *The Sense and Sensibility Screenplay and Diaries.* Rev. ed. New York: Newmarket, 1996.

12

Feminist Implications of
the Silver Screen Austen

Devoney Looser

In January of 1996, *Time* ran a television review with the headline "Sick of Jane Austen Yet?" For many months in 1995 and 1996, British and American viewers found themselves asking, "Why Austen?" and "Why now?" Attempting to answer these questions, as Louis Menand has suggested, "is an invitation to punditry it is probably wise to decline" (15). As the existence of this collection of essays itself demonstrates, however, a number of pundits have happily ignored Menand's advice. Periodicals from *The Progressive* to *The National Review,* from *Rolling Stone* to *Town and Country,* from *People* to *The Wall Street Journal* have recently given over space to Jane Austen. This array of publications alone demonstrates the conflicting ideological forces propelling the Austen revival.

Though I do not pretend to have the key to all Austen mythologies, I argue in this essay that Austen's reemergence demonstrates progressive, feminist elements at work in popular culture, rather than simply tolling neoconservative bells. Austen's popularity has resonance with contemporary Western liberal feminisms, particularly as a result of the ways in which her texts have been consumed and interpreted anew by public intellectuals and mainstream critics alike. Most of the recent Austen adaptations are, to my mind, relatively faithful (albeit decidedly contemporary) interpretations of Austen's women and their feminist leanings. At moments when the adaptations modulate characters differently or when scenes are added or changed, however, we can see precisely how the adaptations contribute to a "mainstreaming" of feminism. Austen herself was involved in mainstreaming feminist ideals when she wrote her novels in the early 1800s. Her return as an ideological factor in big- and small-screen feminist representations in the late twentieth century is not an identical phenomenon, but it is an important similarity that has gone largely unremarked in the popular press.

In trying to answer the "why now" part of the "why Austen" equation, some have claimed that such attention is Austen's birthright, while others have shown that Austen has never exactly disappeared from the public eye. Austen's film and TV repackaging is no grand departure from industry business as usual, promoted by some old-fashioned media hype. James Collins concludes as much: "The BBC is always filming something by Jane Austen. . . . Emma Thompson and Hugh Grant are both English. How remarkable is it that they're making a movie like *Sense and Sensibility?*" (70). Collins remarks that we are not likely to see the headline "ENGLISH ACTORS WEAR PERIOD CLOTHES AND SPEAK WITTY DIALOGUE" anytime soon (70). Though there is truth in this, the headlines have in fact appeared on "Austen-mania"—the record-breaking audiences the BBC attracted in England and that A&E found in the United States. The *Wall Street Journal,* in its front-page assessment, argued that today's Jane-mania is wholly "cash driven" (Stevens 1; see also the response by Johnson A19). Surely, however, our explanations for Austen's popular resurgence must go beyond either the so-called universal appeal of Great Literature or the insidious market forces of late capitalism.

None of these theories seems compelling enough to explain away four feature films, two television miniseries, and bestsellerdom—not to mention the flurry of "Darcy Parties" thrown in the UK in the summer of 1996 (in which groups of women got together to play and replay their videotapes of Colin Firth diving into the lake, *The Guardian* reported). Even the Socialist Workers' Party Marxism '96 Conference got in on the action and featured a session on "what is so great about Jane Austen" alongside its workshops on post-Fordism and flexible labor. If the late Victorian and Edwardian eras provided the locus of cultural nostalgia in the late 1980s and early 1990s, then Regency England seems to have resonance for our own *fin de siècle.*

One glaring difference in the ways Austen adaptations have been written about, compared to those of E.M. Forster, Henry James, Edith Wharton, or even Shakespeare, is the tendency to label the Austen revival as part and parcel of a conservative cultural turn. This phenomenon is worth troubling over. Those who speculate on the cultural forces that contribute to Austen's current popularity often assume that it provides further evidence of her—and our—conservatism. Austen's fictional worlds are seen by many as providing an escape or a form of wish fulfillment (McGrory). Lionel Trilling gave this version a voice two decades ago, when he suspected that his students longed for a course on Austen because, through studying her, they hoped to "in some way transcend [their] sad contemporary existence" (Trilling 209). Many see Austen's popularity as proof that we believe "the past is preferable to now" (Weldon 15).

Whether this "look backward" is seen as itself backward or as a welcome trend has depended on the political perspectives of the critics in question and their apprehension (or lack thereof) of Regency England. Any number of critics could be cited to illustrate today's popular understandings of a conservative Austen, but Camille Paglia's remarks on the topic are worthy of note, not in the least because Paglia herself ranks as an inexplicable media darling. Paglia alternately celebrates and criticizes Austen's revival. In support of the revival, Paglia is "delighted" with the "courtliness of the men" and suspects that women today want to be courted and "maybe that was not so stupid." On the other hand, Paglia also believes that Austen herself was "very conservative" and that Austen's popularity signals a "turning backwards" in the 1990s. For Paglia, Austen's conservative appeal constitutes a "symptom" of the wishes of those who would like to eliminate "ethnics" and who long to go back to a world of white, upper-middle-class gentlemen. According to Paglia, the Austen revival is a "symptom of some deep stirring to go backwards. The sexual problems and political problems and racial problems, social problems, are just out of control in certain ways [today]. I think [the Austen revival] may be a kind of rebound from the OJ trial. It's sort of like, 'Thank god! We don't have to deal with people getting butchered anymore.'" Paglia seizes on an interesting point, though the directions she takes it are predictably troubling. Paglia bizarrely suggests that Austen's world was *not* filled with sexual, political, and racial problems. She talks about the Romantic era as a time when "there were no inconvenient racial problems of any kind. Everything is very homogeneous."

Those of us who know anything of late eighteenth- and early nineteenth-century British history may beg to differ, but Paglia's voice was no anomaly. References to Austen's peaceful, uncomplicated, and morally clear-sighted era abound in the popular press. One must wonder if these critics have really watched the films. Perhaps they have seen director-writer Douglas McGrath's *Emma* (1996), but they have obviously not watched director Roger Michell's *Persuasion* (1995), which is anything but stable and comforting, and they have not watched writer Andrew Davies's *Emma* (1996), with its repeated moonlight chicken-coop thefts. Nor have they, seemingly, read Austen's novels themselves. Even among those who recollect that Austen lived during those halcyon days of the French Revolution, some view her novels as completely outside of such issues or see her as a staunch Tory, surreptitiously trying to hold on to the decaying aristocratic order. Austen's involvement (or lack of it) in political and social history remains a scholarly question mark, but most would now agree that seeing her as ahistorical means ignoring her insights into social, if not political, history.

Austen's insights into history may not have extended to issues of racial equality. With the exception of Amy Heckerling's *Clueless*, which offers a multicultural melting pot of happy-go-lucky rich kids,[1] white characters populate the more faithful of the Austen adaptations in no small part because they populate Austen's novels. Until someone chooses to make a screen version of Austen's unfinished *Sanditon,* which features a mixed-race heiress, this focus on whites in Austen adaptations will likely continue. I leave it to others to settle issues of Austen, race, and empire, rather than taking on those who see the "Jane-train" (Kroll 67) as potentially racist.

Class (or "rank") in Austen's writings and in today's Austen adaptations is a far more mixed bag, though it is true that the "out of sight" poor are rarely present. The charity cases and Gypsies of McGrath's *Emma,* the street beggars of writer Nick Dear's *Persuasion,* and the slightly more economically secure servants of Thompson's *Sense and Sensibility* seem barely a blip in a fairly privileged filmic universe. But these are not worlds populated with upper-class gentleman, as Camille Paglia would have it. Sir Walter Scott referred to Austen's novels as about the "middling classes," as Claudia Johnson points out, and Madame de Staël called them simply "*vulgaire*" (quoted in Johnson, *Jane* xviii). According to Johnson, it was not until our own century that Lord David Cecil tried to "co-opt Austen . . . into the aristocracy" (*Jane* xviii). But anyone who watched the adaptations would see that what motivates the action is neither aristocratic arrogance nor greed. Anxieties about money and status abound in the novels and the adaptations—and not simply to keep up with the Joneses or the de Bourghs.

Despite this economic awareness, Austen's writings hardly give today's audiences a revolutionary, progressive vision of racial and class issues.[2] Her novels are not a call to join abolitionist movements or to break looms, to flout matrimony or compulsory heterosexuality. Some of Austen's appeal today would seem to be related to what Fredric Jameson or Janice Doane and Devon Hodges have discussed as a peculiarly postmodern nostalgia that makes indirect statements about the present by idealizing the past. As Doane and Hodges argue, "Nostalgic writers resist feminism by fixing sexual difference, sometimes appropriating the work of feminists themselves" (142). They suggest that feminists must undermine nostalgic rhetoric by "leaving cultural definitions of masculinity and femininity in play rather than in place" (142). This leads us to ask whether any or all of the Austen adaptations fix sexual difference or if they leave it in play. If they are seen as cementing these definitions, what versions of masculinity and femininity do the films offer? Austen's novels and Austen adaptations are of marginal use to progressive movements for racial and economic equality, but we would be too quick to lump gender into this conclusion. There may be some white middle-class elements that can be appropriated as progressive, perhaps even feminist, in recent Austen adaptations.

It is not my wish to join the uncritical cultural populists for an unquali-fied celebration of Austen's celluloid images. Nor do I wish to suggest that these adaptations necessarily limit viewer identifications only to those I will call "feminist." Regardless of how one labels Austen's characters on a feminist continuum, it must be agreed that her women seem to strike a chord with audiences today. Some of this generation's best actresses have jumped at the chance to play these roles. As McGrath put it, you would not cast Shannen Dougherty as Emma (quoted in Corliss 75). Austen-derived roles have not been filled with merely attractive bosoms, as Fay Weldon would have us believe (H15). These adaptations offer more than what film theorist Laura Mulvey identified two decades ago as moments of narrative of the male gaze and moments of spectacle of the passive female.

Claiming that Austen adaptations present active women would seem almost self-evident, but at least one critic has argued for the conservatism of today's Austen craze by claiming that her female characters demonstrate an elegant passivity—that they are spectacles of passive females in narratives of the male gaze (Rapping 37). I agree that any cultural form that would have us believe women are mere dolls or decorative objects would be a reactionary force. However, this does not seem to be the message of Austen or her present-day adapters. Passivity implies a physical, intellectual, and perhaps moral stasis. In these terms, it is hard not to think of our own era as an incredibly passive one for the middle classes and the privileged alike. In the thoroughly updated *Clueless,* for example, the female characters lounge against a fence during high school PE class, waiting their turn to hit one tennis ball. The Emmalike character, Cher, refuses to learn to parallel park a car because "wherever you go, you have valet" or, it might be added, suburban shopping-mall parking garages. To be fair, there are moments of female passivity even in the more historically accurate Austen adaptations. The adaptations focus relentlessly on female characters in doorways, windows, and mirrors—seem-ingly framed or boxed in. Roger Sales noted this theme in his study of Re-gency representations, concluding that "historic homes and gardens lose some of their conservative meanings if these homes are also visualized as genteel prisons" (25). Recent adaptations also show some men as tied to these do-mestic "prisons." We need only think of Colin Firth's forlorn Darcy in *Pride and Prejudice,* looking out the window at Elizabeth. Despite such exceptions, I have no wish to exonerate Regency England from its restrictive ideologies of gender in making an argument for the adaptations' mainstreaming of femi-nism. As we know, the nineteenth century limited women of the middling classes to marriage and motherhood, unless they were foolish enough to choose the difficult life of a governess or the financially uncertain one of a writer—the two professions most open to women. Women did not have a range of lifestyle options, but this historical fact is not equivalent to passivity or to ubiquitous moments of spectacle in the Austen adaptations.

Women are portrayed as physically active in many of the Austen adaptations, and it will come as a surprise to some that this is not entirely an anachronism. *Pride and Prejudice*'s Elizabeth Bennet, played by Jennifer Ehle, spends a good deal of time jogging from one place to another in the recent BBC production. At times, Ehle verges on being a "Just Do It" advertisement for Nike, but there is evidence of Elizabeth's propensity for running in the novel for those Austen purists who might cry foul (Andreae 16). Marianne Dashwood's walking and Louisa Musgrove's leaping also come to mind as active pursuits faithful to the novels. In fact, Austen seems most harsh in her characterizations of physically passive women. Austen's indolent female characters are second-rate at best and at worst completely unlikable. We might think of *Mansfield Park*'s Mrs. Bertram or of *Persuasion*'s Mary Musgrove.

The Austen adaptations cannot be classed as "soft-focus visions of female passivity," as feminist cultural critic Elayne Rapping has called them (37). Most of the updated Austen narratives have invented activities for female characters in order to show them to be very active. If Rapping means to criticize the Austen adaptations for their intellectually passive women, one can only counter that just about every worthy female character in the films is at least a reader. These readers may be in need of further education, but the fact that they read suggests that they are intellectually engaged and will eventually experience growth. Thompson's Marianne Dashwood reads and recites Shakespeare's sonnets and Sir Walter Scott, and Elinor Dashwood reads in bed. Dear's Anne Elliot, in keeping with the novel, discusses poetry with Captain Benwick. Even *Clueless*'s Cher (Emma) and Tai (Harriet) read, though their choices—*Fit or Fat, Men Are from Mars, Women Are from Venus,* and *Cliff's Notes*—leave something to be desired. To illustrate that the opposite is true, that unworthy women dislike reading, Thompson's Fanny Dashwood complains to her brother Edward Ferrars that Norland's books smell, and Charlotte Palmer thoughtlessly wrinkles her husband's newspaper as he reads it.

If Rapping's complaint alludes to physical passivity, it remains misdirected. To choose just one thematic example, throughout almost all of these adaptations women do their fair share of jabbing at things with sharp objects. These repeated elements need not be interesting for their Freudian connotations alone; they show the female characters to be assertive and engaged with the physical world. We might think of the BBC Mrs. Bennet angrily cutting flowers with a knife or of Elizabeth Bennet teasing a dog with a bone, of the understated passing of umbrellas between Anne Elliot and Frederick Wentworth in the 1995 *Persuasion,* of Margaret Dashwood fencing with Edward Ferrars, Fanny Dashwood pulling Lucy Steele by the nose, or of Marianne Dashwood cutting reeds with Colonel Brandon's knife in Thompson's *Sense and Sensibility.*

Of all of these characters, young Margaret is the most physically active, portrayed as a delightful young tomboy dreaming of travel in the privacy of her tree house. Margaret is, in her make-believe world, a landowner and an explorer. In one early scene in the film, Margaret will not come down from her tree house as her sister Elinor explains to her that houses are passed from father to son, not father to daughter, so that half brother John and his wife Fanny will take over what has been the Dashwood home. Elinor encourages Margaret to come inside and play with her atlas. Margaret replies that it is no longer her atlas; it is now John and Fanny's atlas. This scene, and a later one, in which Elinor and Edward discuss their economic prospects and joke about the wisdom of piracy, is illustrative of the kind of feminism that the film offers. In Thompson's *Sense and Sensibility,* there is often a trenchant critique about the status of women, followed by a joke of subversion, with few gestures toward political action. The way out of this cycle for women, if there is one to be found, rests with Margaret's generation. It is easy to see how, in one critic's eyes, Margaret Dashwood might be compared to the young bluestocking Thomasina Coverly of Tom Stoppard's *Arcadia* (Harris 429)—full of promise for a feminist future.

To consider one last Austen adaptation for its active females, we might recall Emma's mercurial archery skills in a brilliant scene added to Douglas McGrath's film. As she converses with Mr. Knightley, Emma's arrows are dead on when she is focused and completely off when distracted. This scene, lifted and improved from a similar one in the 1940 version of *Pride and Prejudice,* even has the advantage of historical accuracy. In the 1790s, women of the upper classes took to archery as a form of exercise and as a way to display the graces of the female form. Women and men competed against each other in informal events. According to Linda Troost, archery also had a political side. It made a "fashionably radical statement about the equality of the sexes as well as a patriotic endorsement of the moral values of 'manly' England" (14). Female archers were likened to Amazons, and their arrows compared to Cupid's. In this film scene, then, Emma is expressing her spirit and independence, showing off her beauty, and enticing the heart of Mr. Knightley, in one fell swoop. This may all seem quite unexciting when compared to more recent Sigourney Weaver or Linda Hamilton filmic fare, but it is hardly passive. Though we are unlikely to see Maureen Dowd's suggested Austen film sequels, "*Emma 2: Judgment Day* or Sandra Bullock as *Abbey Northanger,* a governess who falls for a ghost" (A23), we must concede that strong, active women are featured in these Austen adaptations.

Today's Austen heroines are not husband-hunting ditzes or passive damsels in distress. Intelligent female leads, grappling with conventions, scandals, rules, and love, are the new Austen norm. Former Austen adaptations fashioned women as unabashedly predatory. On the 1940 *Pride and Prejudice's* studio publicity poster, viewers were warned, "Bachelors Beware! Five Gorgeous Beauties are on a Madcap Manhunt" (quoted in Gold B3). It is difficult to imagine today's adaptations being promoted in such language. The one film that might seem to break the mold is the present-day updating of *Emma, Clueless.* This film has the market cornered on Austen-derived bubbleheads, set as it is in the malls in and around Beverly Hills. But even *Clueless,* with its focus on rich high school girls, has moments of strong womanhood—not just because the script includes references to misogyny, menstruation, and sexual harassment. The Emma Woodhouse character, Cher Horowitz, goes through the film assuming everyone else is clueless. Through most of the film, Cher's approach to life appears to come right out of the pages of Georgette Moschbacher's *Feminine Force,* or the newer how-to-catch-and-keep-a-man bestseller, *The Rules.* Cher spends her time roughly pushing away high school boys, whom she likens to dirty, slobbering, nervous dogs, and screeching, "As if!" She considers grades as "jumping off points" to start negotiations with teachers, just as her father, a $500-an-hour litigator, has taught her.

Cher is charming, and she is not above using the role of a victim to manipulate others, preying on her teacher's feminism to get a better grade. As Cher tells us, "I told my PE teacher an evil male had broken my heart, so she raised my C to a B." The most directly "feminist" moment in *Clueless* could serve as a raison d'être for the film. At one point, Cher's friend, Dionne, chews out her Beverly Hills High boyfriend Murray because he uses the word "woman" to get her attention. Dionne chastises Murray in a firm voice reminding him that she has repeatedly asked him not to call her "woman." Murray responds: "Street slang is an increasingly valid form of expression. Most of the feminine pronouns do have mocking but not necessarily misogynistic undertones," and he sticks out his tongue at her. The film itself may be said to incorporate mocking but not necessarily misogynistic undertones when it comes to its treatment of female characters.

Cher's lesson in the film, like Emma's in the novel, is to recognize that she herself is clueless—which involves, not coincidentally, leaving behind the most egregious of her feminine trappings. Cher recognizes that she loves her ex-stepbrother Josh, who reads Nietzsche and dates women who argue with him about Shakespeare. Cher knows she is going to have to change her mall-rat, manhunting ways to appeal to him. As Cher says, "I mean, ordinarily I'd strut around him and send myself flowers and candy, but I couldn't do that stuff with Josh. . . . I decided I needed a complete makeover. Except this time, I'd makeover my soul." And so begins Cher's transformation into a different kind of Beverly Hills young woman. By the end of the film, gone are Cher's Band-Aid miniskirts. Gone are her spaghetti-strap Calvin Klein dresses. She has turned them in for more practical Capri pants and for dresses with matching bolero jackets, albeit still in powder pink. Cher claims she has become interested in the news and in politics, and she volunteers to serve as the donations captain for the Pismo Beach Disaster Relief Drive. Though Cher is doing these things to impress Josh, her voice-over tells us that these things are making her feel better, too. We are to believe that she has success-fully made over her soul, even if her impetus for doing so was to please a boy.

The final minutes of the film involve the wedding of two high school teachers, Mr. Hall and Miss Geist. Earlier in the film, Cher and her best friend Dionne played matchmaker to bring the two teachers together, suc-ceeding in the goal of making them happy enough to raise everyone's grades. After the ceremony, we see Cher with friends Dionne and Tai at a table with their boyfriends. Dionne and Tai are planning the themes they envision for their own dream weddings, but Cher is strangely silent. When Dionne and Tai rush to the spot where the bouquet will be thrown, Cher smiles and looks on rather than following them. Josh, however, leans over to tell her that the males at the wedding have a $200 pool collected, and it will go to the guy whose girlfriend catches the bouquet. Cher declares that it is "in the bag" and springs into action. In a scene that resembles a pastel football pile-up, Cher emerges triumphantly with the flowers. Though her behavior has not changed very radically, her motivations have. She is in no hurry to get mar-ried. She is driven to catch the bouquet in order to please others and to emerge a winner, as well as by her hardly diminished materialistic impulses. The satirical and feminist elements are hard to extricate. Cher seems to be-come a younger, blonder version of Naomi Wolf as "power feminist." As a result, the film has made critics uncomfortable and uncertain whether we are to understand its message as conservative or progressive.

It would be a mistake to invest *Clueless* with too much seriousness; it is by design, after all, much more lightweight an effort than any of the other Austen adaptations, though not a less successful film for that. As one re-viewer has noted, the film's "'90s Californian materialism has a tang of con-servatism that is both intriguing and repellent" alongside its "nod to femi-nism" (Lipman 46). Strangely, however, even for all of its sartorial flash and feminine status quo, *Clueless* was, according to its director, difficult to bring to fruition because of its female focus. *Clueless* was originally a failed pro-posal for a TV series. When it became a film, 20th Century Fox first owned the rights to the film but dropped them. According to director Amy Heckerling, "They were worried about something that was so female-oriented. . . . They kept pressuring me to create more of a life for the boys in the film, to create more of an ensemble piece, which didn't make sense to me at all" (quoted in Weinraub C18). Paramount stepped in, and the film was made with its focus intact. Although *Clueless* can hardly be called the most feminist of the Austen adaptations, perhaps for its genre its success will change some of the rules.

The power the women wield in the more historically correct Austen film versions is decidedly more complex. Women's influence is to some degree limited—as *Northanger Abbey* notes—to the "power of refusal." But rather than focus on this aspect of the films, which is for the most part faithfully retained from the novels and has been faithfully explicated by many years of literary critics (feminist and otherwise), I will turn to the depiction of women's relationships with other women in the adaptations and the ways in which this aspect, too, can be seen as a feminist turn. There may be no bedroom scenes between the heroine and her hero, but they abound between the heroine and her sister in Davies's *Pride and Prejudice* and Thompson's *Sense and Sensibility.* In the texts in which the heroine has no sister or in which the sisters are flawed, other female companions take their place, and the films show these women on and in each other's arms or whispering in each other's ears.

In Dear's *Persuasion,* only the Admiral's wife, Mrs. Croft, and the poor Mrs. Smith are shown to be affectionate toward heroine Anne Elliot. Mrs. Croft and Anne air the film's most feminist thoughts, both retained from the novel. Mrs. Croft believes that women are "rational creatures" (Dear 33) and perfectly capable of living onboard ships with their naval husbands, and Anne explains that women do not deserve their literary reputation as fickle— a reputation, as she notes, concocted by male writers (Dear 85). At the end of the film, we see that Anne Elliot (now presumably Anne Wentworth) has taken Mrs. Croft's lead and is on board a ship with her new husband, Captain Wentworth, who once opposed the idea of women traveling in that manner. But though *Persuasion* is considered one of Austen's most feminist novels, and though director Michell himself says that Austen offers "a clear-sighted vision of the way the world is tilted against women" (quoted in Rickey), his film version eliminates some of the narrative's feminist elements, including the famous scene of Mrs. Croft taking over the horses' reins. We might ask why this is the case. I would argue that it has more to do with changes in the film's men than in its women, which I take up later in this essay.

The female community is not so warm in *Persuasion* as it is in the other adaptations. Dear's *Persuasion* is exceptional in its painfully dark tone and dour visuals through much of the film. We cannot help but get a sense of how alone Anne Elliot is and how cold her world is; those critics who see the Austen adaptations as stable and comforting (Rapping 38) have not seen

Persuasion. McGrath's *Emma,* then, is quite a contrast for its bright sparkling tone. At her worst, Gwyneth Paltrow's portrayal of Emma fails to respect female community and, as in the novel, makes sport of the poor, garrulous spinster, Miss Bates. In her more charming moments, Emma has her Harriet, as well as a decidedly underdeveloped Mrs. Weston, but this sisterhood would seem little advanced beyond the love displayed in the film for puppies. The failure of women's solidarity, however, is entirely Emma's fault and hers to get beyond. Even *Clueless's* Cher learns that competing with other women will not serve her well, and she embraces her "project," transfer student and rival, Tai, near the end of the film, pledging her friendship.

I do not want to suggest that in Austen's world women must be good to other women. On the contrary, it is not uncommon for women to "be hard on their sex," as Elizabeth Bennet puts it. Some second-wave feminists wanted to see women as morally superior to men—as kinder, gentler humans—but neither Austen's novels nor the films show this to be the case. The dastardly males are more than matched by their manipulative female counterparts. The women we should not like are the ones who openly compete with other female characters, the ones who are "husband hunters" or greedy schemers. They may pretend to be interested in other women but have only their own interests (monetary and/or sexual) at heart. Davies's *Pride and Prejudice* shows Lydia Bennet, once she is married to the philandering Wickham, pulling rank over her unmarried sisters. Lydia claims that she will not have time to write because she is married, though she expects letters from her sisters, who have nothing better to do. Thompson's *Sense and Sensibility* has Lucy Steele as its exemplary conniver, pretending intimacy with Elinor and then Fanny Dashwood to get what she wants—marriage to her reluctant fiancé of five years, Edward Ferrars. Even Dear's *Persuasion* has Elizabeth Elliot, herself a brownnosing snob (depending on the rank of whoever is before her), punished for saying that her sister Anne "is nothing" (Dear 63) to her compared to the sycophantic widow Mrs. Clay. Mrs. Clay runs off with the man whom Elizabeth had been plotting to ensnare, their cousin and heir to Kellynch Hall, Mr. Elliot.

It is women, however, not girls, who are a part of female communities and female solidarity when it exists, perhaps because such communities revolve around romantic and moral issues considered too sensitive for a young girl. Thompson's Margaret Dashwood is forever asking to be admitted to conversations about matters of the heart and is consistently rebuffed, told that she should restrict her conversations to the weather, or asked to fetch something. The only way she can participate is with inappropriately gossipy women like the benign Mrs. Jennings. Margaret's access to female community is having the snarls combed out of her hair in the cold of Barton Cottage or being dragged on walks with her sister Marianne. Without access to conversations of money, romance, or scandal, Margaret realizes that there is little else a female can discuss, unless, as in one scene, her contribution to conversation is practicing her French. It is not a surprise, then, that Margaret should more often imagine herself as a "man"—a traveler obsessed with an atlas, an explorer heading an expedition to China, and a landowner, at least of a tree house.

If Margaret Dashwood is the only female character who imagines herself as a man, the heroes in these adaptations frequently find expression as feminized subjects or "New Men." The celluloid Austen heroes may in fact be the ones most obviously affected by the second wave of the women's movement. Austen adaptations mark male violence and male indifference as signs that one has found the "wrong" man. Far from endorsing the emotionally distant, mysterious male as the pinnacle of masculinity, these adaptations show such men to be the ones heroines must look beyond in order to find truly caring and more equal partners. Austen's heroes have been translated onto the screen as caregivers, as well as rescuers of damsels in distress. Even their modes of rescue speak volumes about them. When Willoughby rescues Marianne with her sprained ankle, he takes off her shoe, in a reverse Cinderella move, and carries her away with extreme pomp and gallantry. Marianne is completely taken in by this enactment of her fantasies of romantic decorum and desire, though they are shot down by Willoughby's later betrayal.

In the mirror image of this scene, when Marianne is rescued from the rain by Colonel Brandon, the maneuver is infused with fewer of the usual romantic frills and furbelows or what Deborah Kaplan refers to as the "harlequinization" of Austen's men in her essay in this volume. In this scene, Brandon is merely doing his duty, without calling undue attention to it. He tramps out into the rain with a purpose and returns having carried out his task. The scene carries a completely different tone—concerned, even tragic, rather than depicting a coup to be congratulated, celebrated, or fussed over. Earlier in the film, when Brandon has left Barton Park to care for his ward, Willoughby pronounces "Frailty thy name is Brandon." As Brandon's later "rescue" of Marianne shows, however, his elision with *woman* proves anything but frail. Instead, Willoughby himself is revealed to have dangerous weaknesses; Brandon's soft spots turn out to be strengths. Austen's heroes are no-nonsense men, but they are not—with the possible exception of the early Darcy—the cold and distant, slightly mysterious heroes of yesterventury (or, in the case of Sylvester Stallone's many incarnations, yesterdecade). In the novel *Pride and Prejudice,* Elizabeth tells us that she marks the moment she fell in love with Darcy to the first time she saw Pemberley. But viewers of the BBC version would be correct to note that Elizabeth changes her attitude toward Darcy once she hears the kind reports of him from his housekeeper, reinforced by his demonstrations of brotherly love for Georgiana.

In Thompson's *Sense and Sensibility,* we are presented with a myriad of significant changes from the original models for the male characters. One of the most striking changes from novel to film is Edward Ferrars's frequently displayed love for children. Edward's filmic relationship with Margaret Dashwood is a completely new addition to Austen's story. Edward discovers Margaret hiding under a table in the library with her atlas in tow. Edward lures sister Elinor to the spot and coaxes Margaret out from under her table with his bogus query about whether or not the Nile is located in South America. As the screenplay notes tell us, in this scene between Edward and Margaret, "*a connection [is] made*" (Thompson 44). According to Elinor, Margaret is "a changed girl" since Edward Ferrars's arrival (Thompson 45). We later see Edward fencing with Margaret in the yard, and it is Margaret who serves as the pretense for Edward's would-be journey to Barton Cottage. He tells Margaret that he will bring her the atlas when he comes to visit the family. When the atlas arrives without Edward, we know there is trouble for Edward and Elinor's romance.

Men's love of children is very much at issue in the films. Dear's *Persuasion* shows Admiral Croft to be a good man for his indulgence of the Musgrove boys, and he makes paper boats with them, which they later sail on the water with Anne's guidance. Thompson's *Sense and Sensibility* has Brandon, too, win young Margaret over upon first meeting her. The screenplay notes that "COLONEL BRANDON *knows what* MARGARET *wants to hear*" when he tells her that in the East Indies, "the air is full of spices" (Thompson 72). As Margaret was to have said, in a line that ended up on the cutting room floor, "I like Colonel Brandon too. He's been to places" (Thompson 74). Further evidence of Brandon's parental inclinations is found in the story of Brandon's ward "Beth" (renamed from the Eliza of the novel). In a scene cut from the film, Brandon visited the squalid flat where Beth was staying in London, only to discover her pregnant with Willoughby's child. This scene, though a new addition to the narrative, is implicit in the novel. Its being retained in the film version would have furthered the portrait of Brandon as a parental figure. Finally, evidence of Brandon's nurturing (and arguably parental) qualities can be found in his attentions to Marianne on her sickbed and during her recovery. In the novel, Brandon is present during Marianne's fever, but Mrs. Jennings seems much closer to the action; Brandon hovers with propriety in the background. In the film, Brandon hovers, but has enough contact with Marianne for her to express her thanks to him. This moment marks the beginning of their filmic courtship.

Not all of the adaptations' or the novels' commentary on male nurturing is positive. Thompson's minor but memorable young father, Mr. Palmer, provides a case in point in *Sense and Sensibility*. Though he is shown to have other redeeming qualities in the film, Mr. Palmer's awkward holding of his son, Thomas, serves as evidence that his curmudgeonly, sarcastic masculinity is far from ideal. This scene also has its origins in the novel, where the narrator tells us that

> Mr. Palmer maintained the common, but unfatherly opinion among his sex, of all infants being alike; and though [Mrs. Palmer] could plainly perceive at different times, the most striking resemblance between this baby and every one of his relations on both sides, there was no convincing his father of it; no persuading him to believe that it was not exactly like every other baby of the same age; nor could he even be brought to acknowledge the simple proposition of its being the finest child in the world. [Austen, *Sense* 248]

This section is clearly a vehicle to establish once again Charlotte Palmer's silly, motherly hubris and cant, but it also shows us Mr. Palmer as "unfatherly" and as representative of his sex in the opinion that all infants are alike—an opinion we might find more horrifying in a father today. The novel's narrator later comments that Mr. Palmer has "no traits at all unusual in his sex and time of life. He was nice in his eating, uncertain in his hours; fond of his child, though affecting to slight it; and idled away the mornings at billiards, which ought to have been devoted to business" (Austen, *Sense* 304-5). The film suggests that Mr. Palmer, rather than being a caricatured version of "everyman," represents a rarity. In the film, Edward and Colonel Brandon have overshadowed the likes of Mr. Palmer as the norm and have made him seem, by extension, even less acceptable for his lack of parental tenderness with his own (albeit crying) son.

Edward's behavior throughout the film is far more in keeping with today's model "New Man." This filmic Edward is also far more easily forgiven than the man we might picture from the novel, which dubs him "highly blameable" (Austen, *Sense* 140)—a sentiment nowhere expressed in the film. Edward and Colonel Brandon are notable not only for their "pleasing manner" and adherence to principles and promises but for their nurturing qualities. In this day of cultural fantasies of Mr. Mom and of what Nancy Chodorow has called equal parenting (218), is it any surprise to see these heroes so updated?[3] The film does not give us an *entirely* new Edward; the seeds of the Edward we see in the film are to some degree located in the novel. For instance, the novel's Edward is said to be fond of family life. Edward is described by Austen's narrator as having "wishes centered in domestic comfort and the quiet of private life" (Austen, *Sense* 16). The film merely fleshes out this portrait to what we might see in a feminist-friendly man today, though eliminating the perhaps still too objectionably effeminate word "domestic" for the more gender-neutral "private" (Thompson 48). Colonel Brandon, as a military man who fights a duel with Willoughby in the novel, displays many more of the trappings of classical manhood, but in the film, even he is shown to have a softer side that is less fully revealed in the novel. This difference between the novel and the film suggests that for these men to be "heroes" in the late twentieth century, they must also be demonstrably more nurturing, caretaking, or in some sense parentally focused, as well as respectful of the inclinations and opinions of the women in whom they take romantic interest.

Most of the Austen adaptations encourage men to reconcile the contradictory demands of manhood to create more just relationships with women and more complete understandings of themselves and their own emotions. As one critic has suggested, "[*Sense and Sensibility*] could easily have been turned into an angry feminist tract, [but] the men survive as real human beings, rather than nasty cardboard cutouts" (Blake 20). The key word in this statement is the word "angry." The feminism that this film and the other Austen adaptations offer is far more conventionally nice. Sometimes it verges on the male-centered status quo, as Davies's *Emma* has Knightley reassure the members of his community (and us) in a final wedding toast that "there will be stability. There will be continuation, though my life is to change." This statement, which should make even the most trepidant feminist reformer wince, is not characteristic of the adaptations *in toto*. What we find in many of the adaptations is a more conciliatory feminism—exactly the kind of depolemicized feminism that the best critics of Austen's novels have seen her as offering in an early nineteenth-century context (Johnson, *Jane*).

Austen's novels, and the Austen adaptations along with them, are not flawless models of feminist narrative, but neither are they conservative propaganda nor another regrettable manifestation of the culture industry. If we are now able to appreciate late eighteenth-century feminists such as Mary Wollstonecraft or Mary Hays, whose "radical" but imperfect ideas were largely castigated and then forgotten by succeeding generations, we should also appreciate texts such as Austen's, which fashioned feminist political platforms into popular and widely palatable terms. If Mary Wollstonecraft's feminism is to be celebrated for its courage in breaking with the past, Jane Austen's, too, should be recognized for its reintegration of her predecessor's gender politics into mainstream language and ideologies.[4] We might argue that a similar need presents itself with Austen adaptations in the 1990s. Though the silver screen Austen might look conservative next to the feminist films of Yvonne

Rainer, Lizzie Borden, or Chantal Ackerman, that is no reason to jettison Austen adaptations to the realm of the patriarchal "fairy tale" fantasy (Rapping 37). If these adaptations offer us Cinderella figures, they are far more complex, meaningful, and hopeful subjects than those we have seen in the past.

The Austen revival is no "unmediated vision of feminism" (Dow and Hogeland 13). However, many of the adaptations gesture further than some mainstream feminist cultural critics. The adaptations move beyond individual problems and self-help solutions. Almost all provide implicit and explicit large-scale social criticism. Of course, it would be foolish to decide that Austen is simply progressive "enough." The Austen revival is not a harbinger of radical change or of certain progress to come. Still, to give Austen over to conservatives as further evidence of their revolution is equally foolish. The adaptations of Austen's novels may not exactly allow feminists to proclaim that we have arrived, but these films offer evidence that women who are subjects rather than objects of male desire are being embraced and fixed as a white middle-class ancestry and future. Furthermore, the Austen revival shows us that the male partners these film women demand are intellectual and moral—if not economic—equals. A feminism that cannot find space to welcome such images, as well as to engage in sustained political critique and action, can hardly be appealing to those of us who prefer to hope for, even to anticipate, some happy endings. Then again, perhaps my essay is more evidence in support of the narrator's quip in *Persuasion:* "How quick come the reasons for approving what we like!" (Austen, *Persuasion* 15).

Notes

1. Andrew Sullivan finds this multiculturalist *Clueless* so free of any conflict or strife that he refers to it as "unicultural."
2. This may say more about the conditions under which Austen wrote. Her popularity may, in fact, speak to the similarity of her cultural situation to our own. Connections between the 1790s and the 1990s have been and will continue to be drawn, both in scholarly and popular media (See Rickey; Johnson, *Jane*).
3. In the novel, women's relationships with children generally serve as commentary on femininity rather than as a test of masculinity. For instance, Lucy Steele's indulgence of the Middleton's children is what wins over Lady Middleton. Lady Middleton is to be disliked for raising spoiled children. Mrs. Jennings's influence on Margaret becomes worrisome to Mrs. Dashwood when Margaret makes inappropriate comments about Elinor's beau in both the novel and the film. But Thompson's *Sense and Sensibility* often uses children as a vehicle to reveal male character, while Austen's novel uses children almost exclusively as a vehicle to reflect on female character.
4. For an argument linking Austen to Wollstonecraft, see Kirkham.

Works Cited

Andreae, Christopher. "In Defense of the Perfect 'Pride and Prejudice.'" *Christian Science Monitor* 6 Dec. 1995: 16.

Austen, Jane. *Northanger Abbey and Persuasion*. Ed. R.W. Chapman. Rev. Mary Lascelles. 3d ed. Vol. 5 of *The Novels of Jane Austen*. 6 vols. Oxford: Oxford UP, 1966.

————. *Sense and Sensibility*. Ed. R.W. Chapman. Rev. Mary Lascelles. 3d ed. Vol. 1 of *The Novels of Jane Austen*. 6 vols. Oxford: Oxford UP, 1966.

Bellafante, Ginia. "Sick of Jane Austen Yet?" *Time* 15 Jan. 1996: 66.

Blake, Richard A. "Plain Jane." Review of *Sense and Sensibility*. *America* 9 Mar. 1996: 20-21.

Chodorow, Nancy. *The Reproduction of Mothering: Psychoanalysis and the Sociology of Gender*. Berkeley: U of California P, 1978.

Clueless. Writer and director Amy Heckerling. With Alicia Silverstone and Paul Rudd. Paramount, 1995.

Collins, James. "Jane Reactions." *Vogue* Jan. 1996: 70-72.

Corliss, Richard. "A Touch of Class." *Time* 29 July 1996: 74-75.

Dear, Nick. *Persuasion*. Methuen Film Series. London: Methuen, 1996.

Doane, Janice, and Devon Hodges. *Nostalgia and Sexual Difference*. New York: Methuen, 1987.

Dow, Bonnie, and Lisa Maria Hogeland. "When Feminism Meets the Press, Our Real Politics Get Lost." *On the Issues* 4.1 (1997): 12-13.

Dowd, Maureen. "Will Jane Nix Pix?" *New York Times* 24 Aug. 1995: A23.

Emma. Writer and director Douglas McGrath. With Gwyneth Paltrow and Jeremy Northam. Miramax, 1996.

Emma. Writer Andrew Davies. Director Diarmuid Lawrence. With Kate Beckinsale and Mark Strong. Meridian (ITV)/A&E, 1996.

Gold, Joel J. "Heady Days for Jane Austen Scholars." *Chronicle of Higher Education* 1 Feb. 1996: B3.

Harris, Jocelyn. "Review of *Sense and Sensibility, Persuasion,* and *Clueless.*" *Eighteenth-Century Fiction* 8 (1996): 427-30.

Johnson, Claudia L. *Jane Austen: Women, Politics, and the Novel*. Chicago: U of Chicago P, 1988.

————. Letter to the Editor: "Nobody Owns Jane Austen." *Wall Street Journal* 18 Apr. 1996: A19.

Kirkham, Margaret. *Jane Austen, Feminism, and Fiction*. Sussex: Harvester; Totowa, N.J.: Barnes and Noble, 1983.

Kroll, Jack. "Jane Austen Does Lunch." *Newsweek* 18 Dec. 1995: 66-68.

Lipman, Amanda. "Clueless." *Sight and Sound* Oct. 1995: 46.

McGrory, Mary. "Jane Austen Joins the Newly Cool." *Indianapolis Business Journal* 1 Jan. 1996: 8B.

Menand, Louis. "What Jane Austen Doesn't Tell Us." *New York Review of Books* 1 Feb. 1996: 13-15.

Paglia, Camille, and Emma Taylor. "Interview with Camille Paglia." *Tripod* 23 Jan. 1996: n.p.

Persuasion. Writer Nick Dear. Director Roger Michell. With Amanda Root and Ciaran Hinds. BBC/WGBH, 1995.

Pride and Prejudice. Writer Andrew Davies. Director Simon Langton. With Jennifer Ehle and Colin Firth. BBC/A&E, 1995.

Rapping, Elayne. "The Jane Austen Thing." *The Progressive* July 1996: 37-38.

Rickey, Carrie. "Jane Austen Is Popping up Again 200 Years Later on Big and Small Screens." *Philadelphia Inquirer* 20 Nov. 1995: Newsbank/Newsfile.

Sales, Roger. *Jane Austen and Representations of Regency England.* London: Routledge, 1996.

Sense and Sensibility. Writer Emma Thompson. Director Ang Lee. With Emma Thompson and Hugh Grant. Mirage-Columbia (Sony), 1995.

Stevens, Amy. "Poor Jane Austen Didn't Live to See 'Sense and Sensibility.'" *Wall Street Journal* 25 Mar. 1996: 1+.

Sullivan, Andrew. "Washington Diarist." *The New Republic* 11 Sept. 1995: 43.

Trilling, Lionel. "Why We Read Jane Austen." In *The Last Decade: Essays and Reviews, 1965-75.* Ed. Diana Trilling. New York: Harcourt, Brace, Jovanovich, 1979. 204-25.

Troost, Linda V. "Diana's Votaries; or, The Fair Toxophilites." *The East-Central Intelligencer* 10.1 (1996): 9-15.

Weinraub, Bernard. "A Surprise Film Hit about Rich Teen-Age Girls." *New York Times* 24 July 1995: C18.

Weldon, Fay. "Jane Austen and the Pride of Purists." *New York Times* 8 Oct. 1995: H15, H24.

13

Mass Marketing Jane Austen

Men, Women, and Courtship in Two Film Adaptations

Deborah Kaplan

Some years ago I was given the "tip sheet"—guidelines for prospective writers—distributed by a well-known publishing house of mass-market contemporary romances.[1] Prescriptions for the characterization of the hero immediately caught my eye: "The hero is 8 to 12 years older than the heroine. He is self-assured, masterful, hot-tempered, capable of violence, passion, and tenderness. He is often mysteriously moody. Heathcliff (*Wuthering Heights*) is a rougher version; Darcy (*Pride and Prejudice*) a more refined one."

The tip sheet thus makes explicit that Jane Austen's *Pride and Prejudice* is one of the models for the late twentieth-century's mass-market romance. To be sure, some of the guidelines have little connection to the world of Austen's novel. The aspiring romance writer is advised that the heroine should have little interest in alcohol and cigarettes and that love scenes should be described sensuously and in detail. Nudity is acceptable, indeed welcome, as long as it is not presented too graphically—"references to pain and blood," the would-be writer is told emphatically, "are out." Nevertheless, if suggestions for the hero's characterization do not give admirers of *Pride and Prejudice* a sense of déjà vu, the tip sheet's plot outline will:

> the action should explore the relationship between the lovers.
> . . . The story usually begins with a clash between the hero and
> the heroine. Often this has to do with misapprehensions each has
> about the other. Sometimes the heroine has heard a great deal
> about the hero and has some reason to resent him before they
> actually meet, or they meet under inauspicious circumstances and
> the heroine is put off by the hero's ruthless, domineering, and
> arrogant manner. Or the hero has formed an opinion of the hero-
> ine before he meets her. [Silhouette]

Jane Austen as one of the mothers of the Harlequin or Silhouette novel? This genealogy should amuse many of Austen's admirers, who know her novels to be much more culturally and linguistically complex than the mass-market romance. And yet, recent popular representations reveal a distinct trend: the harlequinization of Jane Austen's novels. If Austen is one of the ancestors of the paperback romance, recent films of her work are now the heirs of this popular form. The two most explicit descendants in this romance genealogy are the films of *Sense and Sensibility,* adapted by Emma Thompson and directed by Ang Lee, and *Emma,* adapted and directed by Douglas McGrath.

By *harlequinization* I mean that, like the mass-market romance, the focus is on a hero and heroine's courtship at the expense of other characters and other experiences, which are sketchily represented. As the tip sheet suggests, the hero and heroine's plot should begin in the first chapter—no wasting time even with matters as extraneous as the heroine's life before she first encounters the hero. Harlequinization does not require a plot closely patterned on *Pride and Prejudice.* But it does necessitate an unswerving attention to the hero's and heroine's desires for one another and a tendency to represent those desires in unsurprising, even clichéd ways (Radway 122).[2] The mass-market romance suggests that familiarity breeds content. The pleasures of this form are to be found not only in the unfolding of desire and the achievement of gratification but also in the comfortable knowledge of what is to come and how it is to occur.[3] Finally, harlequinization is typified by attention to physical appearances, the result of the subtle and not-so-subtle commodification of persons in this intensely commercial form. Hero and heroine should be both good-looking and sexy. And since much of selfhood is loaded into and expressed by appearance, love at first sight is understandable and appropriate. Clothes, too, are of interest, not only as a means of bringing attention to the bodies of the hero and the heroine but as objects of desire in their own right—another reminder of this highly commercial form.

Since I am going to be critical of some of the films' divergences from the novels, I want to say at the outset that I do not think the medium itself is the culprit. Granted, film inevitably transforms novels. To take an obvious and important example, although Austen's ironic narrators are central to the reader's encounter with her books, most filmmakers wisely reject the amount of voice-over that would be necessary to reproduce the experience of a narrator. Moreover, the transfer to film of a work written in an earlier period also makes film versions radically different. Even had all those involved in making the Austen films worked at rendering the novels as exactly and authentically as possible—and they did not—their efforts would still have been heavily mediated by late twentieth-century minds and bodies. The films were made by writers and directors and for audiences with inescapably modern mental lives. And actors, however good their period-style technique, have been physically shaped by late twentieth-century food, medical treatments, skin and hair care products, sneakers, soft sofas, and weight machines.

A film of a book will always be different from the book itself, but let us also acknowledge that film has the power to show us aspects of Jane Austen's novels in new and revitalizing ways. For example, Ang Lee captures the emotional tension in Barton Cottage after Willoughby leaves for good and the personality differences among the inhabitants in a scene of breathtaking visual beauty, shot looking down a staircase at the three bedroom doors and the landing connecting them. Elinor has pursued her mother up to the landing from below, where they had been arguing about the meaning of Willoughby's sudden departure. Mrs. Dashwood goes into her bedroom weeping and shuts the door. Margaret, who has been trying in vain to get Marianne to open her bedroom door in order to hand her a cup of tea, passes the cup and saucer to Elinor, goes into her bedroom, bursts into tears, and shuts *her* door. Elinor, out on the landing, hears weeping coming from behind all the doors. Sitting down carefully on the stairs, she drinks the tea, an activity evocative of custom and propriety. Emphasizing the solitude of her calm, quiet misery, the scene dramatizes the difference between Elinor and the rest of her family. Moreover, by placing the camera outside the bedroom doors and behind Elinor, the film aligns the audience with Elinor's viewpoint and way of coping.

I am critical then not of film alterations per se—but of alterations made in the service, I presume, of broad commercial appeal. *Sense and Sensibility* cost $15.5 million to make (Gunther 128). While substantially less than the $70-million budget for the 1996 summer blockbuster *Independence Day*, this is still an expenditure necessitating, as cultural critic Louis Menand recently put it, "the maximally profitable economic niche" (4). McGrath's *Emma* cost considerably less to make—only $7 million (Fenster)—and is considered a specialized "boutique film" (Menand 6). Nevertheless, it too has been in search of a profitable market share. Both films have been hyped aggressively, through magazine and television interviews with the films' stars and those seemingly endless, insipid newspaper articles on the making of these films and the reasons for the rash of Jane Austen movies. *Sense and Sensibility*, as of July 1996, had grossed $43 million, and *Emma*, as of early October 1996, had grossed $20 million ("Film"). These are only *domestic* earnings, however. Between February and June 1996, *Sense and Sensibility* opened in ten other countries, including Australia, Brazil, Mexico, and Japan. It has grossed over $125 million worldwide (Gunther 128). Like modern romance paperbacks, the films are mass-market products, and this accounts for their similarities. The conventions of romance have sold well in Harlequin and Silhouette novels, and they have made box-office successes out of mainstream American films.

The medium of film itself may be neutral, but American-produced popular films generally are not. To put Austen novels on film by means of corporations (Columbia Pictures and Miramax) that produce what is now a global popular culture informed by American tastes is to enter a medium shaped by powerful generic conventions of romance. But the films' romantic emphasis also functions as a critique of Austen's writing. Told by a third-person narrator intimate with the consciousness of the female characters and usually at a distance from the mental lives and daily activities of men, Austen's novels, so the films suggest, underrepresent men. The films redress that imbalance by amplifying and glamorizing Austen's heroes, but, as I shall show, doing so prevents them from capturing the nuances of Austen's male characters as well as the teasing ambiguities of the novelist's representations of women and courtship.

The casting of the films' heroes was instrumental in achieving the on-screen romancification of Austen's work. Depicted by Austen's narrator only as "a sensible man" with "a cheerful manner" (*Emma* 9), Mr. Knightley is played in McGrath's film by the dark, good-looking Jeremy Northam. He appears to be older than Gwyneth Paltrow's Emma, but certainly not by Austen's stipulated sixteen years. The actors playing Edward Ferrars (Hugh Grant) and Colonel Brandon (Alan Rickman) are also too physically appealing. Austen's *Sense and Sensibility* emphatically denies these characters striking appearances. "Edward Ferrars," explains the narrator, "was not recommended to their [Mrs. Dashwood and her daughters'] good opinion by any peculiar graces of person or address. He was not handsome, and his manners required intimacy to make them pleasing" (*Sense* 15). Similarly, Colonel Brandon's "face was not handsome" (*Sense* 34). To be sure, both men have gentlemanly behavior, affectionate hearts, and other admirable qualities. But they are made plain in part to contribute to the novel's antiromance argument. The one male character in the novel who is endowed with the dashing looks of a romantic hero, Mr. Willoughby, proves to be not only immoral but also mercenary (a quality at odds with the romantic sensibility).

Judgments of personal attractiveness are, of course, highly subjective, but the stage and film careers of Jeremy Northam, Hugh Grant, and Alan Rickman indicate that all have been widely understood to have at least as much romantic appeal as Greg Wise, who plays the role of Willoughby in the film. Moreover, those prior roles inevitably mediate at least some audience members' perceptions of their characters in the Austen films. Referring to the intertextuality that affects the reception of plays but could apply just as well to films, theater historian Marvin Carlson has noted "that every specific production is composed in large part of elements already encountered elsewhere, that often bring with them as a necessary and inevitable part of reception certain ghosts of these previous encounters" (17). I have already suggested that the mass-market romance is a very important "ghost" affecting the scripting and direction of the films. But some of the actors' past roles also "haunt" their characters in these films. (For the sake of brevity, I will only touch on some of the actors' previous film roles.) Behind Mr. Knightley hovers Jack Devlin, for example, the menacing but seductive figure Northam played in the 1995 movie *The Net.* Colonel Brandon, for some of the audience, would not have escaped the aura of Alan Rickman's charming and charismatic villains, such as the terrorist in *Die Hard* and the Sheriff of Nottingham in *Robin Hood: Prince of Thieves,* or his poignant dead lover in *Truly, Madly, Deeply.* The nervous charm and amorousness of Hugh Grant's character in the film *Four Weddings and a Funeral* may have affected some filmgoers' experience of his Edward Ferrars. (For some viewers, however, that impact was superseded by another memory: Grant's Beverly Hills sex scandal, which occurred in June 1995, while the filming of *Sense and Sensibility* was still in progress but after his scenes had been completed. Incidents in the private lives of public persons may also become ghosts that haunt a particular production.)

The film versions of Austen's men provide sustained dramatizations of their love for the heroines. Colonel Brandon's intense response to Marianne, particularly when she becomes gravely ill, is inflected, according to the novel, by his tragic history with his father's ward, the first Eliza. There is much more than déjà vu, however, in Alan Rickman's interpretation of the character. Like "a man thawing out after having been in a fridge for twenty years" is the way he described his role (quoted in Thompson 251), but he moves rapidly in the part of Brandon from thaw to burn. In the book, Brandon embarks on the journey to bring Mrs. Dashwood to her severely ill daughter, after being requested to do so by Elinor. In the film, she finds him pacing outside Marianne's bedroom in one of his most fetching outfits. He does wear a flannel waistcoat, and for Marianne that article of clothing has symbolized his age and infirmity. But because it is combined with boots, tight breeches, a white shirt with long flowing sleeves, and a thin black scarf draped carelessly around his neck, the romanticism he has quietly repressed in the novel is vividly displayed on his body in the film. His plea to be assigned a useful task—"Give me an occupation, Miss Dashwood, or I shall run mad" (Thompson 181)—combines the conduct-book virtue of industriousness with emotional excess and suggests the hilariously contradictory Laura of Austen's youthful masterpiece *Love and Freindship.* The next scene prolongs this romantic vision of the Colonel, showing him mounting his horse in dashing hat and riding coat, taking a last look toward Marianne's bedroom window, and racing off alone in quest of Mrs. Dashwood.

The affection that Hugh Grant's Edward Ferrars shows toward Elinor in the film also substantially embellishes the novel. Austen's narrator refers to but does not dramatize their "growing attachment" (*Sense* 15). The novelist did not indulge in depictions of hero and heroine falling in love for crucial reasons. First, Austen presents the relationship of Elinor and Edward as one which, however strong their feelings, is conducted with a quiet decorum that surprises her mother and sister and is not, if we can be guided by their reactions, evocative for onlookers. Second, as Edward is already engaged, his affection for Elinor is tinged with guilt and the knowledge that his feelings are hopeless. In the early scenes at Norland Park and during his visit to Barton Cottage (not presented in the film), Austen prefers to focus on his consequent bouts of dejection, perhaps as a way of dealing with the dubious moral stance of a suitor already promised to someone else. The film compensates for Edward's shaky morality by showing him to be sympathetic not only to a family of grieving women, particularly the youngest, Margaret, but to the plight of genteel women in general. That portrait enables the film's indulgence in conventional scenes of courtship, dramatizing Edward's pleasure in looking at Elinor and feeling her gaze upon him, the intimacy of their conversations, and the moments of subtle physical contact, as when he retrieves the end of her shawl and places it around her again.

The dramatized affection of Northam's Mr. Knightley diverges just as much from Austen's writing. Austen set herself a challenging problem in *Emma*. Within a confined community in which marriage is very important, two of the small number of its inhabitants are a lady and gentleman who see each other frequently, are emotionally and socially suited to one another, and are not married. How to explain that they have so far avoided their obvious destiny and how to keep them apart for several chapters? Austen does so by making Mr. Knightley sixteen years older and connecting him by marriage to the Woodhouse family. His age and pseudo-kinship, as well as the paternalistic attitude they license, function to keep the hero and heroine apart. In encounters between them, his stern parental commentary on her behavior is matched by Emma's rebellious resistance to his advice and insistence on the rightness of her own conduct. In addition, although he is to be found frequently in the domestic and social arena, Knightley is portrayed as a man preoccupied with experience elsewhere. Austen does not, in general, represent men away from the company of women. But the novel refers to Mr. Knightley's roles as road improver, farmer, and magistrate frequently enough to create a convincing, albeit "off-stage," world of male work. Finally, Austen's narrator provides, for the most part, Emma's point of view, allowing us little access to other characters' unexpressed thoughts or emotional states. So, while the narrator must account for Emma's blindness to her love for Mr. Knightley, she can leave it to the reader to infer his feelings.

But what happens in the McGrath film? I have already noted that the age gap between Northam and Paltrow is not large enough. Nor does he seem paternalistic. By the time he lectures Emma on her treatment of Miss Bates at Box Hill, that disapproving, judgmental stance can have little impact on the viewer—his distinctly unfatherly ardor for the heroine has already been vividly dramatized. At social gatherings, he frequently comes to her side or meets her eyes in silent mutual accord about the behavior of others. At the Westons' Christmas party, Mr. Elton sits down between Emma and Mr. Knightley, calling attention to the comfortable intimacy of the pair he interrupts. In the book, he sits down between Emma and Mrs. Weston. Although they often argue, as in the novel, McGrath takes some of these conversations out of the drawing room and places them on the lawn of Donwell Abbey, where the two engage in archery, drink tea, or play with one of Mr. Knightley's dogs. Their disputes are undercut by their choice to spend so much time alone together—in the book, Emma's father and others are usually present too—and by the punch lines McGrath gives them. "Try not to kill my dogs," says a wry Mr. Knightley after one of Emma's arrows misses the target and almost pricks a nearby canine. No road improving or cattle-buying for this Mr. Knightley. He has no place else to go and nothing else to do but entertain Emma and, with an attention to dress worthy of Mrs. Elton, try out a variety of fashions, including a straw hat for outdoor parties.

A woman behind me in the movie theater gasped with surprise when Mr. Knightley professed his love for Emma on their walk to Hartfield near the film's end. But surely she belongs to a tiny minority. The filmmakers could have found ways to disguise or mute Mr. Knightley's feelings even without the benefits of a narrator situated at a distance from that character's mental life. They chose not to.

Consistent with their focus on the romantic couple, the films of *Sense and Sensibility* and *Emma* thin out and underpopulate the social world. Sir John Middleton is made a childless widower in Thompson's screenplay. The vulgar Lucy Steele no longer has an even more vulgar sister. In McGrath's film, John and Isabella Knightley do not fall prey to the screenwriter's ax, but they are almost ignored by the camera operators. Does anyone remember what John Knightley looks like in the film? Nor do we have much sense of the elaborate and playful deceptions of Frank Churchill or the intricacies of his social interactions with Jane Fairfax. Even more important, the films' portraits of women's lives lack the complexity with which they are endowed in the novels.

Austen's works have engaged successive generations of readers because of their interpretive richness. None is reducible to a single, simple portrait of courtship (whether or not it is harlequinized). Indeed, many critics have argued that Jane Austen's representations of women challenge the dominance and centrality of the courtship plot. Although some postwar critical commentary about *Emma* has stressed the necessity of the flawed heroine's humiliation by Mr. Knightley and her subsequent reform near the novel's end,[4] more recently, feminist critics have attributed less importance to Emma's marriage to Mr. Knightley. Instead, they have praised Emma Woodhouse's authority and autonomy. In Claudia Johnson's words, for example, the novel presents "positive versions of female power" (*Jane* 126). And feminist and nonfeminist critics alike have been known to applaud Marianne's passionate vitality and independence, preferring it to Elinor's self-suppression. Marianne's champions have generally charged her creator with "betraying" her by marrying her off to the drab Colonel Brandon at the novel's conclusion.[5]

Critics have also argued that, in several of the novels, the friendships of the women characters with one another are at least as important as their relationships with male characters. For *Emma,* this decentering of the courtship plot was accomplished first by critics who took the heroine to task for her infatuations with women.[6] But their homophobic attitudes were subsequently rejected by feminist critics who have since emphasized the value and importance for Emma of her bonds with Harriet Smith and Jane Fairfax. Some critics have also maintained that the strength of Marianne and Elinor's attachment to one another sometimes seems to overshadow *Sense and Sensibility's* courtship plot.

In finding profoundly rendered relationships among women in Austen's novels, critics such as Susan Lanser and Ruth Perry have suggested that Austen was not genuinely committed to the courtship plots that structure her novels.[7] My own book, *Jane Austen among Women,* suggests that Austen's attitude toward and treatment of the courtship plot was more equivocal. It shows the basis in the author's life for her fictional representations of women's loving ties, maintaining that without the support of her sister, Cassandra, and a handful of other female kin and friends, Jane Austen could not have become a novelist. But it suggests that Austen was also sincerely attached to the larger culture of the gentry and specifically to its high valuation of marriage and family life. Hence, *Jane Austen among Women* argues that Austen's novels both endorse and subtly challenge the courtship plot's emphasis on heterosexual romance. Indeed, at least in part it is because they are equivocal that so many diverse interpretations have been and will continue to be generated about the six novels.

Neither of the recent films suggests that female friendships are sufficient to sustain an alternative emotional life for heroines without men. Emma's intense focus on and feelings for Harriet Smith are not given much weight in the film. She and Harriet are "girlfriends" in a modern, trivialized sense, talking about boys or playing with puppies. The film also considerably reduces representations of not only her contacts with but also her thoughts about Jane Fairfax. The presentation of women's relationships is more complex in *Sense and Sensibility*. The filmmakers were concerned that the film not seem to be about "a couple of women waiting around for men" (Doran 14), and so they did emphasize the relationship between Elinor and Marianne.

An early scene in Barton Cottage, invented for the film, illustrates both the discomforts of the Dashwoods' new home and the daily, ongoing intimacy of the sisters. The scene shows Elinor laying another blanket on the bed with Marianne in their small room. She then wraps a shawl around her nightgown, blows out the candle, and seeks the warmth of the bedcovers and Marianne's body heat—only to be greeted by Marianne's complaint that her feet are cold. Elinor jumps out of bed, grabs some stockings, and returns to put them on. The intensity of their bond is also dramatized. At the height of Marianne's illness, Elinor leans over her unconscious sister, runs a hand slowly up the sheet covering her left leg and, in tears, pleads with her: "I cannot do without you. Oh, please, I have tried to bear everything else—I will try—but please, dearest, beloved Marianne, do not leave me alone" (Thompson 184). Although such scenes convey the importance of this relationship, they compete with and are ultimately trumped by other invented scenes between Marianne and Colonel Brandon. His day-to-day presence in Marianne's life is embellished by scenes such as that in which he offers her a knife with which to cut reeds, and her growing love for him is established in one of the film's last scenes, in which he reads to her on the lawn in front of Barton Cottage. Readers who have felt that in marrying Marianne off to the Colonel, Austen was "betraying" her character must surely be placated by this scene and by Rickman's interpretation of this suitor in general. The films of both *Sense and Sensibility* and *Emma* assert not just the appropriateness but also the romantic pleasure of their heroines' marriages.

The recent films of Jane Austen's novels have increased sales of her books. But those who read as well as buy are going to discover that her books are not harlequinized. When they encounter Edward Ferrars's silent despondency and Mr. Knightley's cool sternness, the constant noisy intrusiveness of the Dashwoods' social circle and the loneliness and solitude threatening Emma, and always the self-discipline required for the good manners Jane Austen advocates—will they continue to be enthusiastic about the novelist? We can hope that if some new readers are first escorted to the novels by Jeremy Northam and Alan Rickman, they will stay to appreciate the encounters the books stage between wishes and deeds, glorious dreams and mundane material constraints, and, most of all, simple certainties and interpretive ambiguity.

Notes

This essay first appeared in *Persuasions* 18 (1996): 171-81, in a slightly different form.

1. Dated 1980, the tip sheet outlines novels for Silhouette Romances, which at the time was a Simon & Schuster line. In 1984 Harlequin Enterprises, owned by Toronto's Torstar Corporation, purchased Silhouette. In 1997, Torstar was the world's largest publisher of mass-market paperback romances, offering three lines: Harlequin, Silhouette, and Mira.

2. Radway's well-known study of readers and the mass-market romance confirms the central trait of these novels: "the most striking characteristic of the ideal romance [is] its resolute focus on a single, developing relationship between heroine and hero" (122).

3. Moffat argues that genres in general provide their readers with the satisfaction of being able to predict a work's outcome (48). "Formula fictions," such as mass-market romances, may be said to intensify the satisfactions of predicting a fiction's conclusion.

4. See, for example, Booth (*Rhetoric* 243-66). I am indebted to Johnson's discussion of postwar criticism of *Emma* (*Equivocal* 191-95).

5. See, for example, Kirkham (87) and Tanner (100-2).

6. The most famous work in this vein is Mudrick (181-206).

7. Numerous critics have argued that Austen treats the conventions of the courtship plot ironically and wants her reader, in effect, to read against the grain. See for example, Booth, "Emma."

Works Cited

Austen, Jane. *Emma.* Ed. R.W. Chapman. Rev. Mary Lascelles. 3d ed. Vol. 4 of *The Novels of Jane Austen.* 6 vols. Oxford: Oxford UP, 1966.

———. *Sense and Sensibility.* Ed. R.W. Chapman. Rev. Mary Lascelles. 3d ed. Vol. 1 of *The Novels of Jane Austen.* 6 vols. Oxford: Oxford UP, 1966.

Booth, Wayne C. "*Emma, Emma,* and the Question of Feminism." *Persuasions* 5 (1983): 29-40.

———. *The Rhetoric of Fiction.* 2d ed. Chicago: U of Chicago P, 1983.

Carlson, Marvin. "The Haunted Stage: Recycling and Reception in the Theatre." *Theatre Survey* 35.1 (May 1994): 5-18.

"Film Box Office Report." *Daily Variety* 2 July 1996 and 1 Oct. 1996.

Doran, Lindsay. Introduction to Emma Thompson, *The Sense and Sensibility Screenplay and Diaries.* Rev. ed. New York: Newmarket, 1996. 7-16.

Emma. Writer and director Douglas McGrath. With Gwyneth Paltrow and Jeremy Northam. Miramax, 1996.

Fenster, Bob. "History of Frugal 'Emma' Quite Hectic." *Arizona Republic* 11 Aug. 1996: F8.

Gunther, Mark. "Alas, Poor Sony." *Fortune* 30 Sept. 1996: 128-34.

Johnson, Claudia L. *Equivocal Beings: Politics, Gender, and Sentimentality in the 1790s*. Chicago: U of Chicago P, 1995.

————. *Jane Austen: Women, Politics, and the Novel*. 1983. Chicago: U of Chicago P, 1988.

Kaplan, Deborah. *Jane Austen among Women*. Baltimore: Johns Hopkins UP, 1992.

Kirkham, Margaret. *Jane Austen, Feminism, and Fiction*. 1983. Rpt. New York: Methuen, 1986.

Lanser, Susan. "No Connections Subsequent: Jane Austen's World of Sisterhood." In *The Sister Bond: A Feminist View of a Timeless Connection*. Ed. Toni A.H. McNaron. New York: Pergamon, 1985. 53-67.

Menand, Louis. "Hollywood's Trap." *New York Review of Books* 19 Sept. 1996: 4-6.

Moffat, Wendy. "Identifying with Emma: Some Problems for the Feminist Reader." *College English* 53 (1991): 45-59.

Mudrick, Marvin. *Jane Austen: Irony as Defense and Discovery*. 1952. Rpt. Berkeley: U of California P, 1968.

Perry, Ruth. "Interrupted Friendships in Jane Austen's *Emma*." *Tulsa Studies in Women's Literature* 5 (1986): 185-202.

Radway, Janice. *Reading the Romance: Women, Patriarchy, and Popular Literature*. Chapel Hill: U of North Carolina P, 1984.

Sense and Sensibility. Writer Emma Thompson. Director Ang Lee. With Emma Thompson and Hugh Grant. Mirage-Columbia (Sony), 1995.

Silhouette Books. Tip Sheet. April 1980. In author's possession.

Tanner, Tony. *Jane Austen*. Cambridge: Harvard UP, 1986.

Thompson, Emma. *The Sense and Sensibility Screenplay and Diaries*. Rev. ed. New York: Newmarket, 1996.

Austen Adaptations Available on Video

Emma

1972 (BBC). Writer Denis Constanduros. Director John Glenister. Producer Martin Lisemore. With Doran Godwin (Emma Woodhouse), John Carson (Mr. Knightley), Donald Eccles (Mr. Woodhouse), Robert East (Frank Churchill). Miniseries.

1996 (Miramax). Writer and director Douglas McGrath. Producer Patrick Cassavetti. With Gwyneth Paltrow (Emma Woodhouse), Jeremy Northam (Mr. Knightley), Toni Collette (Harriet Smith), Ewan McGregor (Frank Churchill). Feature film.

1996 (Meridian [ITV] and A&E). Writer Andrew Davies. Director Diarmuid Lawrence. Producer Sue Birtwistle. With Kate Beckinsale (Emma Woodhouse), Mark Strong (Mr. Knightley), Samantha Morton (Harriet Smith), Raymond Coulthard (Frank Churchill). Telefilm.

[*Clueless.*] 1995 (Paramount). Writer and director Amy Heckerling. Producers Scott Rudin and Robert Lawrence. With Alicia Silverstone (Cher), Paul Rudd (Josh), Stacey Dash (Dionne), Brittany Murphy (Tai). Feature film.

Mansfield Park

1983 (BBC). Writer Ken Taylor. Director David Giles. Producer Betty Willingale. With Sylvestra Le Touzel (Fanny Price), Nicholas Farrel (Edmund Bertram), Anna Massey (Aunt Norris), Robert Burbage (Henry Crawford). Miniseries.

Northanger Abbey

1987 (BBC and A&E). Writer Maggie Wadey. Director Giles Foster. Producer Louis Marks. With Katharine Schlesinger (Catherine Morland), Peter Firth (Henry Tilney), Robert Hardy (General Tilney), Googie Withers (Mrs. Allen). Telefilm.

Persuasion

1971 (Granada [ITV]). Writer Julian Mitchell. Director and Producer Howard Baker. With Ann Firbank (Anne Elliot), Bryan Marshall (Captain Wentworth), Basil Dignam (Sir Walter Elliot), Morag Hood (Mary Musgrove). Miniseries.

1995 (BBC and WGBH). Writer Nick Dear. Director Roger Michell. Producers Rebecca Eaton, George Faber, Fiona Finlay. With Amanda Root (Anne Elliot), Ciaran Hinds (Captain Wentworth), Corin Redgrave (Sir Walter Elliot), Sophie Thompson (Mary Musgrove). Telefilm; released as a feature film from Sony Picture Classics.

Pride and Prejudice.

1940 (MGM). Writers Aldous Huxley and Jane Murfin. Director Robert Z. Leonard. Producer Hunt Stromberg. With Greer Garson (Elizabeth Bennet), Laurence Olivier (Mr. Darcy), Maureen O'Sullivan (Jane Bennet), Edmund Gwenn (Mr. Bennet), Edna May Oliver (Lady Catherine de Bourgh). Feature film.

1979 (BBC and A&E). Writer Fay Weldon. Director Cyril Coke. Producer Jonathan Powell. With Elizabeth Garvie (Elizabeth Bennet), David Rintoul (Mr. Darcy), Sabina Franklyn (Jane Bennet), Moray Watson (Mr. Bennet), Judy Parfitt (Lady Catherine de Bourgh). Miniseries.

1995 (BBC and A&E). Writer Andrew Davies. Director Simon Langton. Producer Sue Birtwistle. With Jennifer Ehle (Elizabeth Bennet), Colin Firth (Mr. Darcy), Susannah Harker (Jane Bennet), Benjamin Whitrow (Mr. Bennet), Barbara Leigh-Hunt (Lady Catherine de Bourgh). Miniseries.

Sense and Sensibility

1985 (BBC). Writer Alexander Baron. Director Rodney Bennett. Producer Barry Letts. With Irene Richard (Elinor Dashwood), Bosco Hogan (Edward

Ferrars), Tracy Childs (Marianne Dashwood), Donald Douglas (Sir John Middleton), Peter Woodward (John Willoughby). Miniseries.

1995 (Mirage/Columbia). Writer Emma Thompson. Director Ang Lee. Producer Lindsay Doran. With Emma Thompson (Elinor Dashwood), Hugh Grant (Edward Ferrars), Kate Winslet (Marianne Dashwood), Alan Rickman (Colonel Brandon), Greg Wise (John Willoughby). Feature film.

Selected Reviews, Articles, and Books on the Films, 1995-1997

Allen, Brooke. "Jane Austen for the Nineties." *The New Criterion* Sept. 1995: 15-22.

Alleva, Richard. "Emma Can Read, Too." Review of *Sense and Sensibility*. *Commonweal* 8 Mar. 1996: 15-18.

Amis, Martin. "Jane's World." *The New Yorker* 8 Jan. 1996: 31-35.

Andreae, Christopher. "In Defense of the Perfect 'Pride and Prejudice.'" *Christian Science Monitor* 6 Dec. 1995: 16.

Ansen, David. "In This Fine Romance, Virtue Is Rewarded." Review of *Persuasion*. *Newsweek* 9 Oct. 1995: 78.

"Austen Anew." *The New Yorker* 21-28 Aug. 1995: 55.

Axelrod, Mark. "Once upon a Time in Hollywood: or, The Commodification of Form in the Adaptation of Fictional Texts to the Hollywood Cinema." *Literature/Film Quarterly* 24 (1996): 201-8.

Bellafante, Ginia. "Sick of Jane Austen Yet?" *Time* 15 Jan. 1996: 66.

Birtwistle, Sue, and Susie Conklin. *The Making of Jane Austen's Emma*. London: Penguin, 1996.

———. *The Making of Pride and Prejudice*. London: Penguin, 1995.

Blake, Richard A. "Plain Jane." Review of *Sense and Sensibility*. *America* 9 Mar. 1996: 20-21.

Blandford, Linda. "Beware the Insidious Grip of Darcy Fever." *New York Times* 14 Jan. 1996: H31.

Bowers, Faye. "No Longer Clueless about Austen's Clout." *Christian Science Monitor* 5 Apr. 1996: 7.

Collins, James. "Jane Reactions." *Vogue* Jan. 1996: 70-72.

Corliss, Richard. "A Touch of Class." *Time* 29 July 1996: 74-75.

———. "To Live and Buy in L.A." *Time* 31 July 1995.

Coughlan, Sean. "Surf and Sensibility. *Times Educational Supplement* 22 Sept. 1995: 2.18.

Davies, Andrew. "Austen's Horrible Heroine." Discussion of *Emma*. *The Electronic Telegraph* 23 Nov. 1996. Online at http://www.telegraph.uk.

———. "Picture the Scene." *Times Educational Supplement* 22 Sept. 1995: 2.10-11.

Davies, Caroline. "BBC Pride as 50,000 Buy Austen Video." *The Electronic Tele-graph* 25 Oct. 1995. Online at www.telegraph.co.uk.

Dickson, Jane. "The Older Woman: Greta Scacchi." *The Electronic Telegraph* 14 Sept. 1996. Online at www.telegraph.co.uk.

Doherty, Tom. "Clueless Kids." *Cineaste* 21 (Fall 1995): 14-17.

Doncaster, Peter. "Jane Austen Revival Helps the National Trust." *Britannia.* Online at http://www.britannia.com/newsbits/jausten.html.

Dowd, Maureen. "Will Jane Nix Pix?" *New York Times* 24 Aug. 1995: A23.

Ebert, Roger. Review of *Emma. Chicago Sun-Times* Aug. 1996. Online at http://www.suntimes.com.

———. Review of *Persuasion. Chicago Sun-Times* 27 Oct. 1995. Online at http://www.suntimes.com.

———. Review of *Sense and Sensibility. Chicago Sun-Times* 13 Dec. 1996. Online at http://www.suntimes.com.

"Emma Thompson: A Close Reading." *The New Yorker* 21-28 Aug. 1995: 55-56.

Forde, John Maurice. "Janespotting." *Topic: A Journal of the Liberal Arts* 48 (1997): 11-21.

Foster, Jennifer. "Austenmania, EQ, and the End of the Millenium." *Topic: A Journal of the Liberal Arts* 48 (1997): 56-64.

Francke, Lizzie. Review of *Sense and Sensibility. New Statesman and Society* 23 Feb. 1996: 43.

Giles, Jeff. "Earth Angel." Review of *Emma. Newsweek* 29 July 1996: 66-68.

Greenfield, John R. "Is Emma Clueless? Fantasies of Class and Gender from En-gland to California." *Topic: A Journal of the Liberal Arts* 48 (1997): 31-38.

Grunwald, Henry. "Jane Austen's Civil Society." *Wall Street Journal* 2 Oct. 1996: A14+.

Hannon, Patrice. "Austen Novels and Austen Films: Incompatible Worlds?" *Per-suasions: The Journal of the Jane Austen Society of North America* 18 (1996): 24-32.

Harris, Jocelyn. "Review of *Sense and Sensibility, Persuasion,* and *Clueless.*" *Eigh-teenth-Century Fiction* 8 (1996): 427-30.

James, Caryn. "An *Emma* Both Darker and Funnier." *New York Times* 15 Feb. 1997: 28.

———. "Austen Tale of Lost Love Refound." Review of *Persuasion. New York Times* 27 Sept. 1995: C18.

Kauffmann, Stanley. Review of *Jane Austen's Persuasion. The New Republic* 9 Oct. 1995: 26-27.

———. Review of *Sense and Sensibility. The New Republic* 8 Jan. 1996: 34-35.

Kroll, Jack. "Jane Austen Does Lunch." *Newsweek* 18 Dec. 1995: 66-68.

Lane, Anthony. "Jane's World." *The New Yorker* 25 Sept. 1995: 107-8.

———. "The Dumbing of Emma." *The New Yorker* 5 Aug. 1996: 76-77.

Lee, Susan. "A Tale of Two Movies." *Forbes* 4 Nov. 1996: 391.

Lehmann-Haupt, Christopher. "Pride and Prejudice." *New York Times* 8 Feb. 1997.

Lipman, Amanda. "Clueless." *Sight and Sound* Oct. 1995: 46.

Looser, Devoney. "Jane Austen 'Responds' to the Men's Movement." *Persuasions: The Journal of the Jane Austen Society of North America* 18 (1996): 159-70.

Lyall, Sarah. "'Emma' No. 2 Makes Austen's Heroine Darker and Spikier." *New York Times* 16 Feb. 1997: F4.

Lyons, Donald. Review of *Sense and Sensibility. Film Comment* Jan.-Feb. 1996: 36-42.

Maslin, Janet. "Emma." *New York Times* 2 Aug. 1996. Online at http://www.nytimes.com.

———. "Sense and Sensibility." *New York Times* 13 Dec. 1995. Online at http://www.nytimes.com.

———. "So Genteel, So Scheming, So Austen." Review of *Emma. New York Times* 2 Aug. 1996: C1.

Masters, Kim. "Austen Found: Hollywood Rediscovers the 19th-Century Writer." *Washington Post* 19 Dec. 1995: G1, G7.

McGrory, Mary. "'Clueless' about Jane Austen." *Washington Post* 20 Aug. 1995: C1+.

———. "Dense Insensibility." *Washington Post* 19 Dec. 1995: A2.

Menand, Louis. "Hollywood's Trap." *New York Review of Books* 19 Sept. 1996: 4-6.

———. "What Jane Austen Doesn't Tell Us." *New York Review of Books* 1 Feb. 1996: 13-15.

Morgenstern, Joe. "Persuasion." *Wall Street Journal* 6 Oct. 1995: A8.

———. "Sense and Sensibility." *Wall Street Journal* 15 Dec. 1995: A14.

Nichols, Peter M. "Literary Cycle: Bookshelf, Broadcast, Video Store." *New York Times* 7 Sept. 1997. Online at http://www.nytimes.com.

O'Connor, John. "An England Where the Heart and Purse Are Romantically United." Review of *Pride and Prejudice. New York Times* 13 Jan. 1996: 13, 18.

O'Connor, Suzanne. "Persuasion." *New York Times* 1 Oct. 1995: H26.

Rapping, Elayne. "The Jane Austen Thing." *The Progressive* July 1996: 37-38.

Rochlin, Margy. "Like Emma, Setting Her World All Astir." *New York Times* 28 July 1996: 2.11.

Rothstein, Edward. "Jane Austen Meets Mr. Right." *New York Times* 10 Dec. 1995: 4.1, 4.14.

Sales, Roger. "Afterword" to his *Jane Austen and Representations of Regency England*. New York: Routledge, 1996.

Schwartz, Amy. "'Clued in' to Jane Austen." *Washington Post* 11 Aug. 1995: A23.

Shapiro, Laura, and Carol Hall. "Beyond Sense and Sensibility." *Newsweek* 14 Aug. 1995: 70.

Simon, John. Review of *Jane Austen's Persuasion. National Review* 23 Oct. 1995: 58-59.

———. Review of *Sense and Sensibility. National Review* 29 Jan. 1996: 67.

Sterritt, David. "Emma." *Christian Science Monitor* 2 Aug. 1996: 11.

Stevens, Amy. "Poor Jane Austen Didn't Live to See 'Sense and Sensibility.'" *Wall Street Journal* 25 Mar. 1996: 1+.

Sullivan, Andrew. "Washington Diarist." *The New Republic* 11 Sept. 1995: 43.

Thomas, Evan. "Hooray for Hypocrisy." *Newsweek* 29 Jan. 1996: 61.

Thompson, Emma. *The Sense and Sensibility Screenplay and Diaries.* Rev. ed. New York: Newmarket, 1996.

Troost, Linda. "Jane Austen and Technology." *Topic: A Journal of the Liberal Arts* 48 (1997): iii-v.

Weinraub, Bernard. "A Surprise Film Hit about Rich Teen-Age Girls." *New York Times* 24 July 1995: C10.

Weldon, Fay. "Jane Austen and the Pride of Purists." *New York Times* 8 Oct. 1995: H15, H24.

Contributors

Rachel M. Brownstein is professor of English at the Graduate School of the City University of New York. She is well known for her book *Becoming a Heroine*.

Amanda Collins is a graduate student at the University of Alabama finishing her master's degree. She was graduated from Spring Hill College in 1996, where she was a President's Scholar.

M. Casey Diana is completing a Ph.D. in English literature at the University of Illinois on the rise of addiction in early modern literature. A nontraditional student, she started her academic career after raising a family.

Rebecca Dickson teaches in the Writing Program of the University of Colorado. She has published (with Frank Grady) *Surviving the Day: An American P.O.W. in Japan*. Her field of research is nineteenth-century American literature.

Carol M. Dole is associate professor and chair of the English Department of Ursinus College. She has published articles in *Literature/Film Quarterly*, *English Language Notes*, *Southern Review*, and *Studies in Short Fiction*. Her field of research is Victorian fiction, and she teaches both literature and film.

H. Elisabeth Ellington is completing a Ph.D. at Brandeis. She received her undergraduate degree from Vesalius College, Belgium, and a master's from the University of New Hampshire. She is working on women writers during World War I.

Suzanne Ferriss is associate professor of Liberal Arts at Nova Southeastern University. She has recently published (with Shari Benstock) *On Fashion* and co-edited the forthcoming *Anthology of Literary Feminisms* and *Handbook of Literary Feminisms*.

Sayre Greenfield is assistant professor of English at the University of Pittsburgh at Greensburg. He is the author of *The Ends of Allegory* and of articles published in *Philological Quarterly*, *Criticism*, and *Genre*. His work has also appeared in three collections of biographical essays on women writers.

Lisa Hopkins is senior lecturer at Sheffield Hallam University and earned a first degree from King's College, Cambridge. She is widely published in Renaissance drama, with books on Ford, Shakespeare, and Marlowe, and has many articles in print, including one on Jane Austen and money.

Deborah Kaplan is associate professor of English at George Mason University. She is the author of *Jane Austen among Women* as well as articles in *Criticism*, *Theatre Survey*, *Prose Studies*, and other journals.

Devoney Looser is assistant professor of women's studies at the University of Wisconsin at Whitewater. She is the editor of *Jane Austen and Discourses of Feminism*, coeditor of *Generations*, and author of many articles on Jane Austen.

Nora Nachumi is completing a Ph.D. in English literature at the Graduate Center of the City University of New York. Her dissertation explores the influence of the theater on late-eighteenth-century British women novelists. She recently received a fellowship from the American Association of University Women.

Cheryl Nixon is assistant professor of English at Babson College and recently taught at New Mexico State University. She has published in *Restoration* and is finishing a book on surrogate families, focusing on the guardian/ward relationship in eighteenth-century fiction and law.

Kristin Flieger Samuelian is a visiting assistant professor of English at George Mason University and has published articles in *Nineteenth-Century Studies* and *Victorian Newsletter*. She is finishing a book on women and political fiction in the nineteenth century.

Linda Troost is associate professor of English at Washington and Jefferson College. She is editor of the annual *Eighteenth-Century Women* and has published essays in *Eighteenth-Century Studies*, *Restoration*, *The Dictionary of Literary Biography*, and *The New Grove Dictionary of Opera*.

Index